Introduction

The plays of Shakespeare represent the English climax of a development that had been going on in Christian Europe for about six hundred years. This remarkable evolution of a form had begun with simple dramatizations of New Testament stories; then had come complication and a gradual secularization; and within the secular forms which ultimately became dominant there was a somewhat more rapid growth from rather primitive comedies and tragedies to the complex psychological and philosophical dramas of Shakespeare. The present volume includes examples of relatively early mystery plays, in which the Biblical intention is expanded but not essentially altered; of later Biblical plays in which there is either a considerable intrusion of the secular or an outright dominance of the additions to the original story; of the Morality play, in which the Christian view of life is set forth but set forth in new, imaginative, non-Biblical materials; of early comedy, in which there is a complete liberation from the church but a dependence upon immature materials and techniques; and finally of the comparatively mature late sixteenth-century forms which Shakespeare refined and perfected.[1]

Mystery Plays

The modern student of medieval mystery plays must avoid an excessive emphasis both upon their naïveté, which will be

---

[1] The scope of the present volume does not permit a detailed historical survey of the drama from medieval times to 1590. Rather than use space uneconomically for what would at best be very incomplete history, the editor has limited the introduction to raising a few critical issues concerning the plays in the volume.

most obvious to a reader with little experience of early literature, and upon certain of their achievements, which will be
most obvious to a literary historian. Since we are not going
into large-scale history and are therefore not likely to take
our standards entirely from the age itself, we shall probably
not run the risk of overestimating the accomplishments of the
primitive dramatists. We are, on the contrary, much more
likely to make the charge of naïveté. But we must accept the
naïveté as inevitable in the dramatic transcription, for a popular audience, of myths closely defined in a documentary form
which must have acted coercively upon the intending artist;
and then we must see how obediently the artist accepts the
prescriptions inherent in his task, or how inventively he alters
the nature of the task. It would be an error ever to expect of
him the high independence which we regard as the condition
of artistic creation.

When the unknown writers of the first plays in this volume
undertook to do something more than make transcripts of
Biblical texts, their imaginations took them, in the main, in
two directions. For the most part they attempted an expansion
or intensification, or a wider exploration, of the inherited materials: this is what we find in the *Betrayal* and the *Crucifixion*.
Or occasionally a bare hint in their original led them off into
a presentation of character and action that was only nomi-
nally related to their ostensible theme: thus the secular began
to assume importance, and the didactic rehearsal of the Christian myth was doomed. This is what we find in the *Second
Shepherds' Play*. The *Noah* lies between the two: the husband-
wife farce is all a new venture, trying to dominate the Old
Testament story and yet finally being contained within it.

The author of the *Betrayal* senses the clash between the human and the divine in Christ, and of this he tries to make
drama. He does not, of course, realize the conflict very suc-
cessfully, perhaps because it could be managed better in a lyric
than in the play form to which he is committed. He moves

AN ANTHOLOGY OF ENGLISH DRAMA
BEFORE SHAKESPEARE

An Anthology of English Drama

Before Shakespeare

ℰ

Edited with an Introduction by Robert B. Heilman

THE N. TOWNE BETRAYAL
THE YORK CRUCIFIXION · THE WAKEFIELD NOAH
THE WAKEFIELD SECOND SHEPHERDS' PLAY
EVERYMAN · GAMMER GURTON'S NEEDLE
FRIAR BACON AND FRIAR BUNGAY
THE SPANISH TRAGEDY · DR. FAUSTUS

ℰ

Holt, Rinehart and Winston, Inc.

NEW YORK · CHICAGO · SAN FRANCISCO · ATLANTA · DALLAS
MONTREAL · TORONTO · LONDON · SYDNEY

Introduction copyright, 1952, by Robert B. Heilman
Typography by Stefan Salter

Library of Congress Catalog card number: 52-5607
SBN: 03-008625-6
Printed in the United States of America
90123   68   191817

conventionally on to the arrest of Jesus, but, since he cannot get much beneath the surface, he has less a historic drama than a chronicle in dialogue form. Actually, his leaning is toward pathos rather than conflict—a leaning that appears somewhat in the first part and very conspicuously in the final scene, where he is drawn entirely away from his main "plot."

In their elaboration of the inherited materials, these dramatists move less toward spiritual meanings or symbolic interpretations—such as Marlowe's of the Faust story—than toward psychological filling-in. This is especially apparent in the *Crucifixion*, whose author rather carefully traces the attitudes of the soldiers who raise the Cross and put Christ on it, and presents their brutality with a realism that goes beyond the casual and conventional. Without much overt conflict, the play achieves tension by a relatively subtle kind of clash—that between the attitudes of Christ and the soldiers, and especially that between the soldiers and the recalcitrant materials with which they must deal. While thus exhibiting considerable freedom of imagination, the author confines himself within an elaborate scheme of versification that includes both rhyme and alliteration. He even makes the soldiers speak monotonously in a kind of military order, though when he breaks the order he appears to have a reason for doing so.

In the *Noah* there is a great deal more of tedious exposition, but along with this undramatic rehearsing of Biblical detail, there are notable additions to the Old Testament story. Whereas the *Crucifixion* elaborates the story of Christ, the *Noah* complements the flood story with its own version of domestic farce,[2] and thereby helps create a purely secular tradition of comedy. This tradition is, of course, grounded much more firmly and brilliantly in the *Second Shepherds' Play*. Despite the historically interesting spectacle of the reduction of Biblical origins to a bare framework or afterpiece, what will most

---

[2] For a slightly different version of the same comic theme see the Chester Flood play in J. Q. Adams, *Chief Pre-Shakespearean Dramas*. pp. 111ff.

attract the attention of the critical reader is the technical skill with which the farce is managed—the characterization of Mak, his wife, and the shepherds, who are carefully distinguished; the sense of situation; the growth of tension. Again, the author has a considerable comic range: he has verbal comedy (Mak's southern accent), farce (the situation as a whole), comedy of character (the interaction between the shepherds and Mak), and even comic irony (it is a kindly intention that leads to the discovery of the stolen sheep). But above all, this parasitic growth upon the original is subtly related to the Christ story, for the main comedy is virtually a parody of the Nativity story. There is a "birth," the scene is humble, human being and animal are brought into juxtaposition, and gifts are offered. With these similarities in plan, the shift at the end introduces less an incongruity than a fine contrast in tone.

Fifteenth and Sixteenth Centuries

Everyman and *Gammer Gurton's Needle* can be grouped together only in that they represent a somewhat intermediate position between the early church drama and the fully developed drama of Shakespeare's day. In one we see popular teaching; in the other, popular entertainment.

Considered historically, *Everyman* represents a type of drama that imposes a serious handicap upon the dramatist and yet makes other advantages available to him. The inherent difficulty of the morality play, of which *Everyman* is the most successful extant example, is that the characters are abstractions and generalizations; hence the writer is in danger of producing merely a didactic allegory, undramatic in content and oversimplified in characterization. On the other hand, in the morality play we see a large increase in the materials available to the dramatist—an important advance beyond the farce which was earlier the chief supplement to Biblical themes.

The author of *Everyman* had gifts which permitted him to make the dramatic most of his limited allegorical materials, to rely, not merely upon a lesson-in-dialogue, but upon characterization—Death, Fellowship, and Goods, for instance, are much more than abstractions; humor—some of the excuses made to Everyman by those who will not go with him; a series of climaxes and changes in tension; and even irony—at the grave itself, experience keeps taking a form opposite to the expectations of Everyman.

In *Gammer Gurton's Needle* we have an early instance of a play upon which a clear-cut external form has been imposed— the five-act form, with its careful scene divisions, of the Roman drama. What is more important is the inner form: the drama has essential unity of action, since the major events of the play all spring out of an initial situation which is not clarified until the end. The play gets down to its essential business more rapidly than the *Second Shepherds' Play*, it develops the business much more extensively, and it has the business performed by a larger and more varied cast of characters. All these achievements were necessary to the creation of a mature comic form. But after due allowance has been made for them, it is clear that Mr. S., the author, was not a fundamentally more talented artist than the author of the *Second Shepherds' Play*. He creates lively movement and lively talk (in vulgarity and vituperation he is excellent). But he makes no effort to put together more than a simple farce with simple characters, who, despite various superficial differences, are alike in a naïve ability to be hoodwinked—an ability upon which the dramatist basically relies. Playing opposite them is the trickster Diccon (who probably has both native and Latin sources), whose sole business is to set the others by the ears. Most of the action, then, is the result of mechanical manipulation rather than the spontaneous product of a free relationship among characters of different kinds, as it is in the *Second Shepherds' Play*. And if we compare the irony by which the robbery is discovered in the

Wakefield play with the accident by which the needle is discovered in the play by Mr. S., we see another respect in which
the latter is working on a less sophisticated artistic level.

Shakespeare's Immediate Predecessors

The work of Kyd, Marlowe, and Greene—representatives
of a group of able young men who in the two decades before
Shakespeare helped English drama grow up at a faster rate
than at any previous time—is more nearly adult. The last three
plays in this volume, all written in the neighborhood of 1590,
have obviously a greater freedom from both didacticism and
farce, a less mechanical kind of movement, and a fuller presentation of individual character than do most of the preceding
plays; and one instinctively judges them by more exacting
criteria. The criteria vary with the plays, of course: Kyd and
Marlowe write tragedy, and Greene writes romantic comedy.

The last written of the three plays, *Friar Bacon and Friar
Bungay*, is the least mature. In part this immaturity is due to
the fact that in romantic comedy Greene employs a genre
where the possibilities of a thorough exploration of human
experience are not great. In part the weakness is due to
Greene's inability to give psychological vitality to some of
the conventions which writers of romance inherited. For
instance, there is the convention of the "test": Margaret
receives the unexpected farewell from Lacy, and almost immediately decides to enter a nunnery. Later, in justifying her
choice, she says penitently that she "doted more on him
[Lacy] than on my God." But when Lacy again appears and
demands that she return to him, she gives up her new religious
position as lightly as she had given up Lacy before. The convention is intact; the human reality is largely ignored. Only
in the brief debate between Margaret and her father, who
opposes her entry into a convent, does Greene move toward
an actuality of feeling that transcends the conventional.

If we compare *Friar Bacon and Friar Bungay* with *Gammer Gurton's Needle*, we observe a perceptible move from undiluted farce toward comedy of character. There is, of course, farce in Greene's play. But there is also the Edward-Margaret-Lacy triangle, which develops not by misunderstanding and trickery, but in terms of persons who respond to each other in certain characteristic ways; and which advances not by a series of physical beatings, but by the more subtle kind of action which stems from mind and personality. That is all to the good. But if, on the other hand, we compare *Friar Bacon* with Marlowe's *Faustus*—from which it borrowed much, which it was written to rival, and of which it became a successful theatrical competitor—we see at what a superficial level of interpretation Greene is content to stop. The element which is most obviously common to both plays is the practice of magic and the theatrical spectacle which this makes possible. In *Faustus*, it is true, some of the spectacles seem to be present for mere entertainment value; but even at that we realize that the omnipresent, overarching issue is the fate of Faustus in moral and spiritual terms. In him we see an intense struggle and overpowering anguish. But in Greene's Friar Bacon there is no struggle at all; his repentance in Scene xiii comes as a surprise, and it is as pat and unreal as if the play were purely didactic. The point is, of course, that Greene is not interested in serious matters but in "good theater," and his recipe for good theater is a larger dose of what has worked before (three magicians instead of one), plus a pinch of nearly everything that has ever worked before (romance, the Fool, blockhead comedy, disguise, unhappy love, a series of deaths, and so on). The result is something very much like musical comedy: having breadth instead of depth, variety instead of concentration, and surprise instead of expectation.

The Spanish Tragedy is historically notable as one of the vehicles by which various elements of Senecan tragedy were naturalized in English drama—a declamatory manner, the revenge theme, the ghost—and as a repository of other devices which Shakespeare was to use later: madness, pretended madness, the tardy avenger, the multitude of violent deaths, the play within a play. The important problem, however, is not Kyd's significance in his own time but the extent to which he rose above his historical role and achieved drama interesting as a thing in itself and not merely as a necessary link in a sequence. When we start viewing him in this light, Kyd is none too rewarding. He is, for instance, often praised for his plot making, and it is true that in contrast with the few tragedies which preceded his work, he has a better-developed action, or at least a complication of events in which a movement is traceable, rather than a mere series of dignified speeches. But if his predecessors were short on plot, Kyd has taken a mad plunge in the opposite direction, and the result is a bewildering complexity of actions and events that are difficult to straighten out, not to mention relating them to a coherent pattern of meaning. *King Lear*, too, has unusual complication of plot, but all the parts have a demonstrable bearing upon the theme of cosmic justice, whereas *The Spanish Tragedy* seems merely an accumulation of spectacular happenings; so that, despite one critic who has said that Kyd's work arouses "horror and excitement," the play is far more likely to arouse confusion and astonishment. Kyd has been praised, too, for his characterization, but here again the sharp reader runs into enough problems to curb his potential enthusiasm. Viluppo's villainy is mechanical, unmotivated. Lorenzo is the conventional Machiavellian villain, virtually an allegorization of hardness and treachery; his essential unconvincingness becomes apparent if we set him beside comparable villains like Iago, Goneril, and Regan, who are at once symbols of evil and solid embodiments of human reality. Bel-imperia, as tragic heroine, has some striking resemblances to the amorous wench of the novella; Kyd thus adds a dash of sex to the recipe. Kyd's most conscientious effort, of course, is with Hieronimo; yet, despite some effective moments, his madness is rather superficially conceived and so does not become, as does Lear's, an ironic form of insight.

The tone of the play is pretty well defined by the conclusion, in which the revengers are presented as heroes destined for eternal joys. The failure to carry moral insight beyond this oversimplified black-and-white view of things is the essential mark of melodrama, and that is what the play is. The habits of melodrama appear also in its language, which at any minute is likely to break out into rant. Yet Kyd's dramatic language is not without possibilities. He uses word play (e.g., the last lines of III, xiii), of which Shakespeare made much, and paradox (the opening lines of III, ii), which is important in much poetic language; at times he makes effective use of imagery (the second speech of II, ii). But he does not have a natural, copious command of metaphor; he has difficulty in maintaining the tone of a long speech (in contrast with those of Marlowe's Dr. Faustus, for instance); his characters lean to exclamations, gloomy aphorism, and the balanced syntax of oratory; from these sources, as well as from the dominance of end-stopped lines and the occasional use of stichomythy (I, iii, 77ff.), springs a rather stiff mechanical style.

In Marlowe's "mighty line," as Jonson called it, we have poetry achieved, and not merely hinted at or bordered on. Yet in one important sense Jonson's term is a misnomer, and if it were not a misnomer, Marlowe's poetry would be less good than it is. For it is not the individual line that is mighty, but the series of lines; in the finest passages, the thought and feeling flow from line to line (the end stop is much less frequent than in Kyd), and the images unite all the parts and subordinate them to the whole. In Scene i, after the departure of the Good and Evil Angels, Faustus' language—the recurrence of the pronoun *I*, the images that set forth the marvels that he will work with magic—gives a brilliant picture of a mind ecstatically rejoicing in irresponsible personal power. In

Scene xiv the images of time, the images of punishment, the antiphony of the words *heaven* and *hell*, and the repetition of *soul* (earlier Faustus denied the reality of hell and the soul) all collaborate in transmitting to us the terrible tension of a man overcome by the horror of his fate and yet unable to take the step—repentance—by which he might alter it. Even an occasional short speech which might be taken for an isolated excellence, a "purple passage," turns out to have poetic alliances with other parts of the play. In the middle of Scene xiii the Old Man says to Faustus,

> I can see an angel hovers o'er thy head,
> And, with a vial full of precious grace,
> Offers to pour the same into thy soul.

The same idea is repeated, in Scene xiv, in a comparable image of help that flows from above. Faustus cries,

> See, see, where Christ's blood streams in the firmament!
> One drop would save my soul, half a drop: ah, my Christ!

Faustus, unable to draw upon the vial of grace or the drop of blood—upon spiritual resources—thinks wildly of a physical mode of escape:

> O soul, be changed into little water drops,
> And fall into the ocean, ne'er be found!

All these passages gain something from their association with each other, and, more than that, they work together in another way: they all—grace that can be poured, blood, water—are ways of combating the vast threat that hangs over Faustus, the threat of hell-fire. This form of punishment has become increasingly real to Faustus in the last two scenes; in fact, the best-known speech in the play—the speech beginning "Was this the face that launched a thousand ships"—contains, at a secondary level, an ironic foreshadowing of Faustus' punishment. Helen is at once beautiful and destructive: she "burnt . . . Ilium"; for her, Wittenberg shall "be sacked"; she is like "flaming Jupiter"—who brought Semele to fiery destruction. These images of fire, which are one of the devices that make the passage a unit and not a mere assemblage of "mighty lines," have ironic echoes very near the end of the play, when Faustus futilely suggests "I'll burn my books" and the Chorus comments, "And burned is Apollo's laurel-bough."

This is one example of the way in which Marlowe's poetry creates powerful symbolic patterns. Another, which we cannot do more than sketch here, first appears in Scene i in the multitude of words which suggest the eternal, the heavenly, the divine. Whether he hopes to have godlike power or seeks knowledge of the celestial regions, Faustus is never able to shake himself free from thoughts of heaven: in tracing this central element in his mind, as it appears directly and indirectly in all the serious scenes in the play, the reader can follow not only his inner struggles but his aspirations and their relation to the fundamental convictions of which, by every exercise of logic, he is unable to shake himself free. The poetry, in other words—the whole body of literal and symbolic language which Marlowe uses—is not only brilliant and moving but is important in the structure of the play. Here is where Marlowe approaches Shakespeare.

To say that the language brilliantly exhibits the conflicts in Faustus is, of course, to hint at what should be quite clear—that in Faustus there is the finest characterization achieved by any of the dramatists represented in this volume. Faustus is presented both consistently and profoundly. Though the interpretation of Faustus is addressed primarily to an age which is still deeply Christian and relies upon an awareness of Christian doctrine, it never in its main plot appeals to stock responses—to the love of flattery or reassurance, or the easy tear, or the terror without real danger. Upon a firm, uncompromising characterization, as revealed directly in the action and both directly and indirectly in the poetic language, Marlowe has based the structure of a plot which traces a rich but unstable mind from dissatisfaction with its normal activities to illicit experiment to personality-shaking doubt to a hardened materialism to a final recognition of error that despite the intensity of its emotional accompaniment falls just short of a saving plea for grace.

There are, of course, structural problems in *Dr. Faustus*, chiefly with regard to the comic scenes. To the present editor these episodes seem less out of place than they do to some critics of the play. The Ralph-Robin scenes are not entirely "comic relief"; rather they show, in a diluted form, how the Faustian corruptions can extend down through all the planes of society. The four scenes in which Faustus is shown using his power suggest the trivial uses to which power is likely to be put and thus in a sense justify the conclusion of the play; they give substance to Faustus' phrase "vain pleasure of twenty-four years." Yet these scenes are not entirely satisfactory; the author does not use them unequivocally enough as a commentary upon Faustus' character but lets them degenerate into farce and romance for their own sake.

In the rather loose chronological organization and in the use of the Good and Evil Angels and the Seven Deadly Sins, Marlowe's play looks back toward the medieval. In its portrayal of the grand quest for knowledge and power, the play is the record of Renaissance personality. But we are interested in it neither because it echoes the Middle Ages nor because it records its own times; its suprahistorical success is that it seizes upon a never-ending human conflict—the conflict between the desire for infinite power and freedom, and the limitations which the human being cannot safely transcend, or, more simply, the conflict between the power-lust and virtue. As Faustus, an intellectualized Everyman endeavoring to be a superman, lives through his experiences and meets his Nemesis, we can see his problem presented in both psychological and moral terms: the play is neither a case history nor a mere allegory. The fact that Marlowe creates his remarkable drama out of the same Christian tradition from which sprang the short plays in the early part of this volume underlines the great increase in artistic resourcefulness from the early mystery plays to the beginning of Shakespeare's career.

ROBERT B. HEILMAN

Seattle, Washington
March, 1951

Bibliographical Note

The amount of historical and critical writing on the drama from the beginnings to Shakespeare is so vast that only a small fraction of it can be mentioned here. The titles cited are representative of more recent criticism.

The authoritative work on earlier drama is Karl Young's *The Drama of the Medieval Church* (Oxford, 1933). One of various articles on the wide circulation of the materials in "The Second Shepherds' Play" is Robert C. Cosbey's "The Mak Story and Its Folklore Analogues," *Speculum*, XX (1945), 310–317. Connections between medieval and Elizabethan drama are traced in Willard Farnham's *The Medieval Heritage of Elizabethan Tragedy* (Berkeley, 1936). General introductions to sixteenth-century drama may be found in F. S. Boas, *An Introduction to Tudor Drama* (Oxford, 1933) and T. M. Parrott and R. H. Ball, *A Short View of Elizabethan Drama* (New York, 1943). Works with more specialized interests, as their titles indicate, are E. K. Chambers, *The Elizabethan Stage* (Oxford, 1923), a monumental four-volume study; Alfred Harbage, *Shakespeare's Audience* (New York, 1941); and G. B. Harrison, *Elizabethan Plays and Players* (1940). The presence of two tragedies in the present collection may arouse interest in such works as M. C. Bradbrook, *Themes and Conventions of Elizabethan Tragedy* (Cambridge, 1935) and F. T. Bowers, *Elizabethan Revenge Tragedy* (Princeton, 1940). There is considerable discussion of Kyd's *Spanish Tragedy* in Howard Baker's *Induction to Tragedy* (Baton Rouge, 1939). The most recent study of Marlowe and his works is Paul Kocher's *Christopher Marlowe* (Chapel Hill, 1940).

Of the writers in this volume, Marlowe has evoked most critical interest in our own day—as from T. S. Eliot, whose "Notes on the Blank Verse of Christopher Marlowe" appeared in *The Sacred Wood*. Later essays are Leo Kirschbaum's "Marlowe's *Faustus:* A Reconsideration," *Review of English Studies*, XIX (1943), 225–241, and Robert B. Heilman's "The Tragedy of Knowledge: Marlowe's Treatment of Faustus," *Quarterly Review of Literature*, II (1946), 316–332—the latter a detailed analysis of the imagery of the play. There is further analysis of *Dr. Faustus* and of *Everyman* in Cleanth Brooks and Robert B. Heilman, *Understanding Drama* (New York, 1948).

For the most recent and compact treatment of the early phases of dramatic development, as well as for ample bibliographies, the reader may consult *A Literary History of England*, edited by Albert C. Baugh (New York and London, 1948). The following chapters deal with the period covered in the present anthology: "The Beginnings of the Drama," pp. 273–287; "The Interlude," pp. 358–366; "Elizabethan Comedy," pp. 446–459; "Elizabethan Tragedy," pp. 460–471; and "Christopher Marlowe," pp. 508–518.

Contents

AN ANTHOLOGY OF ENGLISH DRAMA
BEFORE SHAKESPEARE

THE N. TOWNE BETRAYAL*

JESUS	RUFYNE, *a judge*
PETER	JUDAS
ANGEL	GAMALIEL
LEON, *a judge*	MARY

MARY MAGDALENE

Here Jesus goes toward Bethany, and his disciples following with sad countenance, Jesus saying,

Now my dear friends and brethren each one,
Remember the words that I shall say:
The time is come when I must go
For to fulfill the prophecy.

That is said of me that I shall die,   5
The fiend's power from you to flem[1];
Which death I will not deny,
Man's soul my spouse for to redeem.

The oil of mercy is granted plain
By this journey that I shall take;   10
By my father I am sent certain
Between God and man an end[2] to make.

* C. 1425-1450.
[1] Drive away.   [2] Compact.

I

Man for my brother may I not forsake,
Nor show him unkindness in no way;
In suffering for him my body shall shake,   15
And for love of man shall die.

*Here Jesus and his disciples go toward the Mount of Olivet, and
when he comes a little there beside, in a place like to a park, he bids
his disciples await him there; and says to Peter before he goes,*

Peter, with thy fellows here shalt thou abide
And watch till I come again;
I must make my prayer here you beside;
My flesh quaketh for fear and pain.   20

   PETER. Lord, thy request doth me constrain.
In this place I shall abide still,
Nor remove till thou comest again,
In confirming, Lord, of thy will.

*Here Jesus goes to Olivet and sets himself down on his knees and
prays to his Father, thus saying,*

Oh, father, father, for my sake,   25
This great passion thou take from me
Which is ordained that I shall take
If man's soul saved may be;
And if it behoove, father, for me
To save man's soul that should spill,   30
I am ready in each degree
The will of thee to fulfill.

Here Jesus goes to his disciples and finds them sleeping, Jesus thus saying to Peter,

Peter, Peter, thou sleepest fast;
Awake thy fellows and sleep no more.
Of my death ye are not aghast;   35
Ye take your rest, and I suffer sore.

Here Christ goes again the second time to Olivet and says, kneeling,

Father in heaven, I beseech thee,
Remove my anguish by thy great grace,
And let me from this death flee
As I did never no trespass;   40
The water and blood out of my face
Distills for sufferings that I shall take;
My flesh quaketh in fearful case,
As though the joints asunder would shake.

Here Jesus goes again to his disciples and finds them asleep, Jesus thus saying, letting them lie,

Father, the third time I come again   45
Fully my errand for to speed:
Deliver me, Father, from this pain,
Which is brought back with full great dread.
Unto thy son, Father, take heed;
Thou knowest I never did but good;   50
It is not for me this pain I lead,
But for man I sweat both water and blood.

Here an angel descends to Jesus and brings to him a chalice with a host in it.

ANGEL. Hail, both god and man indeed,
The Father hath sent thee this present;
He bad that thou shouldst not dread,   55
But fulfill his intent;
As the parliament of heaven hath meant
That man's soul shall now redeemed be,
From heaven to earth, Lord, thou were sent:
That death appendeth unto thee.   60

This chalice is thy blood, this bread is thy body,
For man's sin ever offered shall be;
To the Father of heaven that is almighty,
Thy disciples and all priesthood shall offer for thee

Here the angel ascends again suddenly.

JESUS. Father, thy will fulfilled shall be;   65
There is nought to say against the case.
I shall fulfill the prophecy
And suffer death for man's trespass.

Here Christ goes again to his disciples and finds them sleeping still.

Awake, Peter, thy rest is full long;
In sleep thou wilt make no delay.   70
Judas is ready, with people strong,
And does his part, me to betray.
Rise up, sirs, I you pray;
Un-close your eyes for my sake.
We shall walk into the way,   75
And see them come that shall me take.

Peter, when thou seest I am forsaken
Among my friends and stand alone,

All the cheer that thou canst make,
Give to thy brethren every one.   80

*Here Jesus with his disciples goes into the place, and there shall
come in persons well arrayed in white harness and body-armour and
some disguised in other garments, with swords, spears, and other
strange weapons, such as cressets with fire and lanterns and torches
lighted, and Judas foremost of all, conveying them to Jesus by
countenance[1]; Jesus thus saying,*

Sirs, in your way ye have great haste
To seek him that will not flee;
Of you I am right nought aghast.
Tell me, sirs, whom seek ye?

LEON. Whom we seek here, I tell thee now: 85
A traitor is worthy to suffer death.
We know he is here among you;
His name is Jesus of Nazareth.

JESUS. Sirs, I am here that will not flee.
Do to me all that ye can;   90
For sooth I tell you I am he,
Jesus of Nazareth, that same man.

*Here all the Jews fall suddenly to the earth when they hear Christ
speak; and when he bids them rise, they rise again, Christ thus
saying,*

Arise, sirs, whom seek ye? Fast have ye gone.
Is aught your coming hither for me?
I stand before you here each one,   95
That you may me both know and see.

[1] Looks, signs.

RUFYNE. Jesus of Nazareth we seek,
If we might him here espy.

JESUS. I told you now, with words meek,
Before you all, that it was I.   100

JUDAS. Welcome, Jesus, my master dear;
I have thee sought in many a place;
I am full glad I find thee here,
For I knew never where thou was.

*Here Judas kisses Jesus, and immediately all the Jews come about
him and lay hands on him and pull him as if they were mad and
make a great cry over him all at once. And after this, Peter says,*

I draw my sword now this sel[1].   105
Shall I smite, master? Fain would I wit[2].

*And forthwith he smites off Malchus's ear, and Malchus cries,
"Help! My ear, my ear!" And Christ blesses it, and it is whole.*

JESUS. Put thy sword in thy sheath fair and well,
For he that smites with sword, with sword shall be smit.

Ah, Judas! This treason counterfeited[3] hast thou,
And that thou shalt full sore repent;   110
Thou hadst better have been unborn now;
Thy body and soul thou hast shent[4].

GAMALIEL. Lo, Jesus, thou mayst not the case refuse[5]:
Both treason and heresy in thee are found.
Study now fast on thy excuse,   115
While that thou goest in cords bound.

---

[1] Time.   [2] Know.   [3] Accomplished, contrived.   [4] Ruined.
[5] Refute.

Thou callest thee king of this world round;
Now let me see thy great power,
And save thyself here, whole and sound,
And bring thee out of this danger.   120

LEON. Bring forth this traitor, spare him not.
On to Caiaphas the judge we shall thee lead;
In many a place we have thee sought,
And to thy works taken good heed.

RUFYNE. Come on, Jesus, and follow me;   125
I am full glad that I thee have.
Thou shalt be hanged upon a tree;
A million of gold shall thee not save.

LEON. Let me lay hand on him on high;
Unto his death I shall him bring.   130
Show forth thy witchcraft and necromancy!
What helpeth thee now all thy false working?

JESUS. Friends, take heed lest ye do un-right,
So unnaturally with cords to bind me here,
And thus to fall on me by night   135
As though I were a thieves' fere[1].
Many times before you I did appear;
Within the temple seen me ye have
The laws of god to teach and lere[2]
To them that will their souls save.   140

Why did ye not me disprove,
If ye heard me preach, both loud and low?

[1] Companion.   [2] Learn, teach.

But now like madmen ye begin to rave
And do things that ye nothing know.

GAMALIEL. Sirs, I charge you not one word more this night,   145
But unto Caiaphas in haste look ye him lead.
Have him forth with great despite,
And to his words take ye no heed.

Here the Jews lead Christ out of the place with great cry and noise,
some drawing Christ forward and some backward, and so leading
forth with their weapons aloft and lights burning. And in the mean-
time Mary Magdalene shall run to our Lady and tell her of our
Lord's taking, thus saying,

Oh, immaculate mother, of all women most meek!
Oh, devoutest, in holy meditation ever abiding!   150
The cause, Lady, that I to your person seek,
Is to know if ye hear any tidings

Of your sweet son and my reverent Lord Jesus,
That was your daily solace, your ghostly[1] consolation.
MARY. I would ye should tell me, Magdalene, if ye knew;   155
For to hear of him, it is all my affection.

MARY MAGDALENE. I would fain tell if I could for weeping,
For sooth, Lady, to the Jews he is sold;
With cords they have him bound and have him in keeping:
They beat him spitefully and have him fast in hold.   160

MARY. Ah! Ah! Ah! How my heart is cold!
Ah! Heart hard as stone, how mayst thou list,

[1] Spiritual.

When these sorrowful tidings are thee told?
So would to God, heart, that thou mightest burst.

Ah, Jesu! Jesu! Jesu! Jesu!   165
Why should ye suffer this tribulation and adversity?
How may they find in their hearts thee to pursue,
That never trespassed in no manner degree?
For never a thing but was good thought ye;
Wherefore, then, should ye suffer this great pain?   170
I suppose verily it is for the trespass of me,
And I knew that my heart should cleave in twain.

For these languors[1] may I sustain,
The sword of sorrow hath so pierced my mind.
Alas, what may I do? Alas, what may I say?   175
These prongs my heart asunder they do rend.

Oh, Father of heaven, where are all thy behests
That thou promised me when a mother thou me made?
Thy blessed son I bore between two beasts,
And now the bright color of his face doth fade.   180

Ah, good Father, why wouldst that thine own dear son shall
    suffer all this?
And acted he never against thy precept but ever was obedient;
And to every creature most pitiful, most gentle, and benign
    iwis[2];
And now for all these kindnesses is now most shamefully shent[3].

Why wilt thou, gracious Father, that it shall be so?   185
May man not else be saved by no other kende[4]?

[1] Sufferings.   [2] Certainly.   [3] Injured.   [4] Creature.

Yet, Lord Father, then that shall comfort my woe,
When man is saved by my child and brought to a good end.

Now, dear son, since thou hast ever been so full of mercy,
That wilt not spare thyself for the love thou hast to men, 190
On all mankind now have thou pity,
And also think on thy mother, that heavy[1] woman.

[1] Sad.

THE YORK CRUCIFIXION*

℣

JESUS   FOUR SOLDIERS

FIRST SOLDIER. Sir knights, take heed hither on high,
This death, untroubled we may not draw[1];
Ye know yourselves as well as I
How lords and leaders of our law
Have given doom that this dotard shall die.   5
SECOND SOLDIER. Sir, all their counsel well we know;
Since we are come to Calvary,
Let each man help now as he ought.
THIRD SOLDIER. We are all ready, lo,
That order to fulfill.   10
FOURTH SOLDIER. Let hear how we shall do,
And go we quick thereto.

FIRST SOLDIER. It may not help here to hone[2],
If we shall any worship win.
SECOND SOLDIER. He must be dead, need be by noon.   15
THIRD SOLDIER. Then it's good time that we begin.
FOURTH SOLDIER. Let strike him down, then he is done;
He shall not damage us with his din.
FIRST SOLDIER. He shall be set and learned[3] soon,
With grief to him and all his kin.   20
SECOND SOLDIER. The foulest death of all
Shall he die for his deeds.
THIRD SOLDIER. That means cross him we shall.
FOURTH SOLDIER. Behold, so right he redes[4].   24

* C. 1375.   [1] Carry out.   [2] Delay.   [3] Placed and taught.
[4] Counsels.

11

FIRST SOLDIER. Then to this work we must take heed,
So that our working be not wrong.

SECOND SOLDIER. No other thing to name is need,
But let us haste him for to hang.

THIRD SOLDIER. And I have gone for gear[1], good speed,
Both hammers and nails large and long.   30

FOURTH SOLDIER. Then may we boldly do this deed;
Come on, let kill this traitor strange.

FIRST SOLDIER. Fair might ye fall in fere[2],
That has wrought in this wise.

SECOND SOLDIER. Us needs naught for to learn,   35
Such cheaters to chastise.

THIRD SOLDIER. Since every thing is right arrayed,
The wiselier now work may we.

FOURTH SOLDIER. The cross on ground is goodly graied[3],
And bored even as it ought to be.   40

FIRST SOLDIER. Look this lad at length be laid
And put for me then upon this tree.

SECOND SOLDIER. For all his acts shall he be flaied[4];
That one assay soon shall ye see.

THIRD SOLDIER. Come forth, thou cursed knave!   45
Thy comfort soon shall cool.

FOURTH SOLDIER. Thy pay here shall thou have.

FIRST SOLDIER. Walk on, now work we well.

JESUS. Almighty God, my Father free,
Let these matters be kept in mind;   50
Thou bad that I should obedient be,
For Adam's guilt for to be pined[5].
Here to death I oblige me

---

[1] Materials.   [2] Company.   [3] Prepared.
[4] Frightened.   [5] Tortured.

From that sin for to save mankind;
And sovereignly beseech I thee,   55
That they for me[1] may favor find;
And from the fiend them fend,
So that their souls be safe
In wellbeing without end;
I keep naught else to crave.   60

FIRST SOLDIER. We! Hark, sir knights, for Mahomet's blood!
Of Adam-kind is all his thought!
SECOND SOLDIER. The wizard waxes worse than mad;
This doleful death dreads he naught.
THIRD SOLDIER. Thou should have mind, with might and
   mood[2],   65
Of wicked works that thou hast wrought.
FOURTH SOLDIER. I think he might have been as good,
Have stopped from sayings that he up brought.
FIRST SOLDIER. Those sayings shall he rue sore,
For all his sauntering, soon.   70
SECOND SOLDIER. Ill speed them that him spare
Till he to death be done!

THIRD SOLDIER. Have done quickly, boy, and make thee
   boune[3],
And bend thy back unto this tree.
FOURTH SOLDIER. Behold, himself has laid him down, 75
Spread out aright as he should be.
FIRST SOLDIER. This traitor here, tainted with treason,
Go fast and fetter him then, ye three.
And since he claimeth kingdom with crown,
Even as a king here shall he be.   80

[1] For my sake.   [2] Thought.   [3] Ready.

SECOND SOLDIER. Now certes I shall not finish
Ere his right hand be fast.

THIRD SOLDIER. The left hand then is mine;
Let see who bears himself best.

FOURTH SOLDIER. His limbs at length than shall I lead,   85
And even unto the bore them bring.

FIRST SOLDIER. Unto his head I shall take heed,
And with my hand help him to hang.

SECOND SOLDIER. Now since we four shall do this deed,
And meddle with this unthriving thing,   90
Let no man spare in special speed
Till that we have made ending.

THIRD SOLDIER. This action may not fail.
Now we are right arrayed.

FOURTH SOLDIER. This boy here in our bale[1]   95
Shall bide full bitter brayde[2].

FIRST SOLDIER. Sir knights, say, how work we now?
SECOND SOLDIER. Yes, certes, I hope I hold this hand.
THIRD SOLDIER. And to the bore I have it brought,
Full obediently, without band.   100

FOURTH SOLDIER. Strike on then hard, for Him who thee
bought[3].

FIRST SOLDIER. Yes, here is a stub that will stiffly stand;
Through bones and sinews it shall be sought[4].
This work is well, I will warrant.

SECOND SOLDIER. Say, sir, how do we there?   105
This bargain may not blynne[5].

---

[1] Sorrow, evil, torment.   [2] Start, quick action.   [3] Redeemed (such
anachronisms are frequent).   [4] Sent, struck; cf. *socked.*
[5] This work must not stop.

THIRD SOLDIER. It fails a foot and more,
The sinews are so gone in[1].

FOURTH SOLDIER. I think that mark amiss be bored.
SECOND SOLDIER. Then must he wait in bitter bale, 110
THIRD SOLDIER. In faith, it was too scantily scored;
That makes it foully for to fail.
FIRST SOLDIER. Why chatter ye so? Fasten on a cord,
And tug him to, by top and tail. 114
THIRD SOLDIER. Yea, thou commands lightly as a lord;
Come help to haul, with ill hail[2]!
FIRST SOLDIER. Now certes that shall I do,
Full surely, as a snail.
THIRD SOLDIER. And I shall tack him to,
Full nimbly with a nail. 120

This work will hold, that dare I hete[3],
For now are bound fast both his hands.
FOURTH SOLDIER. Go we all four, then, to his feet;
So shall our time be speedily[4] spent. 124
SECOND SOLDIER. Let see, what joke his bale might bete[5];
Thereto my back now would I bend.
FOURTH SOLDIER. Oh! This work is all unmeet;
This boring must be all amended.
FIRST SOLDIER. Ah! Peace, man, for Mahomet!
Let no man wot that wonder[6] 130
A rope shall rig him down,
If all his sinews go asunder.

[1] Christ's body has shrunken and does not fit the cross. [2] Exclamation.
[3] Promise. [4] Profitably. [5] Assuage. [6] Concede that the boring must be done over (?).

SECOND SOLDIER. That cord full kindly[1] can I knit,
The comfort of this carl[2] to cool.   134

FIRST SOLDIER. Fasten on then firm that all be fit;
It is no matter how foul he feel.

SECOND SOLDIER. Lug on, ye both, a little yet.

THIRD SOLDIER. I shall not cease, as I have seele[3].

FOURTH SOLDIER. And I shall try him for to hit[4].

SECOND SOLDIER. Oh, halç!

FOURTH SOLDIER.   Ho, now, I haled it well.   140

FIRST SOLDIER. Have done, drive in that nail,
So that no fault be found.

FOURTH SOLDIER. This working would not fail,
If four bulls here were bound.   144

FIRST SOLDIER. These cords have evilly increased his pains,
Ere he were to the borings brought.

SECOND SOLDIER. Yea, asunder are both sinews and veins,
On each side, as have we sought.

THIRD SOLDIER. Now all his tricks nothing him gains;
His sauntering shall with bale be bought[5].   150

FOURTH SOLDIER. I will go say to our sovereigns,
Of all these works how have we wrought.

FIRST SOLDIER. Nay, sirs, another thing
Falls first to you and me:
I say we should him hang   155
On high that men may see.

SECOND SOLDIER. We know well that so their words were;
But, sir, that deed will do us dere[6].

FIRST SOLDIER. It may not mend to argue more;
This harlot[7] must be hanged here.   160

---

[1] Naturally.   [2] Fellow.   [3] Bliss.   [4] Possibly "hit it," i. e., the hole.
[5] Paid for.   [6] Cause us trouble.   [7] Rascal.

SECOND SOLDIER. The mortise is made fit therefore.

THIRD SOLDIER. Fasten on your fingers, then, in fere[1].

FOURTH SOLDIER. I think it will never come there;
We four raise it not right, this year.

FIRST SOLDIER. Say, man, why chatter you so? 165
Thy lifting was but light.

SECOND SOLDIER. He means there must be more,
To heave him to that height.

THIRD SOLDIER. Now certes, I hope it shall not need
To call to us more company; 170
Methinks we four should do this deed
And bear him to yon hill on high.

FIRST SOLDIER. It must be done, without dread[2];
No more, but look ye be ready;
And this part shall I lift and lead; 175
At length he shall no longer lie.
Therefore now make you boune[3];
Let bear him to that hill.

FOURTH SOLDIER. Then will I bend here down,
And attend his toes unto. 180

SECOND SOLDIER. We two shall see to other side,
Or else this work will go all wrong.

THIRD SOLDIER. We are ready. In God, sirs, abide;
And let me first his feet up bring.

SECOND SOLDIER. Why tend ye so to talk this tide? 185

FIRST SOLDIER. Lift up!

FOURTH SOLDIER. Let see!

SECOND SOLDIER. Oh! Lift along!

THIRD SOLDIER. From all this harm, he should him hide,

---

[1] Together. [2] Doubt. [3] Ready.

If he were God.

FOURTH SOLDIER. The devil him hang!

FIRST SOLDIER. For great harm have I hente[1];
My shoulder is asunder.   190

SECOND SOLDIER. And certes I am near schente[2],
So long have I borne under.

THIRD SOLDIER. This cross and I in two must twin[3];
Else breaks my back in sunder soon.   194

FOURTH SOLDIER. Lay it down again and leave off your din;
This deed for us will never be done.

FIRST SOLDIER. Try, sirs, let see if any gin[4],
May help him up, without hone[5];
For here should manly men praise win,
And not with trifles all day to go.   200

SECOND SOLDIER. More manlier men than we,
Full few I hope ye find.

THIRD SOLDIER. This bargain will not be,
For certes I want wind.   204

FOURTH SOLDIER. So wandering in work never we were;
I think this carl some cautels cast[6].

SECOND SOLDIER. My burden sat on me wondrous sore;
Unto the hill I might not last.

FIRST SOLDIER. Lift up, and soon he shall be there;
So fasten on your fingers fast.   210

THIRD SOLDIER. Oh, lift!

FIRST SOLDIER.   We, lo!

FOURTH SOLDIER.   A little more!

SECOND SOLDIER. Hold then!

FIRST SOLDIER.   How now!

[1] Got.   [2] Ruined.   [3] Part.   [4] Device.   [5] Delay.   [6] Played some tricks.

SECOND SOLDIER.   The worst is past!

THIRD SOLDIER. He weighs a wicked weight.

SECOND SOLDIER. So may we all four say,
Ere he was heaved on high,   215
And raised in this array.

FOURTH SOLDIER. He made us stand as any stones[1],
So big was he for to bear.

FIRST SOLDIER. Now raise him nimbly for the nonce,
And set him in this mortise here,   220
And let him fall in all at once,
For certes that pain shall have no peer.

THIRD SOLDIER. Heave up!

FOURTH SOLDIER.   Let down, so all his bones
Are asunder now on sides sere[2].

FIRST SOLDIER. This falling was more cruel   225
Than all the hurts he had;
Now may a man well tell
The least lith[3] of this lad.

THIRD SOLDIER. Methinks this cross will not abide,
Nor stand still in the mortise yet.   230

FOURTH SOLDIER. At the first time was it made over wide;
That makes it waver, thou may well wit.

FIRST SOLDIER. It shall be steadied on each side,
So that it shall no further flit;
Good wedges shall we take this tide,   235
And fasten the foot; then all is fit.

SECOND SOLDIER. Here are wedges arrayed
For that, both large and small.

---

[1] Brought our work to a standstill.   [2] Many.   [3] Limb (cf. "Count all his ribs").

THIRD SOLDIER. Where are our hammers laid
That we should work with, all?   240

FOURTH SOLDIER. We have them here, right at hand.
SECOND SOLDIER. Give me this wedge, I shall it drive.
FOURTH SOLDIER. Here is another yet ordained.
THIRD SOLDIER. Do fasten it for me here belive[1].
FIRST SOLDIER. Lay on then firmly.
THIRD SOLDIER.   Yes, I warrant.
I thrust them together, so may I thrive.   246
Now will this cross full stably stand;
Although he rave, it will not rive.
    FIRST SOLDIER. Say, sir, how like you now
The work that we have wrought?   250
    FOURTH SOLDIER. We pray you, tell us how
Ye feel, or faint ye aught[2]?

    JESUS. All men that walk by way or street,
Take heed ye shall no trouble tine[3];
Behold my head, my hands, my feet,   255
And fully feel now ere ye fine[4],
If any mourning may be meet,
Or mischief measured unto mine.
My Father, that all bales may bete[5],
Forgive these men that cause me pain.   260
What they work, know they not;
Therefore, my Father, I crave
Let never their sins be sought,
But look their souls to save.

    FIRST SOLDIER. We! Hark! He jangles like a jay.   265
    SECOND SOLDIER. Methinks he patters like a magpie.

---

[1] Quickly.   [2] Or, "Before ye faint at all."   [3] Lose.   [4] End.   [5] Allav.

THIRD SOLDIER. He has been doing[1] all this day,
And made great moving of mercy.
FOURTH SOLDIER. Is this the same that did us say
That he was God's son almighty?   270
FIRST SOLDIER. Therefore he feels full fierce affray[2],
And deemed this day to die.
SECOND SOLDIER. Vah! qui destruis templum[3].
THIRD SOLDIER. His sayings were so, certainly.
FOURTH SOLDIER. And sirs, he said to some,   275
He might raise it again.

FIRST SOLDIER. To muster[4] that, he had no might,
For all the cautels that he could cast[5];
Although he were in word so wight[6],
For all his force, now he is fast.   280
As Pilate judged is done and dight[7];
Therefore I say that we go rest.
SECOND SOLDIER. This course[8] must be rehearsed right,
Through the world both east and west.
THIRD SOLDIER. Yea, let him hang here still,   285
And make mouths at the moon.
FOURTH SOLDIER. Then may we wend at will.
FIRST SOLDIER. Nay, good sirs, not so soon,

For certes us needs another note[9]:
This kirtle would I of you crave.   290
SECOND SOLDIER. Nay, nay, sir, we will look by lot
Which of us four it falls to, to have.
THIRD SOLDIER. I say we draw cut for this coat.
Lo, see how now all sides to save.

---

[1] In this situation, enduring (?).   [2] Terror.   [3] See Matthew 27: 40.
[4] Show.   [5] Tricks that he might play.   [6] Strong.   [7] Disposed.
[8] Of events.   [9] Affair, task

FOURTH SOLDIER. The short cut shall win, well ye know't,
Whether it fall to knight or knave.   296
FIRST SOLDIER. Fellows, it needs ye not flyte[1],
For this mantle is mine.
SECOND SOLDIER. Go we then hence tyte[2],
This travail here we tyne[3].   300

---

[1] Scold.   [2] Quickly.   [3] Lose

THE WAKEFIELD NOAH*

❧

NOAH	SECOND SON
GOD	THIRD SON
NOAH'S WIFE	FIRST WIFE
FIRST SON	SECOND WIFE
THIRD WIFE	

NOAH. Mightful God veray[1], Maker of all that is,
Three persons withouten nay, one God in endless bliss,
Thou made both night and day, beast, fowl, and fish,
All creatures that live may, wrought thou at thy wish,
      As thou well might;   5
The sun, the moon, verament[2],
Thou made; the firmament,
The stars also, full fervent,
      To shine thou made full bright.

Angels thou made full even, all orders that is,   10
To have the bliss in heaven. This did thou, more and less,
Full marvelous to neven[3]; yet was there unkindness,
More by folds seven than I can well express.
      For why?
Of all angels in brightness   15
God gave Lucifer most lightness;
Yet proudly he fled his dais,
      And set him even Him by.

He thought himself as worthy as Him that him made;
In brightness, in beauty, therefore He him degraded,   20

* C. 1425-1450.
[1] True.   [2] Truly.   [3] Tell.

23

Put him in a low degree soon after, in a brade[1],
Him and all his company, where he may be unglad
      Forever.
Shall they never win away,
Hence unto Doomsday,   25
But burn in hell for ay;
      Shall they never dissever.

Soon after, that gracious Lord to his likeness made man,
That place to be restored, even as he began,
Of the Trinity by accord, Adam and Eve, that woman. 30
To multiply without discord, in paradise put he them;
      And afterwards to both
Gave in commandment,
On the tree of life to lay no hand;
But yet the false fiend   35
      Made Him with man wroth,

Enticed man to gluttony, stirred him to sin in pride.
But in paradise securely might no sin abide,
And therefore man full hastily was put out in that tide,
In woe and wretchedness to be, pains full unrid[2]   40
      To know,
First on earth, and then in hell
With fiends to dwell.
Unless he his mercy mell[3]
      For those that will him trow.   45

Oil of mercy he us hight[4], as I have heard said,
To every living wight that would love him and dread;
But now before his sight every living leyde[5]

---

[1] Minute.   [2] Cruel.   [3] Mingle.   [4] Promised.   [5] Person.

Most part day and night, sin in word and deed
      Full bold; 50
Some in pride, ire, and envy,
Some in covetousness and gluttony,
Some in sloth and lechery,
      And otherwise many-fold. 54

Therefore I dread lest God on us will take vengeance,
For sin is now requited without any repentance.
Six hundred years and odd have I, without distance[1],
On earth, as any sod, lived with great grievance
      Alway.
And now I grow old, 60
Sick, sorry, and cold;
As muck upon mould,
      I wither away.

But yet will I cry for mercy and call;
Noah thy servant am I, Lord over all! 65
Therefore me and my fry, who shall with me fall,
Save from villainy and bring to thy hall
      In heaven;
And keep me from sin,
This world within; 70
Comely King of mankind,
      I pray Thee, hear my steven[2].

  GOD. Since I have made everything that is living,
Duke, emperor, and king, with my own hand,
For to have their liking by sea and by sand, 75
Every man to my bidding should be bowing
      Full fervent.

---

[1] Dispute.   [2] Voice.

That made man such a creature,
Fairest of favor,
Man must love me par-amour,   80
    By reason, and repent.

Methought I showed man love when I made him to be
All angels above, like to the Trinity;
And now in great reproof full low lies he
On earth, himself to stuff with sin that displeases me   85
    Most of all;
Vengeance will I take
On earth for sin's sake;
My anger thus will I wake
    Against great and small.   90

I repent full sore that ever made I man;
By me he sets no store, and I am his sovereign.
I will destroy, therefore, both beast, man, and woman;
All shall perish, less and more; that bargain may they ban[1],
    That ill has done.   95
On earth I see right nought
But sin that is unsought[2];
Of those that well has wrought
    Find I but a few.

Therefore shall I destroy all this middle-earth   100
With floods that shall flow and run with hideous rerd[3];
I have good cause thereto: for me no man is afeared.
As I say, shall I do—of vengeance draw my sword,
    And make end
Of all that bears life   105
Save Noah and his wife,

---

[1] Regret.   [2] Unexpiated.   [3] Noise.

For they would never strive
    With me nor me offend.

To him in great win[1] hastily will I go,   109
To Noah my servant, ere I blin[2], to warn him of his woe.
On earth I see but sin running to and fro
Among both more and min[3], each one other's foe,
    With all their intent.
All shall I fordo[4]
With floods that shall flow;   115
Work shall I them woe
    That will not repent.

Noah, my friend, I thee command, from cares thee to cool,
A ship to be making of nail and board full well.
Thou was always well working, to me true as steel,   120
To my bidding obedient; friendship shall thou feel
    In reward.
In length thy ship be
Three hundred cubits, warn I thee,
In height even thirty,   125
    Of fifty also in breadth.

Anoint thy ship with pitch and tar without and also within;
The water out to spar[5], this is a noble gin[6].
Look no man thee mar. Three chess[7] chambers begin;
Thou must spend many a spar, this work ere thou win 130
    To end fully.
Make in thy ship also
Parlors one or two,
And houses of office more
    For beasts that there must be.   135

[1] Joy.   [2] Stop.   [3] Less.   [4] Destroy.   [5] Keep.   [6] Device.   [7] Tiers of.

One cubit in height a window shalt thou make;
On the side a door with sleight[1] beneath shall thou take.
With thee shall no man fight, nor do thee no kind wrake[2].
When all is done thus right, thy wife, that is thy make[3],
      Take in to thee;   140
Thy sons of good fame,
Shem, Japhet, and Ham,
Take in also them,
      Their wives also three.

For all shall be fordone that live in land but ye,   145
With floods that from above shall fall, and that plenty;
It shall begin full soon to rain incessantly,
After days seven be done, and endure days forty
      Without fail.
Take to thy ship also   150
Of each kind, beasts two,
Male and female, but no more,
      Ere thou pull up thy sail.

For they may thee avail when all this thing is wrought.
Stuff thy ship with victual, for hunger that ye perish not;
Of beasts, fowl, and cattle, for them have thee in thought;
For them is my counsel, that some succor be sought
      In haste;
They must have corn and hay,
And other meat alway.   160
Do now as I thee say,
      In the name of the Holy Ghost.

[1] Skill.   [2] Kind of injury.   [3] Mate.

NOAH. Ah! Benedicite! What art thou that thus
Tells before what shall be? Thou art full marvelous!
Tell me, for charity, thy name so gracious. 165
   GOD. My name is of dignity and also full glorious
      To know.
I am God most mighty,
One God in Trinity,
Made thee and each man to be; 170
      To love me well thou owe.

   NOAH. I thank thee, Lord so dear, that would vouchsafe
Thus low to appear to a simple knave;
Bless us, Lord, here; for charity I it crave,
The better may we steer the ship that we shall have, 175
      Certain.
   GOD. Noah, to thee and to thy fry
My blessing grant I;
Ye shall wax and multiply
      And fill the earth again, 180

When all these floods are past and fully gone away.
   NOAH. Lord, homeward will I haste as fast as I may;
My wife will I ask what she will say, [*Exit God*]
And I am aghast that we get some fray
      Betwixt us both; 185
For she is full testy,
For little oft angry;
If anything wrong be,
      Soon is she wroth.

     Then he goes to his wife.

God speed, dear wife, how fare ye? 190
   WIFE. Now, as ever might I thrive, the worse I thee see.

Do tell me belive[1], where hast thou thus long be?
To death may we drive, or life for thee[2],
  For want.
When we sweat or swink[3],   195
Thou does what thou think;
Yet of meat and of drink,
  Have we very scant.

NOAH. Wife, we are hard stead with tidings new. 199
 WIFE. But thou were worthy be clad in Stafford blue[4].
For thou art always adread, be it false or true;
But God knows I am led, and that may I rue
  Full ill;
For I dare be thy borrow[5],
From even unto morrow   205
Thou speaks ever of sorrow.
  God send thee once thy fill!

We women may wary[6] all ill husbands.
I have one, by Mary! that loosed me of my bands;
If he is troubled I must tarry, howsoever it stands, 210
With semblance full sorry, wringing both my hands
  For dread.
But yet other while,
What with game and with guile,
I shall smite and smile,   215
  And quit him his meed[7].

NOAH. We! Hold thy tongue, ram-skit, or I shall thee still!
WIFE. By my thrift, if thou smite, I shall turn thee until!

---

[1] Speedily. [2] As far as you are concerned. [3] Labor. [4] Be beaten blue. [5] Pledge. [6] Curse. [7] Pay him his due.

NOAH. We shall assay it tight! Have at thee, Gill!   219
Upon the bone it shall bite!
>WIFE.   Ah, so! Marry, thou smites ill!
>>But I suppose
I shall not in thy debt
Flit from this flet[1]!
Take thee there a languet[2]
>>To tie up thy hose!   225

NOAH. Ah! Wilt thou so? Marry, that is mine.
WIFE. Thou shall have three for two, I swear by God's pain.
NOAH. And I shall repay thee them, in faith, ere syne[3].
WIFE. Out upon thee, ho!
>NOAH.   Thou can both bite and whine
>>With a rerd[4].   230
For all if she strike,
Yet fast will she shriek;
In faith I know none like
>>In all middle-earth.

But I will keep charity, for I have work to do.   235
>WIFE. Here shall no man tarry thee; I pray thee, go to.
Full well may we miss thee, as ever have I ro[5].
To spin will I dress me.
>NOAH.   We! Farewell, lo!
>>But wife,
Pray for me busily,   240
Till again I come unto thee.
>WIFE. Even as thou prays for me,
>>As ever might I thrive.

---

[1] Floor.   [2] Thong.   [3] Long.   [4] Noise.   [5] Peace.

NOAH. I tarry full long from my work, I trow;
Now my gear will I fong[1] and thitherward draw.   245
I may full ill go, the truth for to know;
Unless God help among, I may sit down daw[2]
          To ken;
Now assay will I
How I can of wrightry,   250
In nomine patris et filii,
          Et spiritus sancti, Amen.

To begin of this tree, my bones will I bend;
I trow from the Trinity succor will be sent.   254
It fares full fair, it seems me, this work to my hand;
Now blessed be he that this can amend.
          Lo, here the length,
Three hundred cubits evenly;
In breadth, lo, it is fifty;
The height is even thirty   260
          Cubits full straight.

Now my gown will I cast, and work in my coat;
Make will I the mast, ere I flit one foot.
Ah! My back, I trow, will burst! This is a sorry note!
It is a wonder that I last, such an old dote,   265
          All dulled
To begin such a work!
My bones are so stark[3],
No wonder if they wark[4],
          For I am full old.   270

The top and the sail both will I make,
The helm and the castle also will I take;

---

[1] Take.   [2] Stupid.   [3] Stiff.   [4] Ache.

To drive each single nail will I not forsake;
This gear may never fail, that dare I undertake
>   At once.   275
This is a noble gin,
These nails so they run
Through more and min,
>   These boards each one.

Window and door even as he said,   380
Three chess chambers, they are well made;
Pitch and tar full sure thereupon laid.
This will ever endure; therefore I am paid.
>   For why?
It is better wrought   285
Than I could have thought.
Him that made all of nought,
>   I thank only.

Now will I hie me and nothing be lither[1];
My wife and my family to bring even hither,   290
Attend hither tidily, wife, and consider,
Hence must us flee, all of us together,
>   In haste.
>   WIFE. Why, sir, what ails you?
Who is it that assails you?   295
To flee it avails you,
>   If ye be aghast.

>   NOAH. There is yarn on the reel other, my dame.
>   WIFE. Tell me that every deal, else get ye blame.
>   NOAH. He that cares may keel[2], blessed be his name!   300

---

[1] Slow.   [2] Cool, allay.

He has spoken for our sele[1], to shield us from shame,
    And said,
All this world about,
With floods so stout,
That shall run in a rout,   305
    Shall be overlaid.

He said all shall be slain but only we,
Our sons that obey and their wives three;
A ship he bade me ordain, to save us and our fee[2];
Therefore, with all our main, thank we that free   310
    Healer of sorrow.
Hie us fast, go we thither.
    WIFE. I know never whither,
I daze and I dither,
    For fear of that story.   315

NOAH. Be not afraid, have done. Get together our gear
That we be there ere noon without more dere[3].
    FIRST SON. It shall be done full soon. Brethren, help to bear.
    SECOND SON. Full long shall I not delay, to do my devoir,
        Brother Shem.   320
    THIRD SON. Without any yelp,
With my might shall I help.
    WIFE. Yet for fear of a skelp[4],
        Help well thy dam.

NOAH. Now are we there as we should be;   325
Do get in our gear, our cattle and fee,
Into this vessel here, my children free.
    WIFE. I was never shut ere, as ever might I thee[5],

---

[1] Happiness.   [2] Property.   [3] Hindrance.   [4] Blow.   [5] Thrive.

In such an hostel as this.
In faith I cannot find   330
Which is before, which is behind;
But shall we here be penned,
     Noah, as have thou bliss?

NOAH. Dame, as it is skill[1], here must us abide grace;
Therefore, wife, with good will come into this place.   335
WIFE. Sir, for Jack nor for Gill will I turn my face
Till I have on this hill spun a space
     On my rock[2].
Well were he might get me;
Now will I down set me;   340
Yet counsel I no man let me,
     For dread of a knock.

NOAH. Behold to the heaven the cataracts all
That are open full even, great and small,
And the planets seven left has their stall;   345
These thunders and lightning down make fall
     Full stout
Both halls and bowers,
Castles and towers;
Full sharp are these showers,   350
     That runs about.

Therefore, wife, have done; come into ship fast.
WIFE. Yea, Noah, go patch thy shoes, the better will they last.
FIRST WIFE. Good Mother, come in soon, for all is overcast,
Both the sun and the moon.
SECOND WIFE.   And many winds blast   355
     Full sharp;

[1] Reason.   [2] Distaff.

These floods so they run,
Therefore, Mother, come in.
   WIFE. In faith, yet will I spin;
       All in vain ye carp.   360

   THIRD WIFE. If ye like ye may spin, Mother, in the ship.
   NOAH. Now is this twice. Come in, dame, on my friendship.
   WIFE. Whether I lose or win, in faith, this fellowship
Set I not at a pin. This spindle will I slip
       Upon this hill   365
Ere I stir one foot.
   NOAH. Peter! I trow we dote.
Without any more note
       Come in if ye will.

   WIFE. Yea, water nighs so near that I sit not dry;   370
Into ship with a rush therefore will I hie
For dread that I drown here.
   NOAH.   Dame, securely,
It bes bought full dear, ye abode so long by,
       Out of ship.
   WIFE. I will not, for thy bidding,   375
Go from door to midden[1].
   NOAH. In faith, for your long tarrying,
       You shall lick on the whip.

   WIFE. Spare me not, I pray thee, but even as thou think,
These great words shall not flay me.
   NOAH.   Abide, dame, and drink,
For beaten shall thou be, with this staff till thou stink.   381
Are the strokes good? Say me.
   WIFE.   What say ye, Wat Wink?

---

[1] Dunghill; i. e., do anything you want.

NOAH. Speak!
Cry me mercy, I say!
    WIFE. Thereto say I nay.   385
    NOAH. Unless thou do, by this day,
        Thy head shall I break.

To audience.

    WIFE. Lord, I were at ease and heartily full whole
Might I once have a mess of widow's cole[1];   389
For thy soul, without lies, should I deal penny dole[2];
So would more, no fear, that I see on this sole[3]
        Of wives that are here;
For the life that they lead,
Would their husbands were dead,
For as ever eat I bread,   395
        So would I our sire were.

    NOAH. Ye men that has wives whiles they are young,
If ye love your lives, chastise their tongue;
Methinks my heart rives, both liver and lung,
To see such strifes, wedmen among;   400
        But I
As have I bliss,
Shall chastise this.
    WIFE. Yet may ye miss,
        Nicholl Needy!   405

    NOAH. Now I shall make thee still as stone, beginner of
    blunder!
I shall beat thee back and bone and break all in sonder.
    WIFE. Out, alas, I am gone! Out upon thee, man's wonder!

[1] Fare.   [2] Alms.   [3] Place.

NOAH. See how she can groan, and I lie under!
  But, wife,   410
In this haste let us ho[1],
For my back is near in two.
 WIFE. And I am beat so blue
  That I may not thrive.

Enter Ark.

FIRST SON. Ah! Why fare ye thus? Father and mother both!
SECOND SON. You should not be so spiteful, standing in such a
 woth[2].   416
THIRD SON. These are so hideous, with many a cold coth[3].
NOAH. We will do as ye bid us, we will no more be wroth,
  Dear bairns!
Now to the helm will I bend,   420
And to my ship attend.
 WIFE. I see on the firmament,
  Methinks, the seven stars.

NOAH. This is a great flood. Wife, take heed. 424
 WIFE. So methought, as I stood. We are in great dread,
These waves are so wild.
 NOAH.   Help, God, in this need!
As thou art steersman good, and best, as I rede,
  Of all.
Thou rule us in this race,
As thou me promised has.   430
 WIFE. This is a perilous case;
  Help, God, when we call!

NOAH. Wife, take the steer-tree, and I shall assay
The deepness of the sea that we bear, if I may. 434

[1] Stop. [2] Danger. [3] Disease.

WIFE. That shall I do full wisely; now go thy way,
For upon this flood have we floated many a day,
      With pain.
  NOAH. Now the water will I sound.
Ah! It is far to the ground;
This travail, I expound[1],   440
      I had in vain.

Above all hills bedeyn[2] the flood is risen late
Cubits fifteen; but in a higher state
It may not be, I ween; for this well I wit,   444
This forty days has rain been; it will therefore abate
      Full lele[3].
This water in haste,
Eft will I test;
Now am I aghast,
      It has waned a great deal.   450

Now are the weathers ceased and cataracts quit,
Both the most and the least.
  WIFE.   Methinks, by my wit,
The sun shines in the east. Lo, is not yond it?
We should have a good feast were these floods flit
      So malicious.   455
  NOAH. We have been here, all we,
Three hundred days and fifty.
  WIFE. Yea, now wanes the sea.
      Lord, well is us!   459

  NOAH. The third time will I prove what deepness we bear.
  WIFE. How long shall thou heave? Lay in thy line there.

---

[1] Realize.   [2] Completely; at once.   [3] Loyally.

NOAH. I touch with my sleeve the ground even here.
WIFE. Then begins to grow to us merry cheer.
　　But, husband,
What ground may this be?　　　　　　　　　465
NOAH. The hills of Armenia.
WIFE. Now blessed be he
　　That thus for us can ordain!

NOAH. I see tops of hills high, many at a sight,
Nothing to hinder me, the weather is so bright.　　470
WIFE. These are of mercy, tokens full bright.
NOAH. Dame, thou counsel me what fowl best might
　　And could
With flight of wing
Bring, without tarrying,　　　　　　　　　475
Or mercy some tokening,
　　Either by north or south,

For this is the first day of the tenth moon.
WIFE. The raven, dare I lay, will come again soon;
As fast as thou may cast him forth, have done;　　480
He may happen today come again ere noon
　　Without delay.
NOAH. I will cast out also
Doves one or two:
Go your way, go,　　　　　　　　　　485
　　God send you some prey!

Now are these fowls flown, into several country.
Pray we each one, kneeling on our knee,
To him that is alone worthiest of degree,
That he would send anon our fowls some fee　　490
　　To glad us.

WIFE. They can not fail of land,
The water is so waning.
  NOAH. Thank we God all-wielding,
      That lord that made us. 495

It is a wondrous thing, methinks soothly,
They are so long tarrying, the fowls that we
Cast out in the morning.
  WIFE.   Sir, it may be
They tarry till they bring.
  NOAH.   The raven is a-hungry
      Alway. 500
He is without any reason;
If he find any carrion,
As peradventure may happen,
      He will not away.

The dove is more gentle, her trust I unto, 505
Like unto the turtle, for she is ay true.
  WIFE. Hence but a little she comes. Lo, lo!
She brings in her bill some tidings new.
      Behold!
It is of an olive tree, 510
A branch, thinks me.
  NOAH. It is true, perdy;
      Right so it is called.

Dove, bird full blest, fair might thee befall!
Thou art true for to trust, as stone in the wall. 515
Full well I it wist, thou would come to thy hall.
  WIFE. A true token is't, we shall be saved all.
      For why?
The water, since she came

Of deepness plumb,   520
Is fallen a fathom,
      And more, certainly.

FIRST SON. These floods are gone. Father, behold!
SECOND SON. There is left right none, and so be ye bold.
THIRD SON. As still as a stone, our ship is stalled.   525
NOAH. Upon land here anon that we were, fain I would.
      My children dear,
Shem, Japhet, and Ham,
With glee and with game,
Come, go we all sam[1];   530
      We will no longer abide here.

WIFE. Here have we been, Noah, long enough,
With trouble and teen[2], and 'dured much woe.
NOAH. Behold, on this green neither cart nor plough
Is left, as I ween, neither tree nor bough,   535
      Nor other thing;
But all is away,
Many castles, I say,
Great towns of array.
      Flitted has this flowing.   540

WIFE. These floods, not afright, all this world so wide
Has moved with might, on sea and by side.
NOAH. To death are they dight[3], proudest of pride,
Every single wight that ever was spied
      With sin;   545
All are they slain
And put unto pain.

---

[1] Together.   [2] Grief, difficulty.   [3] Done.

WIFE. From thence again,
   May they never win?   549
 NOAH. Win? No, iwis[1]. Unless he that might has,
Would mind of[2] their miss and admit them to grace.
As he in bale is bliss, I pray him in this space,
In heaven high with his, to purvey us a place,
   That we
With his saints in sight,   555
And his angels bright,
May come to his light.
   Amen, for charity.

---

[1] Certainly. [2] Pay attention to.

THE WAKEFIELD SECOND
SHEPHERDS' PLAY*

❦

FIRST SHEPHERD	GILL, *his wife*
SECOND SHEPHERD	ANGEL
THIRD SHEPHERD	JESUS
MAK	MARY

[*Enter the* FIRST SHEPHERD.]

FIRST SHEPHERD. Lord! What these weathers are cold, and I
    am ill wrapped.
My hands nearly numb, so long have I napped.
My legs they fold, my fingers are chapped;
It is not as I would, for I am all lapped
    In sorrow   5
In storms and tempest,
Now in the east, now in the west,
Woe is him has never rest
    Midday nor morrow!

But we poor shepherds that walk on the moor,   10
In faith, we are near-hands out of the door;
No wonder, as it stands, if we be poor,
For the tilth of our lands lies fallow as the floor,
    As ye ken.
We are so hamyd,   15
For-taxed and ramyd[1];
We are made hand-tamed
    By these gentlery-men.

* C. 1425-1450.
[1] Crippled, taxed to death, ruined.

Thus they rob us of our rest. Our Lady them curse!
These men that are lord-fast, they make the plough tarry.   20
That, men say, is for the best; we find it contrary.
Thus are husbandmen oppressed, in point to miscarry,
    In life.
Thus hold they us under;
Thus they bring us in blunder.   25
It were great wonder
    If ever should we thrive.

For may he get a painted sleeve, or a brooch, now-a-days,
Woe to him that him grieves, or one word gainsays!
Dare no man him reprove, what mastery he has.   30
And yet may no man believe one word that he says,
    No letter.
He can make purveyance[1],
With boast and arrogance;
And all is through maintenance   35
    Of men that are greater.

There shall come a swain as proud as a peacock,
He must borrow my wagon, my plough also,
That I am full fain to grant ere he go.
Thus live we in pain, anger, and woe   40
    By night and day.
He must have if he longéd;
If I should forgang[2] it,
I were better be hanged
    Than once say him nay.   45

It does me good, as I walk thus by mine own,
Of this world for to talk in manner of moan.

[1] Provision.   [2] Do without.

To my sheep will I stalk and hearken anon;
There abide on a ridge, or sit on a stone,
 Full soon.   50
For I trow, pardie,
True men if they be,
We get more company
 Ere it be noon.   [*Moves aside.*]

[*Enter the* SECOND SHEPHERD.]

SECOND SHEPHERD. Ben'c'te[1] and Dominus! What may this
  bemean?   55
Why, fares this world thus, oft have we not seen?
Lord, these weathers are spiteful, and the winds full keen,
And the frosts so hideous, they water my eyes,
 No lie.
Now in dry, now in wet,   60
Now in snow, now in sleet,
When my shoes freeze to my feet,
 It is not all easy.

But as far as I ken, or yet as I go,
We poor wedded men endure much woe;   65
We have sorrow then and then, it falls oft so.
Silly Capel, our hen, both to and fro
 She cackles;
But begin she to croak,
To groan or to cluck,   70
Woe is him, is our cock,
 For he is in the shackles.

These men that are wed have not all their will.
When they are full hard bestead, they sigh full still.

---

[1] Benedicite.

God knows they are led full hard and full ill;   75
In bower nor in bed they say naught theretill,
    This tide.
My part have I found,
I know my lesson.
Woe is him that is bound,   80
    For he must abide.

But now late in our lives—a marvel to me,
That I think my heart rives such wonders to see,
What that destiny drives, it should so be—
Some men will have two wives, and some men three   85
    In store.
Some are woe that has any;
But so far ken I,
Woe is him that has many,
    For he feels sore.   90

But, young men, of wooing, for God that you bought,
Be well ware of wedding, and think in your thought,
"Had I known" is a thing it serves of naught.
Mickle still mourning has wedding home brought,
    And griefs,   95
With many a sharp shower;
For thou may catch in an hour
What shall seem full sour
    As long as thou lives.

For, as ever read I epistle[1], I have one to my fere[2],   100
As sharp as a thistle, as rough as a briar;
She is browed like a bristle, with a sour-laden cheer;
Had she once wet her whistle, she could sing full clear
    Her paternoster.

[1] In the Bible.   [2] Mate.

She is as great as a whale;   105
She has a gallon of gall;
By him that died for us all[1],
   I would I had run till I had lost her!

FIRST SHEPHERD. God, look over the row! Full deafly ye stand.
SECOND SHEPHERD. Yea, the devil in thy maw—so tarrying! 110
Sawest thou anywhere Daw?
FIRST SHEPHERD.   Yea, on a lea-land
Heard I him blow. He comes here at hand,
   Not far.
Stand still.
SECOND SHEPHERD. Why?
FIRST SHEPHERD. For he comes, hope I.   115
SECOND SHEPHERD. He will make us both a lie
   Unless we beware.

       [*Enter* THIRD SHEPHERD, *a boy.*]

THIRD SHEPHERD. Christ's cross me speed, and Saint Nicholas!
Thereof had I need; it is worse than it was.
Whoso could, take heed and let the world pass;   120
It is ever in dread and brittle as glass,
   And slides.
This world fared never so,
With marvels more and moe,
Now in weal, now in woe,   125
   And all things writhes.

Was never since Noah's flood such floods seen,
Winds and rains so rude, and storms so keen;
Some stammered, some stood in doubt, as I ween.
Now God turn all to good! I say as I mean,   130

---

[1] Note the many anachronisms in the play.

　　For ponder.
These floods so they drown,
Both in fields and in town,
And bear all down,
　　And that is a wonder.　　　　135

We that walk in the nights our cattle to keep,
We see sudden sights when other men sleep.
Yet methinks my heart lightens; I see shrews[1] peep.
Ye are two tall wights! I will give my sheep
　　A turn.　　　　140
But full ill have I meant;
As I walk on this land,
I may lightly repent,
　　My toes if I spurn.

[To the other two.]

Ah, sir, God you save, and master mine!　　　　145
A drink fain would I have, and somewhat to dine.
　FIRST SHEPHERD. Christ's curse, my knave, thou art an evil
　　　hind!
　SECOND SHEPHERD. What! the boy likes to rave! Abide until
　　　syne[2]
　　We have made it.
Ill thrift on thy pate!　　　　150
Though the fellow came late,
Yet is he in state
　　To dine—if he had it.

　THIRD SHEPHERD. Such servants as I, that sweats and swinks[3],
Eat our bread full dry, and that me forthinks[4].
　　　　155

---

[1] Rogues.　　[2] After.　　[3] Labors.　　[4] I regret.

We are oft wet and weary when master men winks;
Yet come full late both dinners and drinks.
    But neatly
Both our dame and our sire,
When we have run in the mire,   160
They can nip at our hire,
    And pay us full lately.

But hear my truth, master, for the fare that ye make:
I shall do, hereafter, work as I take[1];
I shall do a little, sir, and between times play,   165
For yet lay my supper never on my stomach
    In fields.
Whereto should I threap[2]?
With my staff can I leap;
And men say "Light cheap   170
    Badly for-yields[3]."

  FIRST SHEPHERD. Thou were an ill lad, to ride a-wooing
With a man that had but little of spending.
  SECOND SHEPHERD. Peace, boy! I bade; no more jangling,
Or I shall make thee a-feared, by the Heaven's King,   175
    With thy gawds[4].
Where are our sheep, boy? We scorn.
  THIRD SHEPHERD. Sir, this same day at morn
I them left in the corn,
    When they rang lauds[5].   180

They have pasture good; they cannot go wrong.
  FIRST SHEPHERD. That is right. By the rood, these nights are
    long!

---

[1] As I am paid.   [2] Talk back.   [3] An easy bargain badly pays back.
[4] Tricks.   [5] Early church service.

Yet I would, ere we go, one gave us a song.

SECOND SHEPHERD. So I thought as I stood, for mirth us among.

THIRD SHEPHERD. I grant.   185

FIRST SHEPHERD. Let me sing the tenory.

SECOND SHEPHERD. And I the treble so high.

THIRD SHEPHERD. Then the mean falls to me.
Let see how ye chant.

[*Enter* MAK, *with a cloak thrown over his smock.*]

MAK. Now, Lord, for thy names seven, that made both moon
and stars,   190
Well more than I can name; thy will, Lord, of me tharns[1].
I am all uneven; that moves oft my brains.
Now would God I were in heaven, for there weep no bairns
So still.

FIRST SHEPHERD. Who is that pipes so poor?   195

MAK. Would God ye knew how I fare!
Lo, a man that walks on the moor,
And has not all his will!

SECOND SHEPHERD. Mak, where hast thou gone? Tell us
tidings.

THIRD SHEPHERD. Is he come? Then everyone take heed to
his things.   200

[*Takes the cloak from* MAK.]

MAK. What! Ich be[2] a yeoman, I tell you, of the king;
The self and the same, sent from a great lording,
And such.
Fie on you! Go hence,
Out of my presence!   205

---

[1] Finds me wanting.   [2] Mak affects southern accent.

I must have reverence.
  Why, who be ich?

FIRST SHEPHERD. Why make ye it so quaint? Mak, ye do
    wrong.
SECOND SHEPHERD. But Mak, list ye saint¹? I trow for that
    you long.
THIRD SHEPHERD. I trow the shrew can paint! The devil might
    him hang!   210
MAK. Ich shall make complaint, and give you all a whang
  At a word,
And tell even how ye doth.
FIRST SHEPHERD. But, Mak, is that truth?
Now take out that southern tooth,   215
  And set in a turd.

SECOND SHEPHERD. Mak, the devil in your eye! A stroke
    would I lend you.
THIRD SHEPHERD. Mak, know ye not me? By God, I could
    'tend to you.
MAK. God, look you all three! Methought I had seen you.
Ye are a fair company.
FIRST SHEPHERD.   Can ye now mean you?²   220
SECOND SHEPHERD. Rascal, jape!
Thus late as thou goes,
What will men suppose?
And thou hast an ill noise³
  Of stealing of sheep.   225

MAK. And I am true as steel, all men wot,
But a sickness I feel that holds me full hot;
My belly fares not well, it is out of state.

---

¹ Do you like to show off?   ² Identify yourself.   ³ Bad reputation.

THIRD SHEPHERD. Seldom lies the devil dead by the gate.

MAK. Therefore   230
Full sore am I and ill;
If I stand stone still,
I eat not a needle
   This month and more.

FIRST SHEPHERD. How fares thy wife? By my hood, how
      fares she?   235

MAK. Lies weltering, by the rood, by the fire, lo!
And a house full of brood. She drinks well, too;
Ill speed other good that she will do!
   But so,
Eats as fast as she can;   240
And every year that comes to man
She brings forth a lakan[1],
   And some years two.

Although I were more gracious and richer by far,
I were eaten out of house and of harbor.   245
Yet she is a foul dowse[2] if ye come near;
There is none that trows nor knows a worse
   Than ken I.
Now will ye see what I proffer—
To give all in my coffer   250
Tomorrow at next to offer
   Her head-mass penny.[3]

SECOND SHEPHERD. I wot so for-wakéd[4] is none in this shire.
I would sleep, if I takéd less to my hire.

THIRD SHEPHERD. I am cold and naked, and would have a fire.

---

[1] Plaything; i. e., child.   [2] Whore.   [3] He will gladly pay for her
requiem mass.   [4] Worn out with watching.

FIRST SHEPHERD. I am weary, for-rakéd[1], and run in the mire.
  Stay awake, thou!   257
SECOND SHEPHERD. Nay, I will lie down by,
For I must sleep, truly.
  THIRD SHEPHERD. As good a man's son was I   260
    As any of you.

But, Mak, come hither! Between shalt thou lie down.
  MAK. Then might I stop you, certain, of that ye would rown[2],
    No dread.
From my top to my toe,   265
Manus tuas commendo,
Pontio Pilato,
    Christ's cross me speed!

    Then he rises, the shepherds being asleep, and says:

Now were time for a man that lacks what he would
To stalk privily then unto a fold,   270
And nimbly to work then, and be not too bold,
For he might pay for the bargain, if it were told,
    At the ending.
Now were time for to begin,
But he needs good counsel   275
That fain would fare well,
    And has but little spending.

But about you a circle as round as a moon,
Till I have done that I will, till that it be noon,
That ye lie stone still till that I have done,   280
And I shall say thereto of good words a few.
    On height

---

[1] Worn out with walking.   [2] Whisper.

Over your heads my hand I lift:
Out go your eyes, foredo your sight!
But yet I must make better shift   285
    If it be right.

Lord, how they sleep hard! That may ye all hear.
I never was a shepherd, but now will I learn.
If the flock be scared, yet shall I nip near.
How! Draw hitherward! Now mends our cheer   290
    From sorrow.
A fat sheep, I dare say;
A good fleece, dare I lay!
Pay back when I may,
    But this will I borrow.   295

      [MAK *crosses the stage to his house.*]

How, Gill, art thou in? Get us some light.
  WIFE. Who makes such din this time of the night?
I am set for to spin; I hope[1] not I might
Rise a penny to win. I curse them on height.
    So fares   300
A housewife that has been
To be rushed thus between;
Here may no work be seen,
    Because of such chores.

  MAK. Good wife, open the hek[2]! Seest thou not what I
    bring?   305
  WIFE. I may let thee draw the snek[3]. Ah, come in, my
    sweeting!
  MAK. Yea, thou dost not reck of my long standing.
  WIFE. By thy naked neck art thou like for to hang.

----

[1] Expect.   [2] Hatch.   [3] Latch.

MAK.   Go way:
I am worthy of my meat,   310
For in a pinch can I get
More than they that swink and sweat
    All the long day.

Thus it fell to my lot, Gill, I had such grace.
    WIFE. It were a foul blot to be hanged for the case.   315
    MAK. I have escaped, Gillot, often as hard a place.
    WIFE. But so long goes the pot to the water, men say,
    At last
Comes it home broken.
    MAK. Well know I the token,   320
But let it never be spoken;
    But come and help fast.

I would he were slain; I like well to eat.
This twelvemonth was I not so fain of one sheep's meat.
    WIFE. Should they come ere he be slain, and hear the sheep
        bleat—   325
    MAK. Then might I be ta'en! That were a cold sweat!
    Go bar
The gate door.
    WIFE.   Yes, Mak,
For if they come at thy back—
    MAK. Then might I pay for all the pack!   330
    The devil of them warn.

    WIFE. A good trick have I spied, since thou ken none.
Here shall we him hide till they be gone—
In my cradle abide. Let me alone,
And I shall lie beside in childbed, and groan.   335
    MAK. Thou hast said;

And I shall say thou was light
Of a male child this night.
   WIFE. Now well is the day bright,
     That ever was I bred.   340

This is a good disguise and a far cast;
Yet a woman's advice helps at the last!
I wot never who spies. Again go thou fast.
   MAK. Unless I come ere they rise, there blows a cold blast!
     I will go sleep.   345

     [MAK *returns to the shepherds and resumes his place.*]

Yet sleeps all this company;
And I shall go stalk privily,
As it never had been I
     That carried their sheep.

FIRST SHEPHERD. *Resurrex a mortruis!* Take hold of my hand.
Judas carnas dominus! I may not well stand;   351
My foot sleeps, by Jesus; and I walter fastand[1].
I thought that we laid us full near England.
   SECOND SHEPHERD. Ah, yea!
Lord, but I have slept well.   355
As fresh as an eel,
As light I me feel
     As leaf on a tree.

THIRD SHEPHERD. Ben'c'te be herein! So my body shakes,
My heart is out of skin, what so it quakes.   360
Who makes all this din? So my brows blacks[2].
To the door will I win. Hark, fellows, wake!
     We were four:

[1] Roll about famishing; cf. *wallow, welter.*   [2] Head aches (?).

See ye aught of Mak now?

FIRST SHEPHERD. We were up ere thou.   365

SECOND SHEPHERD. Man, I give God a vow,

   Yet went he nowhere.

THIRD SHEPHERD. Methought he was lapped in a wolf's skin.

FIRST SHEPHERD. So are many wrapped now—namely, within.

THIRD SHEPHERD. When we had long napped, methought
   with a gin[1]   370

A fat sheep he trapped; but he made no din.

SECOND SHEPHERD. Be still!

Thy dream makes thee mad;

It is but phantom, by the rood.

FIRST SHEPHERD. Now God turn all to good,   375

   If it be his will!

SECOND SHEPHERD. Rise, Mak! For shame! Thou liest right
   long.

MAK. Now Christ's holy name be us among!

What is this? By Saint James, I may not well gang!

I think I be the same. Ah! my neck has lain wrong   380
   Enough.   [*They help* MAK *up.*]

Mickle thank! Since yester even,

Now, by Saint Stephen,

I was flayed with a dream

   That my heart of slough[2].   385

I thought Gill began to croak and travail full sad,

Well nigh at the first cock, of a young lad

For to mend our flock. Then be I never glad;

I have tow on my rock[3] more than ever I had.

   Ah, my head!   390

A house full of young tharnes[4]!

---

[1] Trick.   [2] Slew my heart.   [3] Distaff.   [4] Bellies.

The devil knock out their brains!
Woe is him has many bairns,
    And thereto little bread!

I must go home, by your leave, to Gill, as I thought.   395
I pray you look in my sleeve that I steal naught;
I am loath you to grieve or from you take aught.
  THIRD SHEPHERD. Go forth; ill might thou live! Now would
      I we sought,
  This morn,   400
That we had all our store.
  FIRST SHEPHERD. But I will go before;
Let us meet.
  SECOND SHEPHERD. Where?
  THIRD SHEPHERD.   At the crooked thorn.

      [MAK *crosses to his cottage.*]

  MAK. Undo this door! Who is here? How long shall I stand?
  WIFE. Who makes such a stir? Now walk in the wenyand![1]   405
  MAK. Ah, Gill, what cheer? It is I, Mak, your husband.
  WIFE. Then may we see here the devil in a band,
    Sir Guile.
Lo, he comes with a lote[2]
As he were holden in the throat.   410
I may not sit at my note[3]
    A hand-long while.

  MAK. Will ye hear what to-do she makes to get her a gloze[4]?
She does naught but plays, and wiggles her toes.
  WIFE. Why, who wanders? Who wakes? Who comes? Who
      goes?   415

[5] Waning (of the moon) — supposedly unlucky.   [2] Noise, i. e., as
if he were being hanged.   [3] Work.   [4] Lie, excuse.

Who brews? Who bakes? What makes me thus do?
   And then,
It is ruth to behold,
Now in hot, now in cold,
Full woeful is the household   420
   That wants a woman.

But what end has thou made with the shepherds, Mak?
   MAK. The last word that they said, when I turned my back,
They would look that they had their sheep, all the pack.
I expect they will not be well paid when they their sheep 425
      lack,
   Perdie.
But how so the game goes,
To me they will suppose,
And make a foul noise,
   And cry out upon me.   430

But thou must do as thou hight[1].
   WIFE.   I accord me theretill;
I shall swaddle him right in my cradle.
If it were a greater plight, yet could I help till.
I will lie down straight. Come, cover me.
   MAK.   I will.
   WIFE. Behind!   435
Come Coll and his maroo[2],
They will nip us full narrow.
   MAK. But I may cry "Out, harrow!"
   The sheep if they find.

   WIFE. Hearken aye when they call; they will come anon. 440
Come and make ready all, and sing by thine own;

---

[1] Promised.   [2] Mate.

Sing lullaby thou shall, for I must groan
And cry out by the wall on Mary and John,
 For sore.
Sing lullaby fast   445
When thou hears at the last;
Unless I play a false cast,
 Trust me no more!

 [*The shepherds meet at the crooked hawthorne.*]

THIRD SHEPHERD. Ah, Coll, good morn! Why sleep thou not?
FIRST SHEPHERD. Alas, that ever was I born! We have a foul
  blot.   450
A fat wether have we lorn.
 THIRD SHEPHERD.   Marry, God forbid!
 SECOND SHEPHERD. Who should do us that scorn? That were
  a foul spot.
 FIRST SHEPHERD. Some shrew.
I have sought with my dogs
All Horbury Shrogs,
And of fifteen hogs[1]   455
 Found I but one ewe.

 THIRD SHEPHERD. Now trust me if ye will; by Saint Thomas
  of Kent,
Either Mak or Gill was at that assent.
 FIRST SHEPHERD. Peace, man, be still! I saw when he went. 460
Thou slanders him ill. Thou ought to repent,
 Good speed.
 SECOND SHEPHERD. Now as ever might I thrive,
If I should even here die,
I would say it were he   465
 That did that same deed.

  [1] Year-old sheep.

THIRD SHEPHERD. Go we thither, I rede, and run on our feet.
I shall never eat bread the truth till I wit.

FIRST SHEPHERD. Nor drink, in my heed, with him till I meet.

SECOND SHEPHERD. I will rest in no stead till that I him
greet,   470
    My brother!
One thing I will plight:
Till I see him in sight
Shall I never sleep one night
    Where I do another.   475

    [*At* MAK's *house they hear* GILL *groan and* MAK *sing a
lullaby.*]

THIRD SHEPHERD. Will ye hear how they hack? Our sir likes
    to croon.

FIRST SHEPHERD. Heard I never one crack so clear out of tune!
Call on him.

SECOND SHEPHERD. Mak! Undo your door soon.

MAK. Who is it that spake as it were noon
    On loft?   480
Who is that, I say?

THIRD SHEPHERD. Good fellows, were it day—

MAK. As far as ye may,
    Good, speak soft,

Over a sick woman's head that is at malaise;   485
I had liefer be dead e'er she had any dis-ease.

WIFE. Go to another place! I may not well wheeze.
Each foot that ye tread goes through my nose,
    So high!

FIRST SHEPHERD. Tell us, Mak, if ye may,   490
How fare ye, I say?

MAK. But are ye in this town today?
    How fare ye, I say?

Ye have run in the mire, and are wet yet.
I shall make you a fire if ye will sit.   495
A nurse would I hire, think ye on it.
Well paid is my hire; my dream—this is it,
   In season.
I have bairns, if ye knew,
Well more than enow.   500
But we must drink as we brew,
   And that is but reason.

I would have ye dine ere ye go. Methinks that ye sweat.
  SECOND SHEPHERD. Nay, neither mends our mood, drink nor
     meat.
  MAK. Why, sir, ails you aught but good?
  THIRD SHEPHERD.   Yea, our sheep that we get   505
Are stolen as they go. Our loss is great.
  MAK. Sirs, drink!
Had I been there,
Some should have paid full sore.
  FIRST SHEPHERD. Marry, some men think that ye were;
    And that makes us think.   510

  SECOND SHEPHERD. Mak, some men trows that it should be ye.
  THIRD SHEPHERD. Either ye or your spouse, so say we.
  MAK. Now, if ye have suspicion of Gill or me,
Come and rip our house, and then ye may see   515
    Who had her.
If I any sheep got,
Any cow or stott[1],
And Gill, my wife, rose not
    Since here she laid her,   520

---

[1] Young steer.

As I am true and leal, to God here I pray
That this be the first meal that I shall eat this day.
  FIRST SHEPHERD. Mak, as have I weal, advise thee, I say:
He learned timely to steal that could not say nay.
  WIFE. I swelt[1]!   525
Out, thieves, from my house!
Ye come to rob us, for the nonce.
  MAK. Hear ye not how she groans?
    Your hearts should melt.

  WIFE. Out, thieves, from my bairn! Approach him not there!
  MAK. Knew ye what she had borne, your hearts would be
    sore.   531
Ye do wrong, I you warn, that thus come before
To a woman that has farne[2]. But I say no more.
  WIFE. Ah, my middle!
I pray to God so mild,   535
If ever I you beguiled,
That I eat this child
    That lies in this cradle.

  MAK. Peace, woman, for God's pain, and cry not so!
Thou hurts thy brain, and makes me full of woe.   540
  SECOND SHEPHERD. I think our sheep be slain. What find ye
    two?
  THIRD SHEPHERD. All work we in vain; as well may we go.
    But, hatters[3],
I can find no flesh,
Hard nor nesh[4],   545
Salt nor fresh,
    But two empty platters.

---

[1] Faint.   [2] Fared; i. e., had a child.   [3] Confound it.   [4] Soft.

Live cattle but this, tame nor wild,
None, as have I bliss, so loud as he smelled.
   WIFE. No, so God me bless, and give me joy of my child!
   FIRST SHEPHERD. We have marked amiss; I hold us beguiled. 551
   SECOND SHEPHERD. Sir, done.
Sir, Our Lady him save!
Is your child a knave[1]?
   MAK. Any lord might him have,   555
     This child as his son.

When he wakens he skips, that joy is to see.
   THIRD SHEPHERD. In good time to his hips, and in glee.
Who were his godfathers, so soon ready?
   MAK. So fair fall their lips!
   FIRST SHEPHERD.   Hark now, a lie!   560
   MAK. So God them thank,
Parkin and Gibbon Waller, I say,
And gentle John Horn, in good faith,
He made all the garray[2]
     With his great shank.   565

   SECOND SHEPHERD. Mak, friends will we be, for we are all
     one.
   MAK. We! Now I hold for me, for amends get I none.
Farewell, all three! All glad were ye gone! [*Shepherds go out.*]
   THIRD SHEPHERD. Fair words may there be, but love there
     is none
     This year.   570
   FIRST SHEPHERD. Gave ye the child anything?
   SECOND SHEPHERD. I trow, not one farthing!
   THIRD SHEPHERD. Fast back will I fling;
     Abide ye me here.

---

[1] Boy.   [2] Commotion.

[*Shepherds re-enter.*]

Mak, take it to no grief, if I come to thy bairn.   575

  MAK. Nay, thou does me great reproof; and foul has thou
    fared.

  THIRD SHEPHERD. The child will it not grieve, that little day-
    star.

    Mak, with your leave, let me give your bairn

    But sixpence.

  MAK. Nay, go 'way; he sleeps.   580

  THIRD SHEPHERD. Methinks he peeps.

  MAK. When he wakens he weeps;

    I pray you, go hence!

  THIRD SHEPHERD. Give me leave him to kiss, and lift up the
    clout.

What the devil is this? He has a long snout!   585

  FIRST SHEPHERD. He is marked amiss. We wait ill about.

  SECOND SHEPHERD. "Ill spun weft," ywis, "aye comes foul
    out."

    Aye, so!

He is like to our sheep!

  THIRD SHEPHERD. How, Gib, may I peep?   590

  FIRST SHEPHERD. I trow, nature will creep

    Where it may not go!

  SECOND SHEPHERD. This was a quaint gawd[1] and a far cast!
It was a high fraud!

  THIRD SHEPHERD.   Yea, sirs, was 't.

Let's burn this bawd, and bind her fast.   595
Ah, false scold, hang at the last,

    So shall thou.

Will ye see how they swaddle

---

[1] Trick.

His four feet in the middle?
Saw I never in a cradle   600
    A hornéd lad ere now.

MAK. Peace, bid I! What! Let be your fare!
I am he that him begot, and yon woman him bare.
  FIRST SHEPHERD. After what devil shall he be hatt[1]? "Mak"?
    Lo, God, Mak's heir!
  SECOND SHEPHERD. Let be all that. Now God give him care,
    I say.   606
  WIFE. A pretty child is he
As sits on a woman's knee;
A dilly-downe, perdie,
    To make a man laugh.   610

  THIRD SHEPHERD. I know him by the ear-mark; that is a good
    token.
  MAK. I tell you, sirs, hark! His nose was broken;
Later told me a clerk that he was forespoken[2].
  FIRST SHEPHERD. This is a false work; I would fain be
    wroken[3].
    Get a weapon.   615
  WIFE. He was taken by an elf,
I saw it myself;
When the clock struck twelve
    Was he misshapen.

  SECOND SHEPHERD. Ye two are well gifted, same in a stead.
  THIRD SHEPHERD. Since they maintain their theft, let's do them
    to death.   621
  MAK. If I trespass eft, gird off my head!
With you will I be left.

---

[1] Named.   [2] Enchanted.   [3] Avenged.

FIRST SHEPHERD.   Sirs, take my lead:

    For this trespass

We will neither curse nor fight,   625

Quarrel nor chide,

But have done as tight[1],

    And cast him in canvas.

[They toss him and go back to the fields.]

FIRST SHEPHERD. Lord, what! I am sore in point for to burst.

In faith, I may no more; therefore will I rest.   630

    SECOND SHEPHERD. As a sheep of seven score he weighed in my
        fist.

For to sleep anywhere methinks that I list.

    THIRD SHEPHERD. Now I pray you,

Lie down on this green.

    FIRST SHEPHERD. On these thieves yet I mind.   635

    THIRD SHEPHERD. Whereto should ye strain

    So, I say you?   *[They sleep.]*

An ANGEL *sings "Gloria in excelsis"; then let him say:*

ANGEL. Rise, herd-men kind! For now is he born

That shall take from the fiend what Adam had lorn:

That devil to sheynd[2] this night is he born;   640

God is made your friend now at this morn.

    He behests

At Bethlehem go see,

Where lies the Free

In a crib full poorly   645

    Between two beasts.

FIRST SHEPHERD. This was a wise voice that ever yet I heard.

It is a marvel to name, thus to be scared.

---

[1] Quickly.   [2] Destroy.

SECOND SHEPHERD. Of God's son of heaven he spake upward
All the wood in a levin[1] methought that he made   650
    To appear
THIRD SHEPHERD. He spake of a bairn
In Bethlehem, I you warn.
    FIRST SHEPHERD. That betokens yon star;
    Let us seek. him there.   655

SECOND SHEPHERD. Say, what was his song? Heard ye not
    how he cracked it,
Three briefs to a long?
    THIRD SHEPHERD.   Yea, marry, he hacked it;
Was no crotchet wrong, nor nothing that lacked it.
    FIRST SHEPHERD. For to sing us among, right as he knacked it,
    I can.   660
SECOND SHEPHERD. Let's see how ye croon.
Can ye bark at the moon?
    THIRD SHEPHERD. Hold your tongues, have done!
    FIRST SHEPHERD. Hark after, then!

SECOND SHEPHERD. To Bethlehem he bade that we should
    gang;   665
I am full afeared that we tarry too long.
    THIRD SHEPHERD. Be merry and not sad; o   mirth is our
    song;
Everlasting glad our reward may we fang[2]
    Without noise.
    FIRST SHEPHERD. Therefore thither hie we,   670
If we be wet and weary,
To that child and that lady.
    We have it not to lose.

Lightning.   [2] Take.

SECOND SHEPHERD. We find by the prophecy—let be your
    din—
Of David and Isaiah and more than I mind,   675
They prophesied by clergy that in a virgin
Should he light and lie, to slacken our sin
    And slake it,
Our Race from woe.
For Isaiah said so: 680
"*Ecce virgo*
    Concipiet" a child that is naked.

THIRD SHEPHERD. Full glad may we be, and abide that day
That lovely to see, that all mights may.
Lord, well were me, for once and for aye,   685
Might I kneel on my knee some word for to say
    To that child.
But the angel said,
In a crib was he laid;
He was poorly arrayed,   690
    Both humble and mild.

FIRST SHEPHERD. Patriarchs that have been, and prophets be-
    fore,
They desired to have seen this child that is born.
They are gone full clean; that have they lorn.
We shall see him, I ween, ere it be morn,   695
    To token.
When I see him and feel,
Then know I full well
It is true as steel
    That prophets have spoken: 700

To so poor as we are that he would appear,
First find, and declare by his messenger.

SECOND SHEPHERD. Go we now, let us fare; the place is us
     near.

THIRD SHEPHERD. I am ready, prepared; go we together
     To that bright.   705
Lord, if thy will be—
We are simple all three—
Grant us some kind of glee
     To comfort thy wight.

[*They enter the stable.*]

FIRST SHEPHERD. Hail, comely and clean! Hail, young child!
Hail, maker, as I mean, from a maiden so mild!   711
Thou has cursed, I ween, the devil so wild;
The false guiler of teen[1], now goes he beguiled
     Lo, he merry is!
Lo, he laughs, my sweeting!   715
A welfare meeting!
I have holden my heting[2].
     Have a bob of cherries!

SECOND SHEPHERD. Hail, sovereign Savior, for thou hast us
     sought!
Hail! noble child and flower, that all things has wrought!
Hail, full of favor, that made all of naught!   721
Hail! I kneel and I cower. A bird have I brought
     To my bairn.
Hail, little tiny mop!
Of our creed thou art crop.   725
I would drink of thy cup,
     Little day-star.

THIRD SHEPHERD. Hail, darling dear, full of godhead!
I pray thee be near when that I have need.

[1] Contriver of evil.   [2] Held to my promise.

Hail! Sweet is thy cheer! My heart would bleed   730
To see thee sit here in so poor weed,
   With no pennies.
Hail! Put forth thy dall[1]
I bring thee but a ball:
Have and play thee withal,   735
   And go to the tennis.

MARY. The Father of Heaven, God omnipotent,
That set all in seven days, his Son has sent.
My name could he neven[2] and descend ere he went.
I conceived him full even, through might as he meant;   740
   And now he is born.
Keep he you from woe!
I shall pray him so.
Tell it forth as ye go,
   And mind on this morn.   745

FIRST SHEPHERD. Farewell, lady, so fair to behold,
With thy child on thy knee!
SECOND SHEPHERD.   But he lies full cold.
Lord, well is me. Now we go, thou behold.
THIRD SHEPHERD. Forsooth, already it seems to be told
   Full oft.   750
FIRST SHEPHERD. What grace we have found!
SECOND SHEPHERD. Come forth; now are we won!
THIRD SHEPHERD. To sing are we bound:
   Let take aloft!

EXPLICIT PAGINA PASTORUM

[1] Hand.   [2] Call.

EVERYMAN*

❧

MESSENGER

GOD: *Adonai*

DEATH

EVERYMAN

FELLOWSHIP

COUSIN

KINDRED

GOODS

GOOD DEEDS

KNOWLEDGE

CONFESSION

BEAUTY

STRENGTH

DISCRETION

FIVE WITS

ANGEL

DOCTOR

Here beginneth a treatise how the High Father of Heaven sendeth Death to cummon every creature to come and give account of their lives in this world, and is in manner of a moral play.

[*Enter* MESSENGER *to speak Prologue.*]

MESSENGER. I pray you all give your audience,
And hear this matter with reverence,
By figure a moral play—
The *Summoning of Everyman* called it is,
That of our lives and ending shows   5
How transitory we be all day.
This matter is wondrous precious,
But the intent of it is more gracious,
And sweet to bear away.
The story saith:—Man, in the beginning,   10
Look well, and take good heed to the ending,
Be you never so gay!

* Fifteenth century.

73

Ye think sin in the beginning full sweet,
Which in the end causeth the soul to weep,
When the body lieth in clay.   15
Here shall you see how Fellowship and Jollity,
Both Strength, Pleasure, and Beauty,
Will fade from thee as flower in May.
For ye shall hear how our Heaven King
Calleth Everyman to a general reckoning.   20
Give audience, and hear what he doth say.   [*Exit.*]

                GOD *speaketh* [*from above*].

  GOD. I perceive, here in my majesty,
How that all creatures be to me unkind,
Living without dread in worldly prosperity.
Of ghostly[1] sight the people be so blind,   25
Drowned in sin, they know me not for their God.
In worldly riches is all their mind,
They fear not my rightwiseness, the sharp rod;
My love that I showed when I for them died
They forget clean, and shedding of my blood red;   30
I hanged between two, it cannot be denied;
To get them life I suffered to be dead;
I healed their feet, with thorns hurt was my head.
I could do no more than I did, truly;
And now I see the people do clean forsake me.   35
They use the seven deadly sins damnable;
As pride, covetise, wrath, and lechery,
Now in the world be made commendable;
And thus they leave of angels the heavenly company.
Every man liveth so after his own pleasure,   40
And yet of their life they be nothing sure.
I see the more that I them forbear

  [1] Spiritual.

The worse they be from year to year;
All that liveth appaireth[1] fast.
Therefore I will, in all the haste,   45
Have a reckoning of every man's person;
For, and[2] I leave the people thus alone
In their life and wicked tempests,
Verily they will become much worse than beasts;
For now one would by envy another up eat;   50
Charity they all do clean forget.
I hoped well that every man
In my glory should make his mansion,
And thereto I had them all elect;
But now I see, like traitors deject,   55
They thank me not for the pleasure that I to them meant,
Nor yet for their being that I them have lent.
I proffered the people great multitude of mercy,
And few there be that asketh it heartily;
They be so cumbered with worldly riches,   60
That needs on them I must do justice,
On every man living, without fear.
Where art thou, Death, thou mighty messenger?

[*Enter* DEATH.]

DEATH. Almighty God, I am here at your will,
Your commandment to fulfil.   65
GOD. Go thou to Everyman,
And show him, in my name,
A pilgrimage he must on him take,
Which he in no wise may escape;
And that he bring with him a sure reckoning   70
Without delay or any tarrying.

---

[1] Is impaired.   [2] If (thus frequently throughout the play).

DEATH. Lord, I will in the world go run over all,
And cruelly out search both great and small. [GOD *withdraws.*]
Every man will I beset that liveth beastly
Out of God's laws, and dreadeth not folly.   75
He that loveth riches I will strike with my dart,
His sight to blind, and from heaven to depart,
Except that alms be his good friend,
In hell for to dwell, world without end.
Lo, yonder I see Everyman walking;   80
Full little he thinketh on my coming;
His mind is on fleshly lusts and his treasure;
And great pain it shall cause him to endure
Before the Lord, Heaven King.
Everyman, stand still! Whither art thou going   85
Thus gaily? Hast thou thy Maker forgot?
  EVERYMAN. Why askest thou?
Wouldst thou wete[1]?
  DEATH. Yea, sir, I will show you;
In great haste I am sent to thee   90
From God out of his Majesty.
  EVERYMAN. What, sent to me?
  DEATH. Yea, certainly.
Though thou have forgot him here,
He thinketh on thee in the heavenly sphere,   95
As, ere we depart, thou shalt know.
  EVERYMAN. What desireth God of me?
  DEATH. That shall I show thee;
A reckoning he will needs have
Without any longer respite.   100
  EVERYMAN. To give a reckoning longer leisure I crave;
This blind matter troubleth my wit.

_____
[1] Know.

DEATH. On thee thou must take a long journey;
Therefore thy book of count with thee thou bring;
For turn again thou can not by no way.   105
And look thou be sure of thy reckoning,
For before God thou shalt answer and show
Thy many bad deeds, and good but a few,
How thou hast spent thy life, and in what wise,
Before the Chief Lord of paradise.   110
Have ado[1] that we were in that way,
For, wete thou well, thou shalt make none attorney.
  EVERYMAN. Full unready I am such reckoning to give.
I know thee not. What messenger art thou?
  DEATH. I am Death, that no man dreadeth.   115
For every man I 'rest, and no man spareth;
For it is God's commandment
That all to me should be obedient.
  EVERYMAN. O Death! thou comest when I had thee least in
    mind!
In thy power it lieth me to save,   120
Yet of my goods will I give thee, if thou will be kind;
Yea, a thousand pound shalt thou have,
If thou defer this matter till another day.
  DEATH. Everyman, it may not be, by no way!
I set not by gold, silver, nor riches,   125
Nor by pope, emperor, king, duke, nor princes.
For, and I would receive gifts great,
All the world I might get;
But my custom is clean contrary.
I give thee no respite. Come hence, and not tarry.   130
  EVERYMAN. Alas! shall I have no longer respite?
I may say Death giveth no warning.

---

[1] Get ready.

To think on thee, it maketh my heart sick,
For all unready is my book of reckoning.
But twelve year and I might have abiding,   135
My counting-book I would make so clear,
That my reckoning I should not need to fear.
Wherefore, Death, I pray thee, for God's mercy,
Spare me till I be provided of remedy.

   DEATH. Thee availeth not to cry, weep, and pray;   140
But haste thee lightly that thou were gone that journey,
And prove thy friends if thou can.
For wete thou well the tide abideth no man;
And in the world each living creature
For Adam's sin must die of nature.   145

   EVERYMAN. Death, if I should this pilgrimage take,
And my reckoning surely make,
Show me, for saint charity,
Should I not come again shortly?

   DEATH. No, Everyman; and thou be once there,   150
Thou mayst never more come here,
Trust me verily.

   EVERYMAN. O gracious God, in the high seat celestial,
Have mercy on me in this most need!
Shall I have no company from this vale terrestrial   155
Of mine acquaintance that way me to lead?

   DEATH. Yea, if any be so hardy,
That would go with thee and bear thee company.
Hie thee that thou were gone to God's magnificence,
Thy reckoning to give before his presence.   160
What! weenest thou thy life is given thee,
And thy worldly goods also?

   EVERYMAN. I had weened so, verily.

   DEATH. Nay, nay; it was but lent thee;
For, as soon as thou art gone,   165

Another a while shall have it, and then go therefrom
Even as thou hast done.
Everyman, thou art mad! Thou hast thy wits five,
And here on earth will not amend thy life;
For suddenly I do come.   170
   EVERYMAN. O wretched caitiff! whither shall I flee,
That I might 'scape endless sorrow?
Now, gentle Death, spare me till tomorrow,
That I may amend me
With good advisement.   175
   DEATH. Nay, thereto I will not consent,
Nor no man will I respite,
But to the heart suddenly I shall smite
Without any advisement.
And now out of thy sight I will me hie;   180
See thou make thee ready shortly,
For thou mayst say this is the day
That no man living may 'scape away.   [*Exit* DEATH.]
   EVERYMAN. Alas! I may well weep with sighs deep.
Now have I no manner of company   185
To help me in my journey and me to keep;
And also my writing is full unready.
How shall I do now for to excuse me?
I would to God I had never been gete[1]!
To my soul a full great profit it had be;   190
For now I fear pains huge and great.
The time passeth; Lord, help, that all wrought.
For though I mourn it availeth naught.
The day passeth, and is almost a-go;
I wot not well what for to do.   195
To whom were I best my complaint to make?

[1] Born.

What if I to Fellowship thereof spake,
And showed him of this sudden chance?
For in him is all mine affiance[1],
We have in the world so many a day   200
Been good friends in sport and play.
I see him yonder, certainly;
I trust that he will bear me company;
Therefore to him will I speak to ease my sorrow.
Well met, good Fellowship, and good morrow!   205

[FELLOWSHIP *speaketh*.]

FELLOWSHIP. Everyman, good morrow, by this day!
Sir, why lookest thou so piteously?
If any thing be amiss, I pray thee me say,
That I may help to remedy.
    EVERYMAN. Yea, good Fellowship, yea,   210
I am in great jeopardy.
    FELLOWSHIP. My true friend, show to me your mind;
I will not forsake thee to my life's end
In the way of good company.
    EVERYMAN. That was well spoken, and lovingly.   215
    FELLOWSHIP. Sir, I must needs know your heaviness;
I have pity to see you in any distress;
If any have you wronged, ye shall revenged be,
Though I on the ground be slain for thee,
Though that I know before that I should die.   220
    EVERYMAN. Verily, Fellowship, gramercy.
    FELLOWSHIP. Tush! by thy thanks I set not a straw!
Show me your grief, and say no more.
    EVERYMAN. If I my heart should to you break,
And then you to turn your mind from me,   225

[1] Trust.

And would not me comfort when you hear me speak,
Then should I ten times sorrier be.

FELLOWSHIP. Sir, I say as I will do, indeed.

EVERYMAN. Then be you a good friend at need;
I have found you true here before.   230

FELLOWSHIP. And so ye shall evermore;
For, in faith, and thou go to hell,
I will not forsake thee by the way!

EVERYMAN. Ye speak like a good friend. I believe you well;
I shall deserve it, and I may.   235

FELLOWSHIP. I speak of no deserving, by this day!
For he that will say and nothing do
Is not worthy with good company to go;
Therefore show me the grief of your mind,
As to your friend most loving and kind.   240

EVERYMAN. I shall show you how it is:
Commanded I am to go a journey,
A long way, hard and dangerous,
And give a strict count without delay
Before the high judge, Adonai.   245
Wherefore, I pray you, bear me company,
As ye have promised, in this journey.

FELLOWSHIP. That is matter indeed! Promise is duty;
But, and I should take such a voyage on me,
I know it well, it should be to my pain.   250
Also it maketh me afeared, certain.
But let us take counsel here as well as we can,
For your words would fright a strong man.

EVERYMAN. Why, ye said if I had need,
Ye would me never forsake, quick nor dead,   255
Though it were to hell, truly.

FELLOWSHIP. So I said, certainly,
But such pleasures be set aside, the sooth to say.

And also, if we took such a journey,
When should we come again?   260
  EVERYMAN. Nay, never again till the day of doom.
  FELLOWSHIP. In faith, then will not I come there!
Who hath you these tidings brought?
  EVERYMAN. Indeed, Death was with me here.
  FELLOWSHIP. Now, by God that all hath bought,   265
If Death were the messenger,
For no man that is living today
I will not go that loath journey—
Not for the father that begat me!
  EVERYMAN. Ye promised otherwise, pardie[1].   270
  FELLOWSHIP. I wot well I said so, truly;
And yet if thou wilt eat, and drink, and make good cheer,
Or haunt to women the lusty company,
I would not forsake you while the day is clear,
Trust me verily!   275
  EVERYMAN. Yea, thereto ye would be ready;
To go to mirth, solace, and play,
Your mind will sooner apply
Than to bear me company in my long journey.
  FELLOWSHIP. Now, in good faith, I will not that way. 280
But and thou wilt murder, or any man kill,
In that I will help thee with a good will!
  EVERYMAN. O, that is a simple advice indeed!
Gentle fellow, help me in my necessity;
We have loved long, and now I need,   285
And now, gentle Fellowship, remember me!
  FELLOWSHIP. Whether ye have loved me or no,
By Saint John, I will not with thee go.
  EVERYMAN. Yet, I pray thee, take the labor, and do so much
    for me

---

[1] *Par dieu;* indeed.

To bring me forward, for saint charity, 290
And comfort me till I come without the town.

FELLOWSHIP. Nay, and thou would give me a new gown,
I will not a foot with thee go;
But, and thou had tarried, I would not have left thee so.
And as now God speed thee in thy journey, 295
For from thee I will depart as fast as I may.

EVERYMAN. Whither away, Fellowship? Will you forsake me?

FELLOWSHIP. Yea, by my fay, to God I betake[1] thee.

EVERYMAN. Farewell, good Fellowship! For thee my heart
is sore;
Adieu for ever! I shall see thee no more. 300

FELLOWSHIP. In faith, Everyman, farewell now at the end!
For you I will remember that parting is mourning.

[*Exit* FELLOWSHIP.]

EVERYMAN. Alack! shall we thus depart indeed
(Ah, Lady, help!) without any more comfort?
Lo, Fellowship forsaketh me in my most need. 305
For help in this world whither shall I resort?
Fellowship here before with me would merry make,
And now little sorrow for me doth he take.
It is said, "In prosperity men friends may find,
Which in adversity be full unkind." 310
Now whither for succor shall I flee,
Sith that Fellowship hath forsaken me?
To my kinsmen I will, truly,
Praying them to help me in my necessity;
I believe that they will do so, 315
For "kind will creep where it may not go[2]."
I will go say[3], for yonder I see them go.
Where be ye now, my friends and kinsmen?

---

[1] Commit.   [2] Walk.   [3] Try.

[*Enter* KINDRED *and* COUSIN.]

KINDRED. Here be we now, at your commandment.
Cousin, I pray you show us your intent   320
In any wise, and do not spare.
    COUSIN. Yea, Everyman, and to us declare
If ye be disposed to go any whither,
For, wete you well, we will live and die together.
    KINDRED. In wealth and woe we will with you hold,   325
For over his kin a man may be bold.
    EVERYMAN. Gramercy, my friends and kinsmen kind.
Now shall I show you the grief of my mind.
I was commanded by a messenger
That is a high king's chief officer;   330
He bade me go a pilgrimage, to my pain,
And I know well I shall never come again;
Also I must give a reckoning straight,
For I have a great enemy that hath me in wait[1],
Which intendeth me for to hinder.   335
    KINDRED. What account is that which ye must render?
That would I know.
    EVERYMAN. Of all my works I must show
How I have lived, and my days spent;
Also of ill deeds that I have used   340
In my time, sith life was me lent;
And of all virtues that I have refused.
Therefore I pray you go thither with me,
To help to make mine account, for saint charity.
    COUSIN. What, to go thither? Is that the matter?   345
Nay, Everyman, I had liefer fast bread and water
All this five year and more.
    EVERYMAN. Alas, that ever I was bore!

[1] Lies in wait.

For now shall I never be merry
If that you forsake me.   350
   KINDRED. Ah, sir, what! Ye be a merry man!
Take good heart to you, and make no moan.
But one thing I warn you, by Saint Anne,
As for me, ye shall go alone.
   EVERYMAN. My Cousin, will you not with me go?   355
   COUSIN. No, by our Lady! I have the cramp in my toe.
Trust not to me; for, so God me speed,
I will deceive you in your most need.
   KINDRED. It availeth not us to tice[1].
Ye shall have my maid with all my heart;   360
She loveth to go to feasts, there to be nice[2],
And to dance, and abroad to start;
I will give her leave to help you in that journey,
If that you and she may agree.
   EVERYMAN. Now show me the very effect of your mind.   365
Will you go with me, or abide behind?
   KINDRED. Abide behind? Yea, that will I, and I may!
Therefore farewell till another day.   [*Exit* KINDRED.]
   EVERYMAN. How should I be merry or glad?
For fair promises men to me make,   370
But when I have most need, they me forsake.
I am deceived; that maketh me sad.
   COUSIN. Cousin Everyman, farewell now,
For verily I will not go with you;
Also of mine own life an unready reckoning   375
I have to account; therefore I make tarrying.
Now, God keep thee, for now I go.   [*Exit* COUSIN.]
   EVERYMAN. Ah, Jesus! is all come hereto?
Lo, fair words maketh fools fain[3];

---

[1] Entice, coax.   [2] Wanton.   [3] Glad.

They promise and nothing will do certain.   380
My kinsmen promised me faithfully
For to abide with me steadfastly,
And now fast away do they flee.
Even so Fellowship promised me.
What friend were best me of to provide?   385
I lose my time here longer to abide.
Yet in my mind a thing there is:
All my life I have loved riches;
If that my Goods now help me might,
He would make my heart full light.   390
I will speak to him in this distress.
Where art thou, my Goods and riches?

  GOODS [*From within*]. Who calleth me? Everyman? What,
    hast thou haste?
I lie here in corners, trussed and piled so high,
And in chests I am locked so fast,   395
Also sacked in bags—thou mayst see with thine eye—
I cannot stir; in packs low I lie.
What would ye have? Lightly me say.

  EVERYMAN. Come hither, Goods, in all the haste thou may.
For of counsel I must desire thee.   400

[*Enter* GOODS.]

  GOODS. Sir, and ye in the world have sorrow or adversity,
That can I help you to remedy shortly.

  EVERYMAN. It is another disease that grieveth me;
In this world it is not, I tell thee so.
I am sent for another way to go,   405
To give a strict count general
Before the highest Jupiter of all;
And all my life I have had joy and pleasure in thee;
Therefore I pray thee go with me,

For, peradventure, thou mayst before God Almighty   410
My reckoning help to clean and purify;
For it is said ever among,
That "money maketh all right that is wrong."

GOODS. Nay, Everyman; I sing another song,
I follow no man in such voyages;   415
For, and I went with thee,
Thou shouldst fare much the worse for me;
For because on me thou did set thy mind,
Thy reckoning I have made blotted and blind,
That thine account thou cannot make truly;   420
And that hast thou for the love of me.

EVERYMAN. That would grieve me full sore,
When I should come to that fearful answer.
Up, let us go thither together.

GOODS. Nay, not so! I am too brittle, I may not endure;
I will follow no man one foot, be ye sure.   426

EVERYMAN. Alas! I have thee loved, and had great pleasure
All my life-days on goods and treasure.

GOODS. That is to thy damnation, without lesing[1]!
For my love is contrary to the love everlasting.   430
But if thou had me loved moderately during,
As to the poor to give part of me,
Then shouldst thou not in this dolor be,
Nor in this great sorrow and care.

EVERYMAN. Lo, now was I deceived ere I was ware,   435
And all I may wyte[2] my spending of time.

GOODS. What, weenest thou that I am thine?

EVERYMAN. I had weened so.

GOODS. Nay, Everyman, I say no;
As for a while I was lent thee,   440

---

[1] Lying.   [2] Blame to.

A season thou hast had me in prosperity.
My condition is man's soul to kill;
If I save one, a thousand I do spill;
Weenest thou that I will follow thee
From this world? Nay, verily.   445
   EVERYMAN. I had weened otherwise.
   GOODS. Therefore to thy soul Goods is a thief;
For when thou art dead, this is my guise[1]—
Another to deceive in the same wise
As I have done thee, and all to his soul's reprief[2].   450
   EVERYMAN. O false Goods, curséd thou be!
Thou traitor to God, that hast deceived me
And caught me in thy snare.
   GOODS. Marry! thou brought thyself in care,
Whereof I am right glad.   455
I must needs laugh, I cannot be sad.
   EVERYMAN. Ah, Goods, thou hast had long my heartly love;
I gave thee that which should be the Lord's above.
But wilt thou not go with me indeed?
I pray thee truth to say.   460
   GOODS. No, so God me speed!
Therefore farewell, and have good day.   [*Exit* GOODS.]
   EVERYMAN. O, to whom shall I make my moan
For to go with me in that heavy journey?
First Fellowship said he would with me gone;   465
His words were very pleasant and gay,
But afterward he left me alone.
Then spake I to my kinsmen, all in despair,
And also they gave me words fair,
They lacked no fair speaking,   470
But all forsook me in the ending.

----

[1] Practice, trick.   [2] Reproof.

Then went I to my Goods, that I loved best,
In hope to have comfort, but there had I least;
For my Goods sharply did me tell
That he bringeth many into hell. 475
Then of myself I was ashamed,
And so I am worthy to be blamed;
Thus may I well myself hate.
Of whom shall I now counsel take?
I think that I shall never speed 480
Till that I go to my Good Deeds.
But alas! she is so weak
That she can neither go nor speak.
Yet will I venture on her now.
My Good Deeds, where be you? 485

[GOOD DEEDS *speaks from the ground.*]

GOOD DEEDS. Here I lie, cold in the ground.
Thy sins hath me sore bound,
That I cannot stir.
EVERYMAN. O Good Deeds! I stand in fear;
I must you pray of counsel, 490
For help now should come right well.
GOOD DEEDS. Everyman, I have understanding
That ye be summoned account to make
Before Messias, of Jerusalem King; 494
And you do by me,[1] that journey with you will I take.
EVERYMAN. Therefore I come to you my moan to make;
I pray you that ye will go with me.
GOOD DEEDS. I would full fain, but I cannot stand, verily.
EVERYMAN. Why, is there anything on you fall?
GOOD DEEDS. Yea, sir, I may thank you of all; 500
If ye had perfectly cheered[2] me,

---

[1] Act by my advice.   [2] Cherished.

Your book of count full ready had be.
Look, the books of your works and deeds eke;
Ah, see how they lie under the feet,
To your soul's heaviness.   505
   EVERYMAN. Our Lord Jesus help me!
For one letter here I can not see.
  GOOD DEEDS. There is a blind reckoning in time of distress!
   EVERYMAN. Good Deeds, I pray you, help me in this need,
Or else I am for ever damned indeed;   510
Therefore help me to make my reckoning
Before the Redeemer of all thing,
That King is, and was, and ever shall.
  GOOD DEEDS. Everyman, I am sorry of your fall,
And fain would I help you, and I were able.   515
   EVERYMAN. Good Deeds, your counsel I pray you give me.
  GOOD DEEDS. That shall I do verily;
Though that on my feet I may not go,
I have a sister that shall with you also,
Called Knowledge, which shall with you abide,   520
To help you to make that dreadful reckoning.

[*Enter* KNOWLEDGE.]

  KNOWLEDGE. Everyman, I will go with thee, and be thy guide
In thy most need to go by thy side.
   EVERYMAN. In good condition I am now in every thing,
And am wholly content with this good thing;   525
Thanked be God my Creator.
  GOOD DEEDS. And when he hath brought thee there,
Where thou shalt heal thee of thy smart,
Then go you with your reckoning and your Good Deeds
    together
For to make you joyful at heart   530
Before the blessèd Trinity.

EVERYMAN. My Good Deeds, gramercy!
I am well content, certainly,
With your words sweet.
   KNOWLEDGE. Now go we together lovingly   535
To Confession, that cleansing river.
   EVERYMAN. For joy I weep; I would we were there!
But, I pray you, give me cognition
Where dwelleth that holy man, Confession.
   KNOWLEDGE. In the house of salvation;   540
We shall find him in that place,
That shall us comfort, by God's grace.

   [KNOWLEDGE *leads* EVERYMAN *to* CONFESSION.]

Lo, this is Confession. Kneel down and ask mercy,
For he is in good conceit[1] with God almighty.
   EVERYMAN [*Kneeling*]. O glorious fountain, that all unclean-
      ness doth clarify,   545
Wash from me the spots of vice unclean,
That on me no sin may be seen.
I come, with Knowledge, for my redemption,
Redempt with hearty and full contrition;
For I am commanded a pilgrimage to take,   550
And great accounts before God to make.
Now, I pray you, Shrift, mother of salvation.
Help my Good Deeds for my piteous exclamation.
   CONFESSION. I know your sorrow well, Everyman.
Because with Knowledge ye come to me,   555
I will you comfort as well as I can,
And a precious jewel I will give thee,
Called penance, voider of adversity;
Therewith shall your body chastised be,

[1] Esteem.

With abstinence, and perseverance in God's service.   560
Here shall you receive that scourge of me.

[*Gives* EVERYMAN *a scourge.*]

Which is penance strong, that ye must endure
To remember thy Savior was scourged for thee
With sharp scourges, and suffered it patiently;
So must thou ere thou 'scape that painful pilgrimage.   565
Knowledge, keep him in this voyage,
And by that time Good Deeds will be with thee.
But in any wise be seeker of mercy,
For your time draweth fast, and ye will saved be;
Ask God mercy, and He will grant truly;   570
When with the scourge of penance man doth him bind,
The oil of forgiveness then shall he find. [*Exit* CONFESSION.]
  EVERYMAN. Thanked be God for his gracious work!
For now I will my penance begin;
This hath rejoiced and lighted my heart,   575
Though the knots be painful and hard within.
  KNOWLEDGE. Everyman, look your penance that ye fulfil,
What pain that ever it to you be,
And Knowledge shall give you counsel at will
How your account ye shall make clearly.   580

[EVERYMAN *kneels.*]

  EVERYMAN. O eternal God! O heavenly figure!
O way of rightwiseness! O goodly vision!
Which descended down in a virgin pure
Because he would Everyman redeem,
Which Adam forfeited by his disobedience.   585
O blesséd Godhead! elect and high divine,
Forgive me my grievous offence;
Here I cry thee mercy in this presence.

O ghostly treasure! O ransomer and redeemer!
Of all the world hope and conductor,   590
Mirror of joy, and founder of mercy,
Which illumineth heaven and earth thereby,
Hear my clamorous complaint, though it late be.
Receive my prayers; unworthy in this heavy life.
Though I be a sinner most abominable,   595
Yet let my name be written in Moses' table.
O Mary! pray to the Maker of all thing,
Me for to help at my ending,
And save me from the power of my enemy,
For Death assaileth me strongly.   600
And, Lady, that I may by means of thy prayer
Of your Son's glory to be partner,
By the means of his passion I it crave;
I beseech you, help my soul to save.   [*He rises.*]
Knowledge, give me the scourge of penance.   605
My flesh therewith shall give a quittance.
I will now begin, if God give me grace.
   KNOWLEDGE. Everyman, God give you time and space.
Thus I bequeath you in the hands of our Savior,
Now may you make your reckoning sure.   610
   EVERYMAN. In the name of the Holy Trinity,
My body sore punished shall be.   [*Scourges himself.*]
Take this, body, for the sin of the flesh;
Also thou delightest to go gay and fresh,
And in the way of damnation thou did me bring;   615
Therefore suffer now strokes of punishing.
Now of penance I will wade the water clear,
To save me from purgatory, that sharp fire.

[GOOD DEEDS *rises from floor.*]

   GOOD DEEDS. I thank God, now I can walk and go,
And am delivered of my sickness and woe.   620

Therefore with Everyman I will go, and not spare;
His good works I will help him to declare.
   KNOWLEDGE. Now, Everyman, be merry and glad!
Your Good Deeds cometh now, ye may not be sad;
Now is your Good Deeds whole and sound,   625
Going upright upon the ground.
   EVERYMAN. My heart is light, and shall be evermore.
Now will I smite faster than I did before.
   GOOD DEEDS. Everyman, pilgrim, my special friend,
Blessèd be thou without end.   630
For thee is prepared the eternal glory.
Ye have me made whole and sound,
Therefore I will bide by thee in every stound.[1]
   EVERYMAN. Welcome, my Good Deeds; now I hear thy voice,
I weep for very sweetness of love.   635
   KNOWLEDGE. Be no more sad, but ever rejoice;
God seeth thy living in his throne above.
Put on this garment to thy behoof,
Which is wet with your tears,
Or else before God you may it miss,   640
  When you to your journey's end come shall.
   EVERYMAN. Gentle Knowledge, what do ye it call?
   KNOWLEDGE. It is the garment of sorrow;
From pain it will you borrow;
Contrition it is   645
That getteth forgiveness;
It pleaseth God passing well.
   GOOD DEEDS. Everyman, will you wear it for your heal?

     [EVERYMAN *puts on garment of contrition.*]

   EVERYMAN. Now blessèd be Jesu, Mary's Son,
For now have I on true contrition.   650

  [1] Always.

And let us go now without tarrying;
Good Deeds, have we clear our reckoning?

GOOD DEEDS. Yea, indeed I have it here.

EVERYMAN. Then I trust we need not fear.

Now, friends, let us not part in twain.   655

KNOWLEDGE. Nay, Everyman, that will we not, certain.

GOOD DEEDS. Yet must thou lead with thee
Three persons of great might.

EVERYMAN. Who should they be?

GOOD DEEDS. Discretion and Strength they hight[1],   660
And thy Beauty may not abide behind.

KNOWLEDGE. Also ye must call to mind
Your Five Wits as for your counselors.

GOOD DEEDS. You must have them ready at all hours.

EVERYMAN. How shall I get them hither?   665

KNOWLEDGE. You must call them all together,
And they will hear you incontinent.

EVERYMAN. My friends, come hither and be present;
Discretion, Strength, my Five Wits, and Beauty.

[*Enter* DISCRETION, STRENGTH, FIVE WITS, *and* BEAUTY.]

BEAUTY. Here at your will we be all ready.   670
What will ye that we should do?

GOOD DEEDS. That ye would with Everyman go,
And help him in his pilgrimage.
Advise you, will ye with him or not in that voyage?

STRENGTH. We will bring him all thither,   675
To his help and comfort, ye may believe me.

DISCRETION. So will we go with him all together.

EVERYMAN. Almighty God, lovéd may thou be!
I give thee laud that I have hither brought

[1] Are called.

Strength, Discretion, Beauty, and Five Wits. Lack I naught;
And my Good Deeds, with Knowledge clear,   681
All be in company at my will here.
I desire no more to my business.

STRENGTH. And I, Strength, will by you stand in distress,
Though thou would in battle fight on the ground.   685

FIVE WITS. And though it were through the world round,
We will not depart for sweet nor sour.

BEAUTY. No more will I, unto death's hour,
Whatsoever thereof befall.

DISCRETION. Everyman, advise you first of all;   690
Go with a good advisement and deliberation.
We all give you virtuous monition
That all shall be well.

EVERYMAN. My friends, hearken what I will tell:
I pray God reward you in his heavenly sphere.   695
Now hearken, all that be here,
For I will make my testament
Here before you all present:
In alms half my goods I will give with my hands twain
In the way of charity, with good intent,   700
And the other half still shall remain;
I it bequeath to be returned there it ought to be.
This I do in despite of the fiend of hell,
To go quite out of his peril
Ever after and this day.   705

KNOWLEDGE. Everyman, hearken what I say;
Go to Priesthood, I you advise,
And receive of him in any wise
The holy sacrament and ointment together;
Then shortly see ye turn again hither;   710
We will all abide you here.

FIVE WITS. Yea, Everyman, hie you that ye ready were.

There is no emperor, king, duke, nor baron,
That of God hath commission
As hath the least priest in the world being;   715
For of the blessèd sacraments pure and benign
He beareth the keys, and thereof hath the cure
For man's redemption—it is ever sure—
Which God for our soul's medicine
Gave us out of his heart with great pain,   720
Here in this transitory life, for thee and me.
The blessèd sacraments seven there be:
Baptism, confirmation, with priesthood good,
And the sacrament of God's precious flesh and blood,
Marriage, the holy extreme unction, and penance.   725
These seven be good to have in remembrance,
Gracious sacraments of high divinity.

    EVERYMAN. Fain would I receive that holy body
And meekly to my ghostly[1] father I will go.

    FIVE WITS. Everyman, that is the best that ye can do.   730
God will you to salvation bring,
For priesthood exceedeth all other thing;
To us Holy Scripture they do teach,
And converteth man from sin, heaven to reach;
God hath to them more power given,   735
Than to any angel that is in heaven.
With five words he may consecrate
God's body in flesh and blood to make,
And handleth his Maker between his hands.
The priest bindeth and unbindeth all bands,   740
Both in earth and in heaven;
Thou ministers all the sacraments seven;
Though we kissed thy feet, thou wert worthy;

---

[1] Spiritual.

Thou art the surgeon that cureth sin deadly:
No remedy we find under God   745
But all only priesthood.
Everyman, God gave priests that dignity,
And setteth them in his stead among us to be;
Thus be they above angels, in degree.

[*Exit* EVERYMAN.]

KNOWLEDGE. If priests be good, it is so, surely.   750
But when Jesus hanged on the cross with great smart,
There he gave out of his blessèd heart
The same sacrament in great torment.
He sold them not to us, that Lord omnipotent.
Therefore Saint Peter the Apostle doth say   755
That Jesus' curse hath all they
Which God their Savior do buy or sell,
Or they for any money do take or tell.
Sinful priests giveth the sinners example bad;
Their children sitteth by other men's fires, I have heard;
And some haunteth women's company   761
With unclean life, as lusts of lechery.
These be with sin made blind.
    FIVE WITS. I trust to God no such may we find.
Therefore let us priesthood honor,   765
And follow their doctrine for our souls' succor.
We be their sheep, and they shepherds be
By whom we all be kept in surety.
Peace! for yonder I see Everyman come,
Which hath made true satisfaction.   770
    GOOD DEEDS. Methinketh it is he indeed.

[*Re-enter* EVERYMAN.]

EVERYMAN. Now Jesu be your alder speed[1].
I have received the sacrament for my redemption,
And then mine extreme unction.
Blesséd be all they that counseled me to take it!   775
And now, friends, let us go without longer respite.
I thank God that ye have tarried so long.
Now set each of you on this rod[2] your hand,
And shortly follow me.
I go before, there I would be. God be our guide.   780
  STRENGTH. Everyman, we will not from you go,
Till ye have done this voyage long.
  DISCRETION. I, Discretion, will bide by you also.
  KNOWLEDGE. And though this pilgrimage be never so strong,
I will never part you fro.   785
Everyman, I will be as sure by thee
As ever I did by Judas Maccabee.

[*They go together to the grave.*]

EVERYMAN. Alas! I am so faint I may not stand,
My limbs under me do fold.
Friends, let us not turn again to this land,   790
Not for all the world's gold;
For into this cave must I creep
And turn to earth, and there to sleep.
  BEAUTY. What, into this grave? Alas!
  EVERYMAN. Yea, there shall you consume, more and less.   795
  BEAUTY. And what, should I smother here?
  EVERYMAN. Yea, by my faith, and never more appear.
In this world live no more we shall,
But in heaven before the highest Lord of all.

---

[1] Succor of all of you.   [2] Cross.

BEAUTY. I cross out all this; adieu, by Saint John!   800
I take my cap in my lap and am gone.

EVERYMAN. What, Beauty, whither will ye?

BEAUTY. Peace! I am deaf. I look not behind me,
Not and thou would give me all the gold in thy chest. [*Exit*
   BEAUTY.]

EVERYMAN. Alas, whereto may I trust?   805
Beauty goeth fast away from me;
She promised with me to live and die.

STRENGTH. Everyman, I will thee also forsake and deny.
Thy game liketh me not at all.

EVERYMAN. Why, then ye will forsake me all?   810
Sweet Strength, tarry a little space.

STRENGTH. Nay, sir, by the rood of grace,
I will hie me from thee fast,
Though thou weep till thy heart to-brast[1].

EVERYMAN. Ye would ever bide by me, ye said.   815

STRENGTH. Yea, I have you far enough conveyed.
Ye be old enough, I understand,
Your pilgrimage to take on hand.
I repent me that I hither came.

EVERYMAN. Strength, you to displease I am to blame;   820
Yet promise is debt, this ye well wot.

STRENGTH. In faith, I care not!
Thou art but a fool to complain.
You spend your speech and waste your brain;
Go, thrust thee into the ground.   [*Exit* STRENGTH.]   825

EVERYMAN. I had weened surer I should you have found.
He that trusteth in his Strength
She him deceiveth at the length.
Both Strength and Beauty forsaketh me,

[1] Break into pieces.

Yet they promised me fair and lovingly. 830

DISCRETION. Everyman, I will after Strength be gone;
As for me I will leave you alone.

EVERYMAN. Why, Discretion, will ye forsake me?

DISCRETION. Yea, in faith, I will go from thee;
For when Strength goeth before 835
I follow after evermore.

EVERYMAN. Yet, I pray thee, for the love of the Trinity,
Look in my grave once piteously.

DISCRETION. Nay, so nigh will I not come.
Farewell, every one! [*Exit* DISCRETION.] 840

EVERYMAN. O all thing faileth, save God alone—
Beauty, Strength, and Discretion;
For when Death bloweth his blast,
They all run from me full fast.

FIVE WITS. Everyman, my leave now of thee I take; 845
I will follow the other, for here I thee forsake.

EVERYTHING. Alas! then may I wail and weep,
For I took you for my best friend.

FIVE WITS. I will no longer thee keep;
Now farewell, and there an end. [*Exit* FIVE WITS.] 850

EVERYMAN. O Jesu, help! All hath forsaken me!

GOOD DEEDS. Nay, Everyman; I will bide with thee,
I will not forsake thee indeed;
Thou shalt find me a good friend at need.

EVERYMAN. Gramercy, Good Deeds! Now may I true friends
see. 855
They have forsaken me, every one;
I loved them better than my Good Deeds alone.
Knowledge, will ye forsake me also?

KNOWLEDGE. Yea, Everyman, when ye to death shall go;

But not yet, for no manner of danger.   860
  EVERYMAN. Gramercy, Knowledge, with all my heart.
  KNOWLEDGE. Nay, yet I will not from hence depart
Till I see where ye shall be come.
  EVERYMAN. Methink, alas, that I must be gone
To make my reckoning and my debts pay,   865
For I see my time is nigh spent away.
Take example, all ye that this do hear or see,
How they that I loved best do forsake me,
Except my Good Deeds that bideth truly.
  GOOD DEEDS. All earthly things is but vanity.   870
Beauty, Strength, and Discretion do man forsake,
Foolish friends and kinsmen, that fair spake,
All fleeth save Good Deeds, and that am I.
  EVERYMAN. Have mercy on me, God most mighty;
And stand by me, thou Mother and Maid, holy Mary!   875
  GOOD DEEDS. Fear not, I will speak for thee.
  EVERYMAN. Here I cry God mercy!
  GOOD DEEDS. Short our end, and 'minish our pain.
Let us go and never come again.
  EVERYMAN. Into thy hands, Lord, my soul I commend.   880
Receive it, Lord, that it be not lost.
As thou me boughtest, so me defend,
And save me from the fiend's boast,
That I may appear with that blessèd host
That shall be saved at the day of doom.   885
In manus tuas—of might's most
For ever—*commendo spiritum meum.*[1]

    [EVERYMAN *and* GOOD DEEDS *descend into the grave.*]

  KNOWLEDGE. Now hath he suffered that we all shall endure;
The Good Deeds shall make all sure.

---

[1] "Into thy hands I commend my spirit."

Now hath he made ending. 890
Methinketh that I hear angels sing
And make great joy and melody
Where Everyman's soul received shall be.
   ANGEL [*within*]. Come, excellent elect spouse to Jesu!
Here above thou shalt go 895
Because of thy singular virtue.
Now the soul is taken the body fro,
Thy reckoning is crystal clear.
Now shalt thou into the heavenly sphere,
Unto the which all ye shall come 900
That liveth well before the day of doom.

[*Exit* KNOWLEDGE. *Enter* DOCTOR *for Epilogue.*]

   DOCTOR. This moral men may have in mind:
Ye hearers, take it of worth, old and young,
And forsake Pride, for he deceiveth you in the end,
And remember Beauty, Five Wits, Strength, and Discretion,
They all at the last do Everyman forsake, 906
Save his Good Deeds there doth he take.
But beware, and they be small
Before God he hath no help at all.
None excuse may be there for Everyman. 910
Alas, how shall he do then?
For, after death, amends may no man make,
For then mercy and pity doth him forsake.
If his reckoning be not clear when he doth come,
God will say, "*Ite, maledicti, in ignem aeternum*[1]." 915
And he that hath his account whole and sound,
High in heaven he shall be crowned.
Unto which place God bring us all thither,
That we may live body and soul together.

---

[1] "Go cursed ones, into eternal fire."

Thereto help the Trinity!   920
Amen, say ye, for saint charity.

THUS ENDETH THIS MORAL PLAY OF EVERYMAN.

A RIGHT PITHY, PLEASANT, AND MERRY COMEDY ENTITLED

GAMMER GURTON'S NEEDLE

PLAYED ON STAGE NOT LONG AGO IN CHRIST'S COLLEGE IN CAMBRIDGE. MADE BY MR. S.,* M. A.

❧

THE NAMES OF THE SPEAKERS IN THIS COMEDY:

DICCON, *the Bedlam*
HODGE, *Gammer Gurton's Servant*
TIB, *Gammer Gurton's Maid*
GAMMER GURTON
COCK, *Gammer Gurton's Boy*
DAME CHAT
DOCTOR RAT, *the Curate*
MASTER BAILY
DOLL, *Dame Chat's Maid*
SCAPETHRIFT, *Master Baily's Servant*
MUTES

GOD SAVE THE QUEEN

THE PROLOGUE

As Gammer Gurton with many a wide stitch
Sat piecing and patching of Hodge her man's breech,
By chance or misfortune, as she her gear toss'd,
In Hodge's leather breeches her needle she lost.
When Diccon the Bedlam[1] had heard by report   5

---

* Presumably William Stevenson. The play was probably first presented in 1553-1554.
[1] Beggar.

That good Gammer Gurton was robbed in this sort,
He quietly persuaded with her in that stound[1]
Dame Chat, her dear gossip[2], this needle had found;
Yet knew she no more of this matter, alas,
Than knoweth Tom, our clerk, what the priest saith at mass!
Hereof there ensued so fearful a fray,　　　　　　　　11
Mas. Doctor was sent for, these gossips to stay,
Because he was curate, and esteemed full wise;
Who found that he sought not, by Diccon's device.
When all things were tumbled and clean out of fashion, 15
Whether it were by fortune, or some other constellation,
Suddenly the needle Hodge found by the pricking,
And drew it out of his buttock, where he felt it sticking.
Their hearts then at rest with perfect security,
With a pot of good ale they struck up their plaudite.　　20

THE FIRST ACT. THE FIRST SCENE.
[*Near* GAMMER GURTON'S *house*.]

DICCON. Many a mile have I walked, divers and sundry ways,
And many a good man's house have I been at in my days;
Many a gossip's cup in my time have I tasted,
And many a broach and spit have I both turned and basted,
Many a piece of bacon have I had out of their balks[1],　　5
In running over the country, with long and weary walks;
Yet came my foot never within those door cheeks,
To seek flesh or fish, garlick, onions, or leeks,
That ever I saw a sort[2] in such a plight
As here within this house appeareth to my sight.　　　　10
There is howling and scowling, all cast in a dump,
With whewling and puling, as though they had lost a trump.

---

[1] (line 7) Moment.　　[2] Good friend.

[1] (line 5) Rafters.　　[2] Company.

Sighing and sobbing, they weep and they wail;
I marvel in my mind what the devil they ail.
The old trot sits groaning, with alas and alas!   15
And Tib wrings her hands, and takes on in worse case.
With poor Cock, their boy, they be driven in such fits,
I fear me the folks be not well in their wits.
Ask them what they ail, or who brought them in this stay,
They answer not at all, but, "alack!" and "wellaway!"   20
When I saw it booted not, out at doors I hied me,
And caught a slip of bacon, when I saw none spied me,
Which I intend not far hence, unless my purpose fail,
Shall serve me for a shoeing horn to draw on two pots of ale.

THE FIRST ACT. THE SECOND SCENE.

HODGE, DICCON.

HODGE. See! So cham[1] arrayed with dabbling in the dirt!
She that set me to ditching, ich would she had the squirt!
Was never poor soul that such a life had.
Gog's bones! This vilthy glay[2] has dress'd me too bad!
Gog's soul! See how this stuff tears!   5
Ich were better to be a bearward, and set to keep bears!
By the mass, here is a gash, a shameful hole indeed!
And one stitch tear further, a man may thrust in his head.
DICCON. By my father's soul, Hodge, if I should now be
     sworn,
I cannot choose but say thy breech is foul betorn,   10
But the next remedy in such a case and hap
Is to planch[3] on a piece as broad as thy cap.
HODGE. Gog's soul, man, 'tis not yet two days fully ended,

---

[1] I am. Note also *Ich* for *I*, *Chwould* for *I would*, etc. These southern dialect forms were regularly used for rustic speech. Cf. *Second Shepherds' Play*, ll. 201 ff.
[2] Filthy clay (also dialect forms).   [3] Plank.

Since my dame Gurton, cham sure, these breeches amended;
But cham made such a drudge to trudge at every need,   15
Chwould rend it though it were stitched with sturdy packthread.

DICCON. Hodge, let thy breeches go, and speak and tell me
  soon
What devil aileth Gammer Gurton and Tib her maid to frown.

HODGE. Tush, man, th'art deceived; 'tis their daily look.   19
They cow'r so over the coals, their eyes be blear'd with smoke.

DICCON. Nay, by the mass, I perfectly perceived, as I came
  hither,
That either Tib and her dame hath been by the ears together,
Or else as great a matter, as thou shalt shortly see.

HODGE. Now, ich beseech our Lord they never better agree!

DICCON. By Gog's soul, there they sit as still as stones in the
  street,   25
As though they had been taken with fairies, or else with some
  ill spright.

HODGE. Gog's heart! I durst have laid my cap to a crown
Chwould learn of some prancome[1] as soon as ich came to town.

DICCON. Why, Hodge, art thou inspired? Or didst thou thereof
  hear?

HODGE. Nay, but ich saw such a wonder as ich saw nat this
  seven year.   30
Tom Tankard's cow, by Gog's bones! she set me up her sail,
And flinging about his half acre, fisking with[2] her tail,
As though there had been in her arse a swarm of bees,
And chad not cried "tphrowh, whore," she'd leapt out of his
  leas.

DICCON. Why, Hodge, lies the cunning in Tom Tankard's
  cow's tail?   35

HODGE. Well, ich chave heard some say such tokens do not
  fail.

[1] Strange event.   [2] Frisking.

But ca[n]st thou not tell, in faith, Diccon, why she frowns, or
    whereat?

Hath no man stolen her ducks or hens, or gelded Gib, her cat?

    DICCON. What devil can I tell, man? I could not have one
      word!

They gave no more heed to my talk than thou wouldst to a
    lord.   40

    HODGE. Ich cannot still but muse, what marvellous thing it is.

Chill in and know myself what matters are amiss.

    DICCON. Then farewell, Hodge, a while, since thou dost in-
    ward haste.

For I will into the good wife Chat's, to feel how the ale doth
    taste.

THE FIRST ACT. THE THIRD SCENE.

HODGE. TIB [*enters*].

    HODGE. Cham aghast! By the mass, ich wot not what to do.

Chad need bless me well before ich go them to.

Perchance some felon sprite may haunt our house indeed;

And then chwere but a noddy to venture where cha' no need.

    TIB. Cham worse than mad, by the mass, to be at this stay! 5

Cham chid, cham blam'd, and beaten, all th'hours on the day;

Lamed and hunger-starved, pricked up all in jags,

Having no patch to hide my back, save a few rotten rags!

    HODGE. I say, Tib, if thou be Tib, as I trow sure thou be,

What devil make-a-do is this, between our dame and thee? 10

    TIB. Gog's bread, Hodge, thou had a good turn thou wert
      not here this while!

It had been better for some of us to have been hence a mile;

My gammer is so out of course and frantic all at once,

That Cock, our boy, and I, poor wench, have felt it on our
    bones.

HODGE. What is the matter—say on, Tib—whereat she taketh
    so on? 15

TIB. She is undone, she saith! Alas, her joy and life is gone!
If she hear not of some comfort, she is, faith! but dead;
Shall never come within her lips one inch of meat nor bread.

HODGE. By'r lady, cham not very glad to see her in this dump.
Chold a noble[1] her stool hath fallen, and she hath broke her
    rump. 20

TIB. Nay, and that were the worst, we would not greatly
    care
For bursting of her huckle-bone, or breaking of her chair;
But greater, greater, is her grief, as, Hodge, we shall all feel!

HODGE. Gog's wounds, Tib, my gammer has never lost her
    nee'le?

TIB. Her nee'le!

HODGE.   Her nee'le?

TIB.   Her nee'le! 25
By him that made me, it is true, Hodge, I tell thee.

HODGE. Gog's sacrament! I would she had lost th'heart out
    of her belly!
The devil, or else his dame, they ought[2] her, sure a shame!
How a murrion came this chance, say, Tib! unto our dame?

TIB. My gammer sat her down on her pes[3], and bade me reach
    thy breeches, 30
And by and by—a vengeance in it!—ere she had take two
    stitches
To clout a clout, upon thine arse, by chance aside she leers,
And Gib, our cat, in the milk-pan she spied over head and ears.
"Ah, whore! out, thief!" she cried aloud, and swept the breeches
    down. 34
Up went her staff, and out leapt Gib at doors into the town,

---

[1] I bet a noble.   [2] Owed.   [3] Hassock.

And since that time was never wight could set their eyes
    upon it.
Gog's malison[1] chave Cock and I bid twenty times light
    on it.

  HODGE. And is not then my breeches sewed up, to-morrow
    that I should wear?

  TIB. No, in faith, Hodge, thy breeches lie for all this never
    the near[2].

  HODGE. Now a vengeance light on all the sort, that better
    should have kept it,   40

The cat, the house, and Tib, our maid, that better should have
    swept it!

See where she cometh crawling! Come on, in twenty devils'
    way!

Ye have made a fair day's work, have you not? Pray you, say!

THE FIRST ACT. THE FOURTH SCENE.

GAMMER [*enters*]. HODGE, TIB, COCK.

  GAMMER. Alas, Hodge, alas! I may well curse and ban
This day, that ever I saw it, with Gib and the milk-pan;
For these and ill-luck together, as knoweth Cock, my boy,
Have stuck away my dear nee'le, and robbed me of my joy,
My fair long straight nee'le, that was mine only treasure; 5 ·
The first day of my sorrow is, and last end of my pleasure!

  HODGE (*aside*). Might ha' kept it, when ye had it! But fools
    will be fools still,

Lose that is vast in your hands ye need not, but ye will.

  GAMMER. Go hie thee, Tib, and run, thou whore, to th'end here
    of the town[1]!   9

Didst carry out dust in thy lap? Seek where thou pourest it down;

---

[1] (line 37) Curse.   [2] Not yet repaired.

[1] (line 9) The enclosure about her house.

And as thou sawest me poking, in the ashes where I mourned,
So see in all the heap of dust thou leave no straw unturned.

   TIB. That chall, Gammer, swyth[1] and tite[1], and soon be here
     again!

   GAMMER. Tib, stoop and look down to the ground to it, and
     take some pain.   14

   HODGE. Here is a pretty matter, to see this gear how it goes:

By Gog's soul, I think you would lose your arse, and it were
     loose!

Your nee'le lost? It is pity you should lack care and endless
     sorrow.

Gog's death, how shall my breeches be sewed? Shall I go thus
     to-morrow?

   GAMMER. Ah, Hodge, Hodge! If that ich could find my nee'le,
     by the reed[2],

Ch'ould sew thy breeches, ich promise thee, with full good
     double thread,   20

And set a patch on either knee should last this moneths twain.

Now God and good Saint Sithe[3], I pray to send it home
     again!

   HODGE. Whereto served your hands and eyes, but this your
     nee'le to keep?   23

What devil had you else to do? Ye keep, ich wot, no sheep!

Cham fain abroad to dig and delve, in water, mire, and clay,

Sossing and possing in the dirt still from day to day.

A hundred things that be abroad, cham set to see them well,

And four of you sit idle at home, and cannot keep a nee'le!

   GAMMER. My nee'le, alas! Ich lost it, Hodge, what time ich me
     up hasted

To save the milk set up for thee, which Gib, our cat, hath
     wasted.   30

---

[1] Quickly.   [2] I. e., rood, cross.   [3] St. Osyth (?)

HODGE. The devil he burst both Gib and Tib, with all the rest!
Cham always sure of the worst end, whoever have the best!
Where ha' you been fidging[1] abroad, since you your nee'le lost?

GAMMER. Within the house, and at the door, sitting by this
same post,   35
Where I was looking a long hour, before these folks came here;
But, wellaway, all was in vain, my nee'le is never the near!

HODGE. Set me a candle, let me seek, and grope wherever
it be.
Gog's heart, ye be foolish ich think, you know it not when you
it see!   39

GAMMER. Come hither, Cock! What, Cock, I say!

[*Enter* COCK.]

COCK.   How, Gammer?

GAMMER.   Go, hie thee soon,
And grope behind the old brass pan, which thing when thou
hast done,
There shalt thou find an old shoe, wherein, if thou look well,
Thou shalt find lying an inch of a white tallow candle;
Light it, and bring it tite away.

COCK.   That shall be done anon.

GAMMER. Nay, tarry, Hodge, till thou hast light, and then
we'll seek each one.   45

HODGE. Come away, ye whoreson boy, are ye asleep? Ye
must have a crier!

COCK. Ich cannot get the candle light: here is almost no fire.

HODGE. Chill hold[2] thee a penny, chill make thee come, if
that ich may catch thine ears!
Art deaf, thou whoreson boy? Cock, I say; why, canst not
hear?

GAMMER. Beat him not, Hodge, but help the boy, and come
you two together.   50

---

[1] Fidgeting, moving about.   [2] Bet.

THE FIRST ACT. THE FIFTH SCENE.

GAMMER, TIB. COCK, HODGE [*enter later*].

GAMMER. How now, Tib? Quick, let's hear what news thou
   hast brought hither!

TIB. Chave tost and tumbled yonder heap over and over
   again,

And winnowed it through my fingers, as men would winnow
   grain;

Not so much as a hen's turd, but in pieces I tare it;

Or whatsoever clod or clay I found, I did not spare it,   5

Looking within and eke without, to find your nee'le, alas!

But all in vain and without help! Your nee'le is where it was.

GAMMER. Alas, my nee'le! We shall never meet! Adieu, adieu,
   for aye!

TIB. Not so, Gammer, we might it find, if we knew where
   it lay.

COCK. Gog's cross, Gammer, if ye will laugh, look in but
   at the door,   10

And see how Hodge lieth tumbling and tossing amidst the
   flour,

Raking there some fire to find among the ashes dead,

Where there is not one spark so big as a pin's head;

At last in a dark corner two sparks he thought he sees,   14

Which were indeed nought else but Gib our cat's two eyes.

"Puff!" quod Hodge, thinking thereby to have fire without
   doubt;

With that Gib shut her two eyes, and so the fire was out;

And by and by them opened, even as they were before;

With that the sparks appeared, even as they had done of yore;

And even as Hodge blew the fire, as he did think,   20

Gib, as she felt the blast, straightway began to wink;

Till Hodge fell of swearing, as came best to his turn,
The fire was sure bewitch'd, and therefore would not burn.
At last Gib up the stairs, among the old posts and pins,   24
And Hodge he hied him after, till broke were both his shins;
Cursing and swearing oaths were never of his making,
That Gib would fire the house if that she were not taken.

GAMMER. See, here is all the thought that the foolish urchin
taketh!

And Tib, me think, at his elbow almost as merry maketh.
This is all the wit ye have, when others make their moan.
Come down, Hodge, where art thou? And let the cat alone!

HODGE. Gog's heart, help and come up! Gib in her tail hath
fire,

And is like to burn all, if she get a little higher!
Come down, quoth you? Nay, then you might count me a
patch[1],
The house cometh down on your heads, if it take once the
thatch.   25

GAMMER. It is the cat's eyes, fool, that shineth in the dark.

HODGE. Hath the cat, do you think, in every eye a spark?

GAMMER. No, but they shine as like fire as ever man see.

HODGE. By the mass, and she burn all, you sh' bear the blame
for me!

GAMMER. Come down and help to seek here our nee'le, that
it were found.   40

Down, Tib, on the knees, I say! Down, Cock, to the ground!
To God I make a vow, and so to good Saint Anne,
A candle shall they have a-piece, get it where I can,
If I may my nee'le find in one place or in other.

HODGE. Now a vengeance on Gib light, on Gib and Gib's
mother,   45
And all the generation of cats both far and near!

[1] Fool.

Look on the ground, whoreson, thinks thou the nee'le is here?
  COCK. By my troth, Gammer, methought your nee'le here
    I saw,
But when my fingers touch'd it, I felt it was a straw.
  TIB. See, Hodge, what's this? May it not be within it?   50
  HODGE. Break it, fool, with thy hand, and see and thou canst
    find it.
  TIB. Nay, break it you, Hodge, according to your word.
  HODGE. Gog's sides! Fie, it stinks! It is a cat's turd!
It were well done to make thee eat it, by the mass!
  GAMMER. This matter amendeth not; my nee'le is still where
    it was.   55
Our candle is at an end, let us all in quite,
And come another time, when we have more light.

THE SECOND ACT.

First a SONG.

> *Back and side go bare, go bare,*
>   *Both foot and hand go cold;*
> *But, belly, God send thee good ale enough,*
>   *Whether it be new or old.*

> *I cannot eat but little meat,*   5
>   *My stomach is not good;*
> *But sure I think that I can drink*
>   *With him that wears a hood.*
> *Though I go bare, take ye no care,*
>   *I am nothing a-cold;*   10
> *I stuff my skin so full within*
>   *Of jolly good ale and old.*
>   *Back and side go bare, go bare, etc.*

I love no roast but a nut-brown toast
  And a crab[1] laid in the fire.   15
A little bread shall do me stead:
  Much bread I not desire.
No frost nor snow, no wind, I trow,
  Can hurt me if I would;
I am so wrapt, and thoroughly lapt   20
  Of jolly good ale and old.
Back and side go bare, etc.

And Tib my wife, that as her life
  Loveth well good ale to seek,
Full oft drinks she till ye may see   25
  The tears run down her cheek;
Then doth she troll to me the bowl
  Even as a malt-worm should;
And saith, "Sweet heart, I took my part
  Of this jolly good ale and old."   30
    Back and side go bare, etc.

Now let them drink till they nod and wink,
  Even as good fellows should do;
They shall not miss to have the bliss
  Good ale doth bring men to;   35
And all poor souls that have scoured bowls,
  Or have them lustily troll'd,
God save the lives of them and their wives,
  Whether they be young or old.
Back and side go bare, etc.   40

---

[1] Roasted crab-apple, dropped into the ale.

THE SECOND ACT. THE FIRST SCENE.

DICCON [*enters from* DAME CHAT'S *alehouse*].

HODGE [*enters later*].

DICCON. Well done, by Gog's malt! Well sung and well said!
Come on, mother Chat, as thou art true maid,
One fresh pot of ale let's see, to make an end
Against this cold weather my naked arms to defend!   4
This gear it warms the soul! Now, wind, blow on thy worst!
And let us drink and swill till that our bellies burst!
Now were he a wise man by cunning could define
Which way my journey lieth, or where Diccon will dine!
But one good turn I have: be it by night or day,
South, east, north, or west, I am never out of my way!   10
   HODGE. Chim goodly rewarded, cham I not, do you think?
Chad a goodly dinner for all my sweat and swink!
Neither butter, cheese, milk, onions, flesh, nor fish,
Save this poor piece of barley-bread: 'tis a pleasant costly dish!
   DICCON. Hail, fellow Hodge, and well to fare with thy meat,
      if thou have any: 15
But by thy words, as I them smelled, thy daintrels[1] be not
      many.
   HODGE. Daintrels, Diccon? Gog's soul, man, save this piece
      of dry horsebread,
Cha bit no bit this livelong day, no crumb come in my head:
My guts they yawl-crawl, and all my belly rumbleth,   19
The puddings[2] cannot lie still, each one over other tumbleth.
By Gog's heart, cham so vexed, and in my belly penn'd,
Chould one piece were at the spital-house, another at the
      castle end!

[1] Delicacies.   [2] Viscera.

DICCON. Why, Hodge, was there none at home thy dinner
for to set?

HODGE. Gog's bread, Diccon, ich came too late, was nothing
there to get!

Gib—a foul fiend might on her light!—licked the milk-pan so
clean, 25

See, Diccon, 'twas not so well washed this seven year, as ich
ween!

A pestilence light on all ill-luck! Chad thought, yet, for all this,

Of a morsel of bacon behind the door at worst should not
miss:

But when ich sought a slip to cut, as ich was wont to do, 29

Gog's souls, Diccon! Gib, our cat, had eat the bacon too!

Which bacon DICCON *stole, as is declared before.*

DICCON. Ill-luck, quod he? Marry, swear it, Hodge! this day,
the truth tell,

Thou rose not on thy right side, or else blessed thee not well.

Thy milk slopped up, thy bacon filched! That was too bad
luck, Hodge!

HODGE. Nay, nay, there was a fouler fault, my Gammer ga'
me the dodge;

Seest not how cham rent and torn, my heels, my knees, and
my breech? 35

Chad thought, as ich sat by the fire, help here and there a stich;

But there ich was pouped[1] indeed.

DICCON.   Why, Hodge?

HODGE.   Boots not,
man, to tell.

Cham so drest amongst a sort of fools, chad better be in hell.

My Gammer, cham ashamed to say, by God, served me not
well.

---

[1] Fooled, cheated.

DICCON. How so, Hodge?

HODGE.   Has she not gone, trowest now,
and lost her nee'le?   40

DICCON. Her eel, Hodge? Who fished of late? That was a
dainty dish!

HODGE. Tush, tush, her nee'le, her nee'le, her nee'le, man!
'Tis neither flesh nor fish;

A little thing with an hole in the end, as bright as any
sil'er,

Small, long, sharp at the point, and straight as any pillar.

DICCON. I know not what a devil thou meanest; thou bring'st
me more in doubt.   45

HODGE. Knowest not with what Tom Tailor's man sits
broaching through a clout[1]?

A nee'le, a nee'le, a nee'le! My Gammer's nee'le is gone.

DICCON. Her nee'le, Hodge! Now I smell thee! That was a
chance alone!

By the mass, thou hast a shameful loss, and it were but for thy
breeches.

HODGE. Gog's soul, man, chould give a crown chad it but
three stitches.   50

DICCON. How sayest thou, Hodge? What should he have,
again thy Needle got?

HODGE. By m'father's soul, and chad it, chould give him a
new groat.

DICCON. Canst thou keep counsel in this case?

HODGE.   Else chwold
my tongue were out.

DICCON. Do thou but then by my advice, and I will fetch
it without doubt.

HODGE. Chill run, chill ride, chill dig, chill delve,   55
Chill toil, chill trudge, shalt see;

---

[1] Piercing through a cloth.

Chill hold, chill draw, chill pull, chill pinch,
  Chill kneel on my bare knee;
Chill scrape, chill scratch, chill sift, chill seek,
  Chill bow, chill bend, chill sweat,   40
Chill stoop, chill stir, chill cap, chill kneel,
  Chill creep on hands and feet;
Chill be thy bondman, Diccon, ich swear by sun and moon,
And channot somewhat to stop this gap, cham utterly undone!

Pointing behind to his torn breeches.

DICCON. Why, is there any special cause thou takest hereat
  such sorrow?   65
HODGE. Kirstian Clack, Tom Simpson's maid, by the mass,
  comes hither to-morrow,
Cham not able to say, between us what may hap;
She smiled on me the last Sunday, when ich put off my cap.
DICCON. Well, Hodge, this is a matter of weight, and must
  be kept close,   69
It might else turn to both our costs, as the world now goes.
Shalt swear to be no blab, Hodge?
HODGE.   Chill, Diccon.
DICCON.   Then go to,
Lay thine hand here; say after me, as thou shalt hear me do.
Hast no book?
HODGE.   Cha' no book, I.
DICCON.   Then needs must force us both,
Upon my breech to lay thine hand, and there to take thine
  oath.
        HODGE. I, Hodge, breechless   75
        Swear to Diccon, rechless[1],
        By the cross that I shall kiss,
        To keep his counsel close,

[1] Reckless.

And always me to dispose
To work that his pleasure is.   80

Here he kisseth DICCON's *breech.*

DICCON. Now, Hodge, see thou take heed,
And do as I thee bid;
For so I judge it meet;
This needle again to win,
There is no shift therein,   85
But conjure up a spreet.
  HODGE. What, the great devil, Diccon, I say?
  DICCON. Yea, in good faith, that is the way.
Fet[1] with some pretty charm.
  HODGE. Soft, Diccon, be not too hasty yet,   90
By the mass, for ich begin to sweat!
Cham afraid of some harm.
  DICCON. Come hither, then, and stir thee not
One inch out of this circle plat,
But stand as I thee teach.   95
  HODGE. And shall ich be here safe from their claws?
  DICCON. The master-devil with his long paws
Here to thee cannot reach.
Now will I settle me to this gear.
  HODGE. I say, Diccon, hear me, hear!   100
Go softly to this matter!
  DICCON. What devil, man? Art afraid of nought?
  HODGE. Canst not tarry a little thought
Till ich make a courtesy of water?
  DICCON. Stand still! to it! Why shouldest thou fear him? 105
  HODGE. Gog's sides, Diccon, me think ich hear him!
And tarry, chall mar all!
  DICCON. The matter is no worse than I told it.

---

[1] Fetched.

HODGE. By the mass, cham able no longer to hold it!
Too bad! ich must beray[1] the hall!   110
 DICCON. Stand to it, Hodge! Stir not, you whoreson!
What devil, be thine arse-strings brusten?
Thyself a while but stay,
The devil (I smell him) will be here anon.
 HODGE. Hold him fast, Diccon, cham gone!   115
Chill not be at that fray!

THE SECOND ACT. THE SECOND SCENE.

DICCON. CHAT [*enters later*].

DICCON. Fie, shitten knave, and out upon thee!
    Above all other louts, fie on thee!
    Is not here a cleanly prank?
    But thy matter was no better,
    Nor thy presence here so sweeter,   5
    To fly I can thee thank.

    Here is a matter worthy glosing[1],
    Of Gammer Gurton's needle losing,
    And a foul piece of work!
    A man I think might make a play,   10
    And need no word to this they say,
    Being but half a clerk[2].

    Soft, let me alone, I will take the charge
    This matter further to enlarge
    Within a time short.   15
    If ye will mark my toys, and note,
    I will give ye leave to cut my throat
    If I make not good sport.

---

[1] (line 110) Befoul.

---

[1] (line 7) Commenting on.   [2] Learned man.

Dame Chat, I say, where be ye? Within?

   CHAT. Who have we there maketh such a din? 20

   DICCON. Here is a good fellow, maketh no great danger.

   CHAT. What, Diccon? Come near, ye be no stranger.

We be fast set at trump, man, hard by the fire;

Thou shalt set on the king, if thou come a little nigher.

   DICCON. Nay, nay, there is no tarrying; I must be gone

     again. 25

But first for you in counsel I have a word or twain.

   CHAT. Come hither, Doll! Doll, sit down and play this game,

And as thou sawest me do, see thou do even the same.

There is five trumps besides the queen, the hindmost thou shalt

     find her. 29

Take heed of Sim Glover's wife, she hath an eye behind her!

Now, Diccon, say your will.

   DICCON.   Nay, soft a little yet;

I would not tell it my sister, the matter is so great.

There I will have you swear by Our Dear Lady of Boulogne,

Saint Dunstan, and Saint Dominic, with the three Kings of

     Cologne,

That ye shall keep it secret.

   CHAT.   Gog's bread! that will I do! 35

As secret as mine own thought, by God and the devil too!

   DICCON. Here is Gammer Gurton, your neighbour, a sad and

     heavy wight:

Her goodly fair red cock at home was stole this last night.

   CHAT. Gog's soul! her cock with the yellow legs, that nightly

     crowed so just?

   DICCON. That cock is stolen.

   CHAT.   What, was he fet out of the

     hen's roost? 40

   DICCON. I cannot tell where the devil he was kept, under key

     or lock;

But Tib hath tickled in Gammer's ear, that you should steal
    the cock.
    CHAT. Have I, strong whore? By bread and salt!—
    DICCON.   What,
    soft, I say, be still!
Say not one word for all this gear.
    CHAT.   By the mass, that I will!
I will have the young whore by the head, and the old trot by
    the throat.   45
    DICCON. Not one word, Dame Chat, I say; not one word,
    for my coat!
    CHAT. Shall such a beggar's brawl[1] as that, thinkest thou, make
    me a thief?
The pox light on her whore's sides, a pestilence and mischief!
Come out, thou hungry needy bitch! O, that my nails be short!
    DICCON. Gog's bread, woman, hold your peace! This gear
    will else pass sport!   50
I would not for an hundred pound this matter should be
    known,
That I am author of this tale, or have abroad it blown!
Did ye not swear ye would be ruled, before the tale I told?
I said ye must all secret keep, and ye said sure ye would.
    CHAT. Would you suffer, yourself, Diccon, such a sort to
    revile you,   55
With slanderous words to blot your name, and so to defile you?
    DICCON. No, Goodwife Chat, I would be loath such drabs
    should blot my name,
But yet ye must so order all that Diccon bear no blame.
    CHAT. Go to, then, what is your reed[2]? Say on your mind,
    ye shall me rule herein.
    DICCON. Godamercy to Dame Chat! In faith thou must the
    gear begin.   60

---

[1] Brat.   [2] Counsel.

It is twenty pound to a goose-turd, my gammer will not tarry,
But hitherward she comes as fast as her legs can her carry,
To brawl with you about her cock; for well I heard Tib say
The cock was roasted in your house to breakfast yesterday;
And when ye had the carcass eaten, the feathers ye outflung,
And Doll, your maid, the legs she hid a foot-deep in the dung.

CHAT. O gracious God! My heart it bursts!

DICCON.   Well, rule your-
self a space;   67
And Gammer Gurton when she cometh anon into this place,
Then to the quean, let's see, tell her your mind, and spare not.
So shall Diccon blameless be; and then, go to, I care not! 70

CHAT. Then, whore, beware her throat! I can abide no longer.
In faith, old witch, it shall be seen which of us two be stronger!
And, Diccon, but at your request, I would not stay one hour.

DICCON. Well, keep it till she be here, and then out let it
pour!   74
In the meanwhile get you in, and make no words of this.
More of this matter within this hour to hear you shall not
miss;
Because I know you are my friend, hide it I could not, doubtless.
Ye know your harm; see ye be wise about your own business!
So fare ye well.

CHAT.   Nay, soft, Diccon, and drink! What, Doll,
I say!   79
Bring here a cup of the best ale; let's see, come quickly away!

THE SECOND ACT. THE THIRD SCENE.

HODGE, DICCON.

DICCON. Ye see, masters, that one end tapp'd of this my
short device!
Now must we broach th'other too, before the smoke arise;

And by the time they have a while run, I trust ye need not
    crave it.

But look, what lieth in both their hearts, ye are like, sure, to
    have it.

HODGE. Yea, Gog's soul, art alive yet? What, Diccon, dare
    ich come? 5

DICCON. A man is well hied[1] to trust to thee; I will say
    nothing but mum;

But and ye come any nearer, I pray you see all, be sweet!

HODGE. Tush, man, is Gammer's nee'le found? That chould
    gladly weet[2].

DICCON. She may thank thee it is not found, for if you had
    kept thy standing,

The devil he would have fet it out, ev'n, Hodge, at thy com-
    manding. 10

HODGE. Gog's heart! and could he tell nothing where the nee'le
    might be found?

DICCON. Ye foolish dolt, ye were to seek, ere we had got
    our ground;

Therefore his tale so doubtful was that I could not perceive it.

HODGE. Then ich see well something was said; chope one day
    yet to have it. 14

But Diccon, Diccon, did not the devil cry "ho, ho, ho"?

DICCON. If thou hadst tarried where thou stood'st, thou
    wouldst have said so!

HODGE. Durst swear of a book, cheard him roar, straight
    after ich was gone.

But tell me, Diccon, what said the knave? Let me hear it anon.

DICCON. The whoreson talked to me, I know not well of
    what.

One while his tongue it ran and paltered of a cat, 20

---

[1] Paid (?)   [2] Know.

Another while he stammered still upon a rat;
Last of all, there was nothing but every word, Chat, Chat;
But this I well perceived before I would him rid,
Between Chat, and the rat, and the cat, the needle is hid.
Now whether Gib, our cat, hath eat it in her maw,   25
Or Doctor Rat, our curate, have found it in the straw,
Or this Dame Chat, your neighbour, hath stolen it, God he
knoweth!
But by the morrow at this time, we shall learn how the matter
goeth.

HODGE. Canst not learn to-night, man? Seest not what is
here?

Pointing behind to his torn breeches.

DICCON. 'Tis not possible to make it sooner appear.   30

HODGE. Alas, Diccon, then chave no shift; but—lest ich tarry
too long—
Hie me to Sim Glover's shop, there to seek for a thong,
Therewith this breech to thatch and tie as ich may.

DICCON. To-morrow, Hodge, if we chance to meet, shall see
what I will say.

THE SECOND ACT. THE FOURTH SCENE.

DICCON, GAMMER.

DICCON. Now this gear must forward go, for here my
Gammer cometh.
Be still a while, and say nothing; make here a little romth[1].

GAMMER. Good lord, shall never be my luck my nee'le again
to spy?
Alas, the while, 'tis past my help! Where 'tis, still it must lie!

DICCON. Now, Jesus! Gammer Gurton, what driveth you to
this sadness?   5

---

[1] Room.

I fear me, by my conscience, you will sure fall to madness.

  GAMMER. Who is that? What, Diccon? Cham lost, man!
    fie, fie!

  DICCON. Marry, fie on them that be worthy! But what should
    be your trouble?

  GAMMER. Alas! the more ich think on it, my sorrow it waxeth
    double.

My goodly tossing spurrier's¹ nee'le chave lost ich wot not
    where.   10

  DICCON. Your nee'le? When?

  GAMMER.   My nee'le, alas, ich might full
    ill it spare,

As God himself he knoweth, ne'er one beside chave.

  DICCON. If this be all, good Gammer, I warrant you all is safe.

  GAMMER. Why, know you any tidings which way my nee'le
    is gone?   14

  DICCON. Yea, that I do, doubtless, as ye shall hear anon,

 A see a thing this matter toucheth within these twenty hours,

Even at this gate, before my face, by a neighbour of yours.

She stooped me down, and up she took up a needle or a pin.

I durst be sworn it was even yours, by all my mother's kin.

  GAMMER. It was my nee'le, Diccon, ich wot; for here, even
    by this post,   20

Ich sat, what time as ich up start, and so my nee'le it lost;

Who was it, leve² son? Speak, ich pray thee, and quickly tell
    me that!

  DICCON. A subtle quean as any in this town, your neighbour
    here, Dame Chat.

  GAMMER. Dame Chat, Diccon! Let me be gone, chill thither
    in post haste.

  DICCON. Take my counsel yet or ye go, for fear ye walk in
    waste,   25

---

¹ First-class harness-maker's.   ² Dear.

It is a murrain crafty drab, and froward to be pleased;
And ye take not the better way, our needle yet ye lose it.
For when she took it up, even here before your doors,
"What, soft, Dame Chat," quoth I, "that same is none of
    yours."
"Avaunt," quoth she, "sir knave! What pratest thou of that
    I find?   30
I would thou hast kiss'd me I wot where"; she meant, I know,
    behind;
And home she went as brag[1] as it had been a body-louse,
And I after, as bold as it had been the good-man of the house.
But there and ye had heard her, how she began to scold!
The tongue it went on pattens[2], by him that Judas sold!   35
Each other word I was a knave, and you a whore of whores,
Because I spake in your behalf, and said the nee'le was yours.
    GAMMER. Gog's bread, and thinks that callet thus to keep my
      nee'le me fro?
    DICCON. Let her alone, and she minds none other but even
      to dress you so.
    GAMMER. By the mass, chill rather spend the coat that is on
      my back!   40
Thinks the false quean by such a sleight[3], that chill my nee'le
    lack?
    DICCON. Slip not your gear, I counsel you, but of this take
      good heed:
Let not be known I told you of it, how well soever ye speed.
    GAMMER. Chill in, Diccon, a clean apron to take and set
      before me;   44
And ich may my nee'le once see, chill sure remember thee!

---

[1] Proud.   [2] Wooden shoes; noisily.   [3] Cf. sleight-of-hand.

THE SECOND ACT. THE FIFTH SCENE.

DICCON.

DICCON. Here will the sport begin; if these two once may
    meet,
Their cheer, durst lay money, will prove scarcely sweet.
My gammer, sure, intends to be upon her bones
With staves, or with clubs, or else with cobble stones.
Dame Chat, on the other side, if she be far behind,   5
I am right far deceived; she is given to it of kind[1].
He that may tarry by it awhile, and that but short,
I warrant him, trust to it, he shall see all the sport.
Into the town will I, my friends to visit there,
And hither straight again to see th'end of this gear.   10
In the meantime, fellows, pipe up; your fiddles, I say, take
    them,
And let your friends hear such mirth as ye can make them.

THE THIRD ACT. THE FIRST SCENE.

HODGE.

HODGE. Sim Glover, yet gramercy! Cham meetly well-sped
    now,
Th'art even as good a fellow as ever kiss'd a cow!
Here is a thong indeed, by the mass, though ich speak it;
Tom Tankard's great bald curtal[2], I think, could not break it!
And when he spied my need to be so straight and hard,   5
Has lent me here is nawl[3], to set the gib forward[4];
As for my gammer's nee'le, the flying fiend go wi' it!
Chill not now go to the door again with it to meet.
Chould make shift good enough and chad a candle's end;
The chief hole in my breech with these two chill amend.   10

---

[1] By nature.   [2] A "curtailed" horse.   [3] Awl.   [4] Help things out.

THE THIRD ACT. THE SECOND SCENE.

GAMMER, HODGE.

GAMMER. Now Hodge, may'st now be glad, cha news to tell
thee;

Ich know who has my nee'le; ich trust soon shall it see.

HODGE. The devil thou does! Hast heard, gammer, indeed,
or dost but jest?

GAMMER. 'Tis as true as steel, Hodge.

HODGE.   Why, knowest well
where didst lose it?

GAMMER. Ich know who found it, and took it up! Shalt see
ere it be long.   5

HODGE. God's Mother dear! If that be true, farewell both
nawl and thong!

But who has it, gammer? Say on; should fain hear it disclosed.

GAMMER. That false vixen, that same Dame Chat, that counts
herself so honest.

HODGE. Who told you so?

GAMMER.   That same did Diccon the bedlam, which saw it done.

HODGE. Diccon? It is a vengeable knave, Gammer, 'tis a
bonable[1] whoreson,   10

Can do mo things than that, els cham deceived evil:

By the mass, ich saw him of late call up a great black devil!

O, the knave cried "*ho, ho!*" He roared and he thundered,

And ye 'ad been here, cham sure you'ld murrainly[2] ha'
wondered.

GAMMER. Was not thou afraid, Hodge, to see him in this
place?   15

HODGE. No, and chad come to me, should have laid him on
the face,

---

[1] Abominable.   [2] Plaguily, confoundedly.

Chould have, promised him!

GAMMER. But, Hodge, had he no horns
    to push?

HODGE. As long as your two arms. Saw ye never Friar Rush[1]
Painted on a cloth, with a side-long cow's tail,
And crooked cloven feet, and many a hooked nail?   20
For all the world, if I should judge, chould reckon him his
    brother.
Look, even what face Friar Rush had, the devil had such another.

GAMMER. Now, Jesus' mercy, Hodge! Did Diccon in him
    bring?

HODGE. Nay, Gammer, hear me speak, chill tell you a greater
    thing.
The devil (when Diccon had him, ich heard him wondrous
    well)   25
Said plainly here before us, that Dame Chat had your nee'le.

GAMMER. Then let us go, and ask her wherefore she minds
    to keep it;
Seeing we know so much, 'twere a madness now to slip it.

HODGE. Go to her, Gammer; see ye not where she stands in
    her doors?   29
Bid her give you the nee'le, 'tis none of hers but yours.

THE THIRD ACT. THE THIRD SCENE.

GAMMER, CHAT, HODGE [*at a distance*].

GAMMER. Dame Chat, chould pray thee fair, let me have that
    is mine!
Chill not these twenty years take one fart that is thine;
Therefore give me mine own, and let me live beside thee.

CHAT. Why, art thou crept from home hither, to mine own
    doors to chide me?

---

[1] Character in a popular story.

Hence, doting drab, avaunt, or I shall set thee further!   5
Intends thou and that knave me in my house to murther?

GAMMER. Tush, gape not so on me, woman! Shalt not yet
eat me,
Nor all the friends thou hast, in this shall not entreat me!
Mine own goods I will have, and ask thee no by-leave:
What, woman! Poor folks must have right, though the thing
you aggrieve.   10

CHAT. Give thee thy right, and hang thee up, with all thy
beggar's brood!
What, wilt thou make me a thief, and say I stole thy good?

GAMMER. Chill say nothing, ich warrant thee, but that ich
can prove it well.
Thou fet my good even from my door, cham able this to tell!

CHAT. Did I, old witch, steal aught was thine? How should
that thing be known?   15

GAMMER. Ich cannot tell; but up thou tookest it as though it
had been thine own.

CHAT. Marry, fie on thee, thou old gib[1], with all my very
heart!

GAMMER. Nay, fie on thee, thou ramp[2], thou rig[2], with all
that take thy part!

CHAT. A vengeance on those lips that layeth such things to
my charge!

GAMMER. A vengeance on those callet's hips, whose conscience
is so large!   20

CHAT. Come out, hog!

GAMMER.   Come out, hog, and let have me
right!

CHAT. Thou arrant witch!

GAMMER.   Thou bawdy bitch, chill make
thee curse this night!

---

[1] Cat.   [2] Strumpet.

CHAT. A bag and a wallet!

GAMMER.   A cart for a callet!

CHAT.   Why, weenest
thou thus to prevail?
I hold thee a groat, I shall patch thy coat!

GAMMER.   Thou wert as good
kiss my tail!
Thou slut, thou cut[1], thou rakes[2], thou jakes[3]! will not shame
make thee hide [thee]?   25

CHAT. Thou skald[4], thou bald, thou rotten, thou glutton! I
will no longer chide thee;
But I will teach thee to keep home.

GAMMER.   Wilt thou, drunken beast?

They fight.

HODGE. Stick to her, Gammer, take her by the head; chill
warrant you this feast!
Smite, I say, Gammer! Bite, I say, Gammer! I trow ye will
be keen!
Where be your nails? Claw her by the jaws, pull me out both
her eyen.   33
Gog's bones, Gammer, hold up your head!

CHAT.   I trow, drab, I shall
dress thee.
Tarry, thou knave, I hold thee a groat! I shall make these hands
bless thee!
Take thou this, old whore, for amends, and learn thy tongue
well to tame,
And say thou met at this bickering, not thy fellow but thy
dame!

HODGE. Where is the strong stewed whore? Chill gi'r a whore's
mark!   35

---

[1] Gelding.   [2] Cf. "rakehell".   [3] Low wretch.   [4] Scurvy person.

Stand out one's way, that ich kill none in the dark!

Up, Gammer, and ye be alive! Chill fight now for us both.

Come no near me, thou scald callet! To kill thee ich were loth.

    CHAT. Art here again, thou hoddypeke[1]? What, Doll, bring
      me out my spit.

    HODGE. Chill broach thee with this; by m'father's soul, chill
      conjure that foul spreet.   40

Let door stand, Cock! Why com'st indeed? Keep door, thou
  whoreson boy!

    CHAT. Stand to it, thou dastard, for thine ears; ise teach
      thee, a sluttish toy!

    HODGE. Gog's wounds, whore, chill make thee avaunt!

Take heed, Cock, pull in the latch!   [*He flees.*]

    CHAT. I'faith, Sir Loose-breech, had ye tarried, ye should have
      found your match!   45

    GAMMER. Now 'ware thy throat, losel[2], thou'se pay for all!

    HODGE.   Well said,
  Gammer, by my soul.

Hoise[3] her, souse[3] her, bounce her, trounce her, pull her throat-
  bole![4]

    CHAT. Com'st behind me, thou withered witch? And I get
      once on foot,

Thou'se pay for all, thou old tar-leather! I'll teach thee what
  longs to it!

Take thee this to make up thy mouth, till time thou come by
  more!   50

    HODGE. Up, Gammer, stand on your feet; where is the old
      whore?

Faith, would chad her by the face, chould crack her callet crown!

    GAMMER. Ah, Hodge, Hodge, where was thy help, when
      vixen had me down?

---

[1] Fool.   [2] Good-for-nothing.   [3] Hit.   [4] Choke her.

HODGE. By the mass, Gammer, but for my staff Chat had
gone nigh to spill you!

Ich think the harlot had not cared, and chad not come, to kill
you.   55

But shall we lose our nee'le thus?

GAMMER.   No, Hodge, chwere loath
to do so.

Thinkest thou chill take that at her hand? No, Hodge, ich tell
thee no.

HODGE. Chould yet this fray were well take up, and our
nee'le at home,

'Twill be my chance else some to kill, wherever it be or
whom!

GAMMER. We have a parson, Hodge, thou knows, a man
esteemed wise,   60

Mast' Doctor Rat; chill for him send, and let me hear his
advice.

He will her shrive for all this gear, and give her penance straight;

Wese[1] have our nee'le, else Dame Chat comes ne'er within
heaven-gate.

HODGE. Yea, marry, Gammer, that ich think best; will you
now for him send?   64

The sooner Doctor Rat be here, the sooner wese ha' an end.

And here, Gammer! Diccon's devil, as ich remember well,

Of cat, and Chat, and Doctor Rat, a felonious tale did tell.

Chold you forty pound, that is the way your nee'le to get
again.

GAMMER. Chill ha' him straight! Call out the boy, wese
make him take the pain.

HODGE. What, Cock, I say! Come out! What devil! Can'st
not hear?   70

COCK. How now, Hodge? How does Gammer? Is yet the
weather clear?

[1] We'll.

What would chave me to do?

GAMMER.   Come hither, Cock, anon!

Hence swith[1] to Doctor Rat, hie thee that thou were gone,

And pray him come speak with me, cham not well at ease.

Shalt have him at his chamber, or else at Mother Bee's;   75

Else seek him at Hob Filcher's shop, for as cheard it reported,

There is the best ale in all the town, and now is most resorted.

COCK. And shall ich bring him with me, Gammer?

GAMMER.   Yea, by

and by[2], good Cock.

COCK. Shalt see that shall be here anon, else let me have on
the dock[3].

HODGE. Now, Gammer, shall we two go in, and tarry for
his coming?   80

What devil, woman! Pluck up your heart, and leave off all
this glooming.

Though she were stronger at the first, as ich think ye did
find her,

Yet there ye dress'd the drunken sow, what time ye came
behind her.

GAMMER. Nay, nay, cham sure she lost not all, for, set th'end
to the beginning,   84

And ich doubt not but she will make small boast of her winning.

THE THIRD ACT.   THE FOURTH SCENE.

TIB, HODGE, GAMMER. COCK [*enters later*].

TIB. See, Gammer, Gammer, Gib, our cat, cham afraid what
she aileth;

She stands me gasping behind the door, as though her wind
her faileth:

---

[1] Quickly.   [2] Right now.   [3] Tail, rear.

Now let ich doubt what Gib should mean, that now she doth
    so dote.

    HODGE. Hold hither! I chould twenty pound, your nee'le is
    in her throat.

Grope her, ich say. Methinks ich feel it; does not prick your
    hand?   5

    GAMMER. Ich can feel nothing.

    HODGE.   No? Ich know there's not
    within this land

A murrainer[1] cat than Gib is, betwixt the Thames and Tyne;
Sh'as as much wit in her head almost as ch'ave in mine.

    TIB. Faith, sh'as eaten something, that will not easily down;
Whether she gat it at home, or abroad in the town   10
Ich cannot tell.

    GAMMER.   Alas, ich fear it be some crooked pin!

And then farewell Gib! She is undone, and lost all save the skin!

    HODGE. 'Tis your nee'le, woman, I say! Gog's soul! give me
    a knife,

And chill have it out of her maw, or else chall lose my life!

    GAMMER. What! Nay, Hodge, fie! Kill not our cat, 'tis all
    the cats we ha' now.   15

    HODGE. By the mass, Dame Chat has me so moved, ich care
    not what I kill, ma[2] God a vow!

Go to, then, Tib, to this gear! Hold up her tail and take her!
Chill see what devil is in her guts! Chill take the pains to
    rake her!

    GAMMER. Rake a cat, Hodge! What wouldest thou do?

    HODGE.   What,
    think'st that cham not able?

Did not Tom Tankard rake his curtal t'o'er day standing in
    the stable?   20

---

[1] More cursed.   [2] I make.

GAMMER. Soft! Be content, let's hear what news Cock bringeth
    from Mast' Rat.

COCK. Gammer, chave been there as you bad, you wot well
    about what.

'Twill not be long before he come, ich durst swear off a book,

He bids you see ye be at home, and there for him to look.

GAMMER. Where didst thou find him, boy? Was he not
    where I told thee? 25

COCK. Yes, yes, even at Hob Filcher's house, by Him that
    bought and sold me!

A cup of ale had in his hand, and a crab lay in the fire;

Chad much a-do to go and come, all was so full of mire.

And, Gammer, one thing I can tell: Hob Filcher's nawl was lost,

And Doctor Rat found it again, hard beside the door-post.

I chold a penny can say something, your nee'le again to fet.

GAMMER. Cham glad to hear so much, Cock; then trust he
    will not let 32

To help us herein best he can; therefore, till time he come

Let us go in; if there be ought to get, thou shalt have some.

THE FOURTH ACT. THE FIRST SCENE.

DOCTOR RAT, GAMMER GURTON [*enters later*].

DOCTOR RAT. A man were better twenty times be a bandog[1]
    and bark,

Than here among such a sort be parish priest or clerk,

Where he shall never be at rest one pissing while a day,

But he must trudge about the town, this way and that way;

Here to a drab, there to a thief, his shoes to tear and rent, 5

And that which is worst of all, at every knave's commandment!

I had not sit the space to drink two pots of ale,

---

[1] A dog that must be tied up.

But Gammer Gurton's sorry boy was straight-way at my tail,
And she was sick, and I must come, to do I wot not what!
It once her finger's-end but ache— trudge, call for Doctor Rat!
And when I come not at their call, I only thereby lose;   11
For I am sure to lack therefore a tithe-pig or a goose.
I warrant you, when truth is known, and told they have their
    tale,
The matter whereabout I come is not worth a halfpennyworth
    of ale;   14
Yet must I talk so sage and smooth, as though I were a gloser[1]
Else ere the year come at an end, I shall be sure the loser.
What work ye, Gammer Gurton? How, here is your friend
    M[ast'] Rat.
> GAMMER. Ah! good M[ast'] Doctor! cha troubled, cha trou-
> bled you, chwot well that.
> DOCTOR RAT. How do ye, woman? Be ye lusty, or be ye not
> well at ease?
> GAMMER. By Gis[2], Master, cham not sick, but yet chave a
> disease.   20
Chad a foul turn now of late, chill tell it you, by Gigs!
> DOCTOR RAT. Hath your brown cow cast her calf, or your
> sandy sow her pigs?
> GAMMER. No, but chad been as good they had as this, ich
> wot well.
> DOCTOR RAT. What is the matter?
> GAMMER.   Alas, alas! 'cha lost my
> good nee'le!   24
My nee'le, I say, and wot ye what, a drab came by and spied
    it,
And when I asked her for the same, the filth flatly denied it.
> DOCTOR RAT. What was she that—

---

[1] Flatterer.   [2] Cf. Jeez.

GAMMER. A dame, ich warrant you! She began to scold and
  brawl—
Alas, alas! Come hither, Hodge! This wretch can tell you all.

THE FOURTH ACT. THE SECOND SCENE.

HODGE, DOCTOR RAT, GAMMER. DICCON [*enters later*].

HODGE. Good morrow, Gaffer Vicar.
DOCTOR RAT.   Come on, fellow, let
  us hear!
Thy dame hath said to me, thou knowest of all this gear;
Let's see what thou canst say.
HODGE.   By m' fay, sir, that ye shall,
What matter soever here was done, ich can tell your ma'-
  ship [all]:
    My Gammer Gurton here, see now,   5
      Sat her down at this door, see now;
    And, as she began to stir her, see now,
      Her nee'le fell in the floor, see now;
    And while her staff she took, see now,
      At Gib her cat to fling, see now,   10
    Her nee'le was lost in the floor, see now—
      Is not this a wondrous thing, see now?
    Then came the quean, Dame Chat, see now,
      To ask for her black cup, see now:
    And even here at this gate, see now,   15
      She took that nee'le up, see now:
    My gammer then she yede[1], see now,
      Her nee'le again to bring, see now,
    And was caught by the head, see now—
      Is not this a wondrous thing, see now?   20
    She tare my gammer's coat, see now,

---

[1] Went.

And scratched her by the face, see now;
 Chad thought sh'ad stopp'd her throat, see now—
  Is not this a wondrous case, see now?
 When ich saw this, ich was wroth, see now, 25
  And start between them twain, see now;
 Else ich durst take a book-oath, see now,
  My gammer had been slain, see now.

GAMMER. This is even the whole matter, as Hodge has plainly
 told;
And chould fain be quiet for my part, that chould. 30
But help us, good Master, beseech ye that ye do:
Else shall we both be beaten and lose our nee'le too.

DOCTOR RAT. What would ye have me to do? Tell me, that
 I were gone;
I will do the best that I can, to set you both at one.
But be ye sure Dame Chat hath this your nee'le found? 35

GAMMER. Here comes the man, that see her take it up off
 the ground.
Ask him yourself, Master Rat, if ye believe not me;
And help me to my nee'le, for God's sake and Saint
 Charity!

DOCTOR RAT. Come near, Diccon, and let us hear what thou
 can express.
Wilt thou be sworn thou seest Dame Chat this woman's
 nee'le have? 40

DICCON. Nay, by Saint Benet, will I not! Then might ye
 think me rave!

GAMMER. Why, did'st not thou tell me so even here? Canst
 thou for shame deny it?

DICCON. Ay, marry, Gammer; but I said I would not abide
 by it.

DOCTOR RAT. Will you say a thing, and not stick to it to
 try it?

DICCON. "Stick to it," quoth you, Master Rat? Marry, sir,
    I defy it! 45
Nay, there is many an honest man, when he such blasts hath
    blown
In his friend's ears, he would be loath the same by him were
    known.
If such a toy be used oft among the honesty,
It may beseem a simple man of your and my degree.
    DOCTOR RAT. Then we be never the nearer, for all that you
        can tell! 50
    DICCON. Yea, marry, sir, if ye will do by mine advice and
        counsel.
If Mother Chat see all us here, she knoweth how the matter
    goes;
Therefore I reed[1] you three go hence, and within keep close,
And I will into Dame Chat's house, and so the matter use,
That ere ye could go twice to church I warrant you hear news.
She shall look well about her, but, I durst lay a pledge, 56
Ye shall of Gammer's nee'le have shortly better knowledge.
    GAMMER. Now, gentle Diccon, do so; and, good sir, let us
        trudge.
    DOCTOR RAT. By the mass, I may not tarry so long to be
        your judge.
    DICCON. 'Tis but a little while, man. What! Take so much
        pain! 60
If I hear no news of it, I will come sooner again.
    HODGE. Tarry so much, good Master Doctor, of your
        gentleness!
    DOCTOR RAT. Then let us hie us inward; and, Diccon, speed
        thy business.
    DICCON. Now, sirs, do you no more, but keep my counsel
        just,

[1] Advise.

And Doctor Rat shall thus catch some good, I trust;   65
But Mother Chat, my gossip, talk first withal I must,
For she must be chief captain to lay the Rat in the dust.

THE FOURTH ACT.   THE THIRD SCENE.

DICCON, CHAT.

DICCON. Good even, Dame Chat, in faith, and well-met in
   this place!

CHAT. Good even, my friend Diccon; whither walk ye this
   pace?

DICCON. By my truth even to you, to learn how the world
   goeth.

Heard ye no more of the other matter? Say me now, by your
   troth!

CHAT. O yes, Diccon, here the old whore and Hodge, that
   great knave—   5

But, in faith, I would thou hadst seen—O Lord, I drest them
   brave!

She bare me two or three souses behind in the nape of the
   neck,

Till I made her old weasand to answer again, "Keck!"

And Hodge, that dirty dastard, that at her elbow stands—   9

If one pair of legs had not been worth two pair of hands,

He had had his beard shaven if my nails would have served,

And not without a cause, for the knave it well deserved.

DICCON. By the mass, I can thee thank, wench, thou didst
   so well acquit thee!

CHAT. And th' adst seen him, Diccon, it would have made
   thee beshit thee   14

For laughter.   The whoreson dolt at last caught up a club,

As though he would have slain the master-devil, Belzabub.

But I set him soon inward.

DICCON.   O lord, there is the thing
That Hodge is so offended! That makes him start and fling!
  CHAT. Why? Makes the knave any moiling[1], as ye have seen
    or heard?   19
  DICCON. Even now I saw him last, like a mad man he far'd,
And sware by heaven and hell he would a-wreak his sorrow,
And leave you never a hen alive by eight of the clock to-
    morrow;
Therefore mark what I say, and my words see that ye trust.
Your hens be as good as dead, if ye leave them on the roost.
  CHAT. The knave dare as well go hang himself, as go upon
    my ground.   25
  DICCON. Well, yet take heed, I say. I must tell you my tale
    round.
Have you not about your house, behind your furnace or lead[2],
A hole where a crafty knave may creep in for need?
  CHAT. Yes, by the mass, a hole broke down, even within
    these two days.
  DICCON. Hodge he intends this same night to slip in there-
    aways.   30
  CHAT. O Christ, that I were sure of it! In faith, he should
    have his meed!
  DICCON. Watch well, for the knave will be there as sure as
    is your creed.
I would spend myself a shilling to have him swinged well.
  CHAT. I am as glad as a woman can be of this thing to hear tell.
By Gog's bones, when he cometh, now that I know the matter,
He shall sure at the first skip to leap in scalding water,   36
With a worse turn besides; when he will, let him come.
  DICCON. I tell you as my sister; you know what meaneth
    "mum"!

---

[1] Ado.   [2] Brewing vat.

THE FOURTH ACT.   THE FOURTH SCENE.

DICCON, DOCTOR RAT.

DICCON. Now lack I but my doctor to play his part again.
And lo, where he cometh towards, peradventure to his pain!

DOCTOR RAT. What good news, Diccon, fellow? Is Mother
Chat at home?

DICCON. She is, sir, and she is not, but it please her to whom;
Yet did I take her tardy, as subtle as she was.   5

DOCTOR RAT. The thing that thou went'st for, hast thou
brought it to pass?

DICCON. I have done that I have done, be it worse, be it better,
And Dame Chat at her wit's end I have almost set her.

DOCTOR RAT. Why, hast thou spied the nee'le? Quickly, I
pray thee, tell!   9

DICCON. I have spied it, in faith, sir, I handled myself so well;
And yet the crafty quean had almost take my trump.
But, ere all came to an end, I set her in a dump!

DOCTOR RAT. How so, I pray thee, Diccon?

DICCON.   Marry, sir, will
ye hear?
She was clapp'd down on the backside, by Cock's mother dear,
And there she sat sewing a halter or a band,   15
With no other thing save Gammer's needle in her hand.
As soon as any knock, if the filth be in doubt,
She needs but once puff, and her candle is out:
Now I, sir, knowing of every door the pin,
Came nicely, and said no word, till time I was within;   20
And there I saw the nee'le, even with these two eyes;
Whoever say the contrary, I will swear he lies.

DOCTOR RAT. O Diccon, that I was not there then in thy
stead!

DICCON. Well, if ye will be ordered, and do by my reed,
I will bring you to a place, as the house stands,   25
Where ye shall take the drab with the nee'le in her hands.

DOCTOR RAT. For God's sake do so, Diccon, and I will gage
   my gown
To give thee a full pot of the best ale in the town.   28

DICCON. Follow me but a little, and mark what I will say;
Lay down your gown beside you, go to, come on your way!
See ye not what is here? A hole wherein ye may creep
Into the house, and suddenly unawares among them leap;
There shall ye find the bitch-fox and the nee'le together.
Do as I bid you, man; come on your ways hither!

DOCTOR RAT. Art thou sure, Diccon, the swill-tub stands not
   hereabout?   35

DICCON. I was within myself, man, even now; there is no
   doubt.
Go softly, make no noise; give me your foot, sir John,
Here will I wait upon you, till you come out anon.

                   DOCTOR RAT *climbs in.*

DOCTOR RAT [*from within*]. Help, Diccon! Out alas! I shall
   be slain among them!

DICCON. If they give you not the needle, tell them that ye
   will hang them.   40
Ware that! How, my wenches! Have ye caught the fox,
That used to make revel among your hens and cocks?
Save his life yet for his order, though he sustain some pain.
Gog's bread! I am afraid they will beat out his brain.   [*Exit.*]

DOCTOR RAT. Woe worth the hour that I came here!   45
And woe worth him that wrought this gear!
A sort of drabs and queans have me blest!
Was ever creature half so evil drest?
Whoever it wrought and first did invent it
He shall, I warrant him, ere long repent it!   50

I will spend all I have without[1] my skin
But he shall be brought to the plight I am in!
Master Baily[2], I trow, and he be worth his ears,
Will snaffle these murderers, and all that them bears:
I will surely neither bite nor sup   55
Till I fetch him hither, this matter to take up.

THE FIFTH ACT.   THE FIRST SCENE.

MASTER BAILY, DOCTOR RAT.

BAILY. I can perceive none other, I speak it from my heart,
But either ye are in all the fault, or else in the greatest part.
DOCTOR RAT. If it be counted his fault, besides all his griefs,
When a poor man is spoiled, and beaten among thieves,
Then I confess my fault herein, at this season;   5
But I hope you will not judge so much against reason.
BAILY. And, methinks, by your own tale, of all that ye name,
If any played the thief, you were the very same.
The women they did nothing, as your words made probation,
But stoutly withstood your forcible invasion.   10
If that a thief at your window to enter should begin,
Would you hold forth your hand and help to pull him in?
Or you would keep him out?   I pray you answer me.
DOCTOR RAT. Marry, keep him out, and a good cause why!
But I am no thief, sir, but an honest learned clerk.   15
BAILY. Yea, but who knoweth that, when he meets you in
    the dark?
I am sure your learning shines not out at your nose!
Was it any marvel, though the poor woman arose
And start up, being afraid of that was in her purse?
Methink you may be glad that you[r] luck was no worse. 20

---

[1] Except.   [2] Bailiff.

DOCTOR RAT. Is not this evil enough, I pray you, as you
think?

Showing his broken head.

BAILY. Yea, but a man in the dark, if chances do wink,
As soon he smites his father as any other man,
Because for lack of light discern him he ne can.
Might it not have been your luck with a spit to have been
slain?   25

DOCTOR RAT. I think I am little better, my scalp is cloven to
the brain.
If there be all the remedy, I know who bears the knocks.

BAILY. By my troth, and well worthy besides to kiss the
stocks!
To come in on the back side, when ye might go about!
I know none such, unless they long to have their brains
knock'd out.   30

DOCTOR RAT. Well, will you be so good, sir, as talk with
Dame Chat
And know what she intended? I ask no more but that.

BAILY. Let her be called, fellow, because of Master Doctor,
                                                    [*to* SCAPETHRIFT]
I warrant in this case she will be her own proctor;
She will tell her own tale in meter or in prose,   35
And bid you seek your remedy, and so go wipe your nose.

THE FIFTH ACT. THE SECOND SCENE.

M. BAILY, CHAT, D. RAT. GAMMER, HODGE, DICCON [*enter later*].

BAILY. Dame Chat, Master Doctor upon you here complained
That you and your maids should him much misorder,
And taketh many an oath, that no word be feigned,
Laying to your charge, how you thought him to murder;

And, on his part again, that same man saith furder,   5
He never offended you in word nor intent.
To hear you answer hereto, we have now for you sent.
   CHAT. That I would have murdered him? Fie on him, wretch!
And evil mought he thee[1] for it, our Lord I beseech.
I will swear on all the books that opens and shuts,   10
He feigneth this tale out of his own guts;
For this seven weeks with me, I am sure, he sat not down.
[*To* RAT.] Nay, ye have other minions, in the other end of the
   town,
Where ye were liker to catch such a blow,
Than anywhere else, as far as I know!   15
   BAILY. Belike, then Master Doctor, yon stripe there ye got
      not!
   DOCTOR RAT. Think you I am so mad that where I was beat
      I wot not?
Will ye believe this quean, before she hath tried it?
It is not the first deed she hath done, and afterward denied it.
   CHAT. What, man, will you say I broke your head?   20
   DOCTOR RAT. How canst thou prove the contrary?
   CHAT. Nay, how provest thou that I did the deed?
   DOCTOR RAT. Too plainly, by St Mary,
This proof, I trow, may serve, though I no word spoke!
                  Showing his broken head.   24
   CHAT. Because thy head is broken, was it I that it broke?
I saw thee, Rat, I tell thee, not once within this fortnight.
   DOCTOR RAT. No, marry, thou sawest me not; for why[2] thou
      hadst no light;
But I felt thee for all the dark, beshrew thy smooth cheeks!
And thou groped me, this will declare any day this six weeks,
                  Showing his head.

----

[1] Thrive.   [2] Because.

BAILY. Answer me to this, M[ast'] Rat: when caught you
this harm of yours? 30

DOCTOR RAT. A while ago, sir. God he knoweth, within less
than these two hours.

BAILY. Dame Chat, was there none with you (confess, i' faith)
about that season?

What, woman? Let it be what it will, 'tis neither felony nor
treason.

CHAT. Yes, by my faith, Master Baily, there was a knave
not far

Who caught one good filip on the brow with a door-bar, 35
And well was he worthy, as it seemed to me;
But what is that to this man, since this was not he?

BAILY. Who was it then? Let's hear!

DOCTOR RAT.   Alas, sir, ask you that?

Is it not made plain enough by the own mouth of Dame Chat?
The time agreeth, my head is broken, her tongue cannot lie,
Only upon a bare nay she saith it was not I. 41

CHAT. No, marry, was it not indeed! Ye shall hear by this
one thing:

This afternoon a friend of mine for good-will gave me warning,
And bad me well look to my roost, and all my capons' pens,
For if I took not better heed, a knave would have my hens
Then I, to save my goods, took so much pains as him to watch;
And as good fortune served me, it was my chance him for
to catch.

What strokes he bare away, or other what was his gains,
I wot not, but sure I am he had something for his pains!

BAILY. Yet tell'st thou not who it was.

CHAT.   Who it was? A false
thief, 50

That came like a false fox, my pullen[1] to kill and mischief!

[1] Poultry.

BAILY. But knowest thou not his name?

CHAT.   **I know it, but what**
then?

It was that crafty cullion[1] Hodge, my Gammer Gurton's man.

BAILY. Call me the knave hither, he shall sure kiss the stocks.

I shall teach him a lesson for filching hens or cocks!   55

DOCTOR RAT. I marvel, Master Baily, so bleared be your eyes;

An egg is not so full of meat, as she is full of lies:

When she hath played this prank, to excuse all this gear,

She layeth the fault in such a one as I know was not there.

CHAT. Was he not there? Look on his pate; that shall be his
witness!   60

DOCTOR RAT. I would my head were half so whole; I would
seek no redress!

BAILY. God bless you, Gammer Gurton!

GAMMER.   God yield[2] ye,
master mine!

BAILY. Thou hast a knave within thy house—Hodge, a servant
of thine;

They tell me that busy knave is such a filching one,   64

That hen, pig, goose or capon, thy neighbour can have none.

GAMMER. By God, cham much a-meved[3] to hear any such
report!

Hodge was not wont, ich trow, to 'have him in that sort.

CHAT. A thievisher knave is not on-live, more filching, nor
more false;

Many a truer man than he has hanged up by the halse[4];   69

And thou, his dame—of all his theft thou art the sole receiver;

For Hodge to catch, and thou to keep, I never knew none better!

GAMMER. Sir reverence of your masterdom, and you were
out a-door,

---

[1] Rascal. French *couillon*, testicle.   [2] Reward.   [3] Moved, upset.
[4] Neck.

Chould be so bold, for all her brags, to call her arrant whore;
And ich knew Hodge as bad as t'ou, ich wish me endless sorrow
And chould not take the pains to hang him up before to-
morrow! 75

CHAT. What have I stolen from thee or thine, thou ill-favor'd
old trot?

GAMMER. A great deal more, by God's blest, than chever by
thee got!
That thou knowest well, I need not say it.

BAILY. Stop there, I say,
And tell me here, I pray you, this matter by the way, 79
How chance Hodge is not here? Him would I fain have had.

GAMMER. Alas, sir, he'll be here anon; ha' be handled too bad.

CHAT. Master Baily, sir, ye be not such a fool, well I know
But ye perceive by this lingering there is a pad[1] in the straw.

Thinking that HODGE *his head was broke, and
that* GAMMER *would not let him come before them.*

GAMMER. Chill show you his face, ich warrant thee; lo, now
where he is! 84

BAILY. Come on, fellow. It is told me thou art a shrew, i-wis:
Thy neighbour's hens thou takest, and plays the two-legged fox;
Their chickens and their capons too, and now and then their
cocks.

HODGE. Ich defy them all that dare it say; cham as true as
the best!

BAILY. Wert not thou take within this hour in Dame Chat's
hens'-nest?

HODGE. Take there? No, master; chould not do't for a house
full of gold! 90

CHAT. Thou, or the devil in thy coat—swear this I dare
be bold.

---

[1] Toad.

DOCTOR RAT. Swear me no swearing, quean. The devil he give thee sorrow!
All is not worth a gnat, thou canst swear till to-morrow!
Where is the harm he hath? Show it, by God's bread! 94
Ye beat him with a witness, but the stripes light on my head!

HODGE. Beat me! Gog's blessed body, chould first, ich trow, have burst thee!
Ich think, and chad my hands loose, callet, chould have crust[1] thee!

CHAT. Thou shitten knave, I trow thou knowest the full weight of my fist;
I am foully deceived unless thy head and my door-bar kissed.

HODGE. Hold thy chat, whore; thou criest so loud, can no man else be heard. 100

CHAT. Well, knave, and I had thee alone, I would surely rap thy costard!

BAILY. Sir, answer me to this: Is thy head whole or broken?

CHAT. Yea, Master Baily, blest be every good token.

HODGE. Is my head whole! Ich warrant you, 'tis neither scurvy nor scald[2]!
What, you foul beast, does think 'tis either peeled or bald? 105
Nay, ich thank God, chill not for all that thou may'st spend
That chad one scab on my narse as broad as thy finger's end

BAILY. Come nearer here!

HODGE.   Yes, that ich dare.

BAILY.   By our Lady, here is no harm,
Hodge's head is whole enough, for all Dame Chat's charm.

CHAT. By Gog's blest, however the thing he cloaks or smolders[3], 110

---

[1] Crushed.   [2] Scabby.   [3] Smothers.

I know the blows he bare away, either with head or shoulders.

Camest thou not, knave, within this hour, creeping into my
    pens,

And there was caught within my house, groping among my
    hens?

    HODGE. A plague both on the hens and thee! A cart, whore,
      a cart[1]!

Chould I were hanged as high as a tree, and chwere as false
    as thou art!   115

Give my gammer again her washical[2] thou stole away in thy
    lap!

    GAMMER. Yea, Master Baily, there is a thing you know not
      on, mayhap;

This drab she keeps away my good, the devil he might her
    snare.

Ich pray you that ich might have a right action on her.   119
    CHAT. Have I thy good, old filth, or any such old sow's?

I am as true, I would thou knew, as skin between thy brows.
    GAMMER. Many a truer hath been hanged, though you escape
      the danger!

    CHAT. Thou shalt answer, by God's pity, for this thy foul
      slander!

    BAILY. Why, what can you charge her withal? To say so ye
      do not well.

    GAMMER. Marry, a vengeance to her heart! The whore has
      stol'n my nee'le!   125

    CHAT. Thy needle, old witch! How so? It were alms thy soul
      to knock!

So didst thou say the other day, that I had stol'n thy cock.

And roasted him to my breakfast, which shall not be forgotten,

The devil pull out thy lying tongue and teeth that be so rotten!

---

[1] To haul her through the streets, according to custom.   [2] What-you-
call-it.

GAMMER. Give me my nee'le! As for my Cock, chould be
very loath 130
That chould hear tell he should hang on thy false faith and
troth.

BAILY. Your talk is such, I can scarce learn who should be
most in fault.

GAMMER. Yet shall ye find no other wight, save she, by bread
and salt!

BAILY. Keep ye content a while, see that your tongues ye
hold.

Methinks you should remember this is no place to scold. 135
How knowest thou, Gammer Gurton, Dame Chat thy needle
had?

GAMMER. To name you, sir, the party, chould not be very
glad.

BAILY. Yea, but we must needs hear it, and therefore say it
boldly.

GAMMER. Such one as told the tale full soberly and coldly,
Even he that looked on—will swear on a book— 140
What time this drunken gossip my fair long nee'le up took,
Diccon, Master, the Bedlam, cham very sure ye know him.

BAILY. A false knave, by God's pity! Ye were but a fool to
trow[1] him.

I durst aventure well the price of my best cap,
That when the end is known, all will turn to a jape, 145
Told he not you that besides she stole your cock that tide[2]?

GAMMER. No, master, no indeed; for then he should have lied.
My cock is, I thank Christ, safe and well a-fine.[3]

CHAT. Yea, but that rugged colt, that whore, that Tib of
thine, 149
Said plainly thy cock was stol'n, and in my house was eaten.
That lying cut[4] is lost that she is not swinged and beaten,

---

[1] Believe.   [2] Time.   [3] At the end.   [4] Gelding, as term of abuse.

And yet for all my good name it were a small amends!
I pick not this gear, hear'st thou, out of my fingers' ends;
But he that heard it told me, who thou of late didst name,
Diccon, whom all men knows, it was the very same.   155

BAILY. This is the case: you lost your nee'le about the doors,
And she answers again, she has no cock of yours;
Thus in you[r] talk and action, from that you do intend,
She is whole five mile wide, from that she doth defend.
Will you say she hath your cock?   160

GAMMER. No, marry, sir, that chill not.

BAILY.   Will you confess her
nee'le?

CHAT.   Will I? No, sir, will I not.

BAILY.   Then there lieth all the
matter.

GAMMER. Soft, master, by the way!
Ye know she could do little, and she could not say nay.

BAILY. Yea, but he that made one lie about your cock-
stealing,   165
Will not stick to make another, what time lies be in dealing.
I ween the end will prove this brawl did first arise
Upon no other ground but only Diccon's lies.

CHAT. Though some be lies, as you belike have espied them,
Yet other some be true, by proof I have well tried them.   170

BAILY. What other thing beside this, Dame Chat?

CHAT.   Marry, sir, even this.
The tale I told before, the self-same tale it was his;
He gave me, like a friend, warning against my loss,
Else had my hens be stol'n each one, by God's cross!
He told me Hodge would come, and in he came indeed,   175
But as the matter chanced, with greater haste than speed.
This truth was said, and true was found, as truly I report.

BAILY. If Doctor Rat be not deceived, it was of another sort.

DOCTOR RAT. By God's mother, thou and he be a couple of
  subtle foxes!

Between you and Hodge I bear away the boxes. 180

Did not Diccon appoint the place, where thou should'st stand
  to meet him?

CHAT. Yes, by the mass, and if he came, bad me not stick
  to spit him.

DOCTOR RAT. God's sacrament! The villain knave hath dress'd
  us round about!

He is the cause of all this brawl, that dirty shitten lout!

When Gammer Gurton here complained, and made a rueful
  moan, 185

I heard him swear that you had gotten her needle that was
  gone;

And this to try, he further said, he was full loth; howbeit

He was content with small ado to bring me where to see it.

And where ye sat, he said full certain, if I would follow his reed,

Into your house a privy way he would me guide and lead,

And where ye had it in your hands, sewing about a clout,

And set me in the back-hole, thereby to find you out: 192

And whiles I sought a quietness, creeping upon my knees,

I found the weight of your door-bar for my reward and fees.

Such is the luck that some men gets, while they begin to mell[1].

In setting at one such as were out, minding to make all well.

HODGE. Was not well blest, Gammer, to 'scape that stour[2]?
  And chad been there,

Then chad been dress'd[3], belike, as ill, by the mass, as Gaffer
  Vicar.

BAILY. Marry, sir, here is a sport alone; I looked for such
  an end. 199

If Diccon had not play'd the knave, this had been soon amend.

---

[1] Meddle.   [2] Tumult.   [3] Served, treated.

My Gammer here he made a fool, and dress'd her as she was;
And goodwife Chat he set to scold, till both parts cried, alas!
And D[octor] Rat was not behind, whiles Chat his crown did
　　pare.
I would the knave had been stark blind, if Hodge had not his
　　share.

　HODGE. Cham meetly well-sped already among's, cham
　　dress'd like a colt! 　　　　　　　　　　　　　　205
And chad not had the better wit, chad been made a dolt.

　BAILY. Sir knave, make haste Diccon were here; fetch him,
　　wherever he be!

　CHAT. Fie on the villain, fie, fie! That makes us thus agree!

　GAMMER. Fie on him, knave, with all my heart! Now fie, and
　　fie again!

　DOCTOR RAT. Now "fie on him!" may I best say, whom he
　　hath almost slain. 　　　　　　　　　　　　　　210

　BAILY. Lo, where he cometh at hand; belike he was not far!
Diccon, here be two or three thy company cannot spare.

　DICCON. God bless you, and you may be bless'd, so many all
　　at once!

　CHAT. Come, knave, it were a good deed to geld thee, by
　　Cock's bones!
Seest not thy handiwork? Sir Rat, can ye forbear him? 　215

　DICCON. A vengeance on those hands light, for my hands
　　came not near him.
The whoreson priest hath lift the pot in some of these alewives'
　　chairs,
That his head would not serve him, belike, to come down the
　　stairs.

　BAILY. Nay, soft! thou may'st not play the knave, and have
　　this language too! 　　　　　　　　　　　　　　219
It thou thy tongue bridle a while, the better may st thou do.
Confess the truth, as I shall ask, and cease a while to fable;

And for thy fault I promise thee thy handling shall be reasonable.
Hast thou not made a lie or two, to set these two by the ears?

DICCON. What if I have? Five hundred such have I seen within these seven years;

I am sorry for nothing else but that I see not the sport 225
Which was between them when they met, as they themselves report.

BAILY. The greatest thing—Master Rat, ye see how he is dress'd!

DICCON. What devil need he be groping so deep, in goodwife Chat's hens'-nest?

BAILY. Yea, but it was thy drift to bring him into the briars.

DICCON. God's bread! Hath not such an old fool wit to save his ears? 230

He showeth himself herein, ye see, so very a cox[1],
The cat was not so madly allured by the fox
To run into the snares was set for him, doubtless;
For he leapt in for mice, and this Sir John for madness.

DOCTOR RAT. Well, and ye shift no better, ye losel[2], lither[3] and lazy, 235

I will go near for this to make ye leap at a daisy.[4]
In the king's name, Master Baily, I charge you set him fast.

DICCON. What? Fast at cards or fast on sleep? It is the thing I did last.

DOCTOR RAT. Nay, fast in fetters, false varlet, according to thy deeds.

BAILY. Master Doctor, there is no remedy; I must entreat you, needs, 240
Some other kind of punishment.

DOCTOR RAT.   Nay, by All-Hallows!
His punishment, if I may judge, shall be nought else but the gallows.

[1] Fool.   [2] Ne'er do well.   [3] Low.   [4] Be hanged.

BAILY. That were too sore; a spiritual man to be so extreme!

DOCTOR RAT. Is he worthy any better, sir? How do you judge and deem?

BAILY. I grant him worthy punishment, but in no wise so great. 245

GAMMER. It is a shame, ich tell you plain, for such false knaves entreat.

He has almost undone us all—that is as true as steel—

And yet for all this great ado cham never the near my nee'le!

BAILY. Canst thou not say anything to that, Diccon, with least or most?

DICCON. Yea, marry, sir, thus much I can say well, the nee'le is lost. 250

BAILY. Nay, canst not thou tell which way that needle may be found?

DICCON. No, by my fay, sir, though I might have an hundred pound.

HODGE. Thou liar, lickdish, didst not say the nee'le would be gitten?

DICCON. No, Hodge; by the same token you were that time beshitten

For fear of hobgoblin—you wot well what I mean; 255

As long as it is since, I fear me yet ye be scarce clean.

BAILY. Well, Master Rat, you must both learn and teach us to forgive.

Since Diccon hath confession made, and is so clean shreve[1],

If ye to me consent, to amend this heavy chance,

I will enjoin him here some open kind of penance, 260

Of this condition—where ye know my fee is twenty pence

For the bloodshed, I am agreed with you here to dispense—

Ye shall go quit[2], so that ye grant the matter now to run

To end with mirth among us all, even as it was begun.

---

[1] Shriven.   [2] Absolved.

CHAT. Say yea, Master Vicar, and he shall sure confess to be
 your debtor,   265
And all we that be here present will love you much the better.

DOCTOR RAT. My part is the worst; but since you all hereon
 agree,
Go even to, Master Baily! Let it be so for me!

BAILY. How say'st thou, Diccon? Art content this shall on me
 depend?

DICCON. Go to, M[ast'] Baily, say on your mind, I know ye
 are my friend.   270

BAILY. Then mark ye well: To recompense this thy former
 action—
Because thou hast offended all, to make them satisfaction—
Before their faces here kneel down, and as I shall thee teach—
For thou shalt take an oath of Hodge's leather breech:
First, for Master Doctor, upon pain of his curse,   275
Where he will pay for all, thou never draw thy purse;
And when ye meet at one pot he shall have the first pull,
And thou shalt never offer him the cup but it be full.
To goodwife Chat thou shalt be sworn, even on the same
 wise,
If she refuse thy money once, never to offer it twice. 280
Thou shalt be bound by the same, here as thou dost take it,
When thou may'st drink of free cost, thou never forsake it.
For Gammer Gurton's sake, again sworn shalt thou be,
To help her to her needle again if it do lie in thee;
And likewise be bound, by the virtue of that,   285
To be of good a-bearing to Gib her great cat.
Last of all, for Hodge the oath to scan,
Thou shalt never take him for fine gentleman.

HODGE. Come on, fellow Diccon, chall be even with thee
 now!

BAILY. Thou wilt not stick to do this, Diccon, I trow? 290

DICCON. No, by my father's skin, my hand down I lay it!
Look, as I have promised, I will not denay it.
But, Hodge, take good heed now, thou do not beshit me!

And gave him a good blow on the buttock.

HODGE. Gog's heart! Thou false villain, dost thou bite me?
BAILY. What, Hodge, doth he hurt thee ere ever he begin?
HODGE. He thrust me into the buttock with a bodkin or
a pin.   296

He discovers the needle.

I say, Gammer! Gammer!
GAMMER.   How now, Hodge, how now?
HODGE. God's malt, Gammer Gurton!
GAMMER.   Thou art mad, ich
trow!
HODGE. Will you see the devil, Gammer?
GAMMER.   The devil, son!
God bless us!
HODGE. Chould, [if] ich were hanged, Gammer—
GAMMER.   Marry,
see, ye might dress us—   300
HODGE. Chave it, by the mass, Gammer!
GAMMER.   What, not my
nee'le, Hodge?
HODGE. Your nee'le, Gammer! your nee'le!
GAMMER.   No, fie, dost but
dodge!
HODGE. Ch' a found your nee'le, Gammer, here in my hand
be it!
GAMMER. For all the loves on earth, Hodge, let me see it!
HODGE. Soft, Gammer!
GAMMER.   Good Hodge!

HODGE.   Soft, ich say; tarry a
while!   305

GAMMER. Nay, sweet Hodge, say truth and not me beguile!

HODGE. Cham sure on it, ich warrant you; it goes no more
astray.

GAMMER. Hodge, when I speak so fair, wilt still say me
nay?

HODGE. Go near the light, Gammer, this—well, in faith,
good luck!—

Ch'was almost undone, 'twas so far in my buttock!   310

GAMMER. 'Tis mine own dear nee'le, Hodge, sikerly I wot!

HODGE. Cham I not a good son, Gammer, cham I not?

GAMMER. Christ's blessing light on thee, hast made me for
ever!

HODGE. Ich knew that ich must find it, else chould a' had it
never!

CHAT. By my troth, Gossip Gurton, I am even as glad 315
As though I mine own self as good a turn had!

BAILY. And I, by my conscience, to see it so come forth,
Rejoice so much at it, as three needles be worth.

DOCTOR RAT. I am no whit sorry to see you so rejoice.

DICCON. Nor I much the gladder for all this noise;   320
Yet say, "Gramercy, Diccon!" for springing of the game.

GAMMER. Gramercy, Diccon, twenty times! O, how glad
cham!

If that chould do so much, your masterdom to come hither,
Master Rat, Gloodwife Chat, and Diccon together,
Cha but one halfpenny, as far as ich know it,   325
And chill not rest this night, till ich bestow it.
If ever ye love me, let us go in and drink.

BAILY. I am content, if the rest think as I think.
Master Rat, it shall be best for you if we so do,
Ten shall you warm you and dress yourself too.   330

DICCON. Soft, sirs, take us with you, the company shall be
   the more!
As proud comes behind, they say, as any goes before!
But now, my good masters, since we must be gone,
And leave you behind us here all alone;
Since at our last ending thus merry we be,   335
For Gammer Gurton's needle sake, let us have a plaudite.

THE HONORABLE HISTORY OF FRIAR BACON AND FRIAR BUNGAY*

ROBERT GREENE

DRAMATIS PERSONÆ

KING HENRY THE THIRD

EDWARD, PRINCE OF WALES, *his son*

EMPEROR OF GERMANY

KING OF CASTILE

LACY, *Earl of Lincoln*

WARREN, *Earl of Sussex*

ERMSBY, *a gentleman*

RALPH SIMNELL, *the King's Fool*

FRIAR BACON

MILES, *Friar Bacon's poor scholar*

FRIAR BUNGAY

JAQUES VANDERMAST

BURDEN,
MASON, } *Doctors of Oxford*
CLEMENT,

A DEVIL, *a fiend like* HERCULES

LAMBERT,
SERLSBY, } *gentlemen*

TWO SCHOLARS, *sons to Lambert and Serlsby*

KEEPER *of Fressingfield*

THOMAS,
RICHARD, } *Country clowns*

CONSTABLE, POST, LORDS, COUNTRY CLOWNS, *etc.*

ELINOR, *daughter to the King of Castile*

MARGARET, *the Keeper's daughter (of Fressingfield)*

JOAN, *a farmer's daughter*

HOSTESS *of the Bell at Henley*

A DRAGON, *shooting fire, etc.*

[Scene I. *Framlingham.*]

Enter PRINCE EDWARD *malcontented, with* LACY, WARREN, ERMSBY, *and* RALPH SIMNELL, *the Fool.*

LACY. Why looks my lord like to a troubled sky
When heaven's bright shine is shadowed with a fog

* 1582-1592.

Alate[1] we ran the deer, and through the lawns
Stripped[2] with our nags the lofty frolic bucks
That scudded 'fore the teasers[3] like the wind.　　　　5
Ne'er was the deer of merry Fressingfield
So lustily pulled down by jolly mates,
Nor shared the farmers such fat venison,
So frankly dealt, this hundred years before;
Nor have I seen my lord more frolic in the chase,　　10
And now—changed to a melancholy dump.

WARREN. After the prince got to the Keeper's lodge,
And had been jocund in the house awhile,
Tossing off ale and milk in country cans,
Whether it was the country's sweet content,　　　　15
Or else the bonny damsel filled us drink
That seemed so stately in her stammel[4] red,
Or that a qualm did cross his stomach then,
But straight he fell into his passions.

ERMSBY. Sirrah Ralph, what say you to your master,　　20
Shall he thus all amort[5] live malcontent?

RALPH. Hearest thou, Ned?—Nay, look if he will speak to me!

PRINCE EDWARD. What say'st thou to me, fool?

RALPH. I prithee, tell me, Ned, art thou in love with the
Keeper's daughter?　　　　25

PRINCE EDWARD. How if I be, what then?

RALPH. Why, then, sirrah, I'll teach thee how to deceive Love.

PRINCE EDWARD. How, Ralph?

RALPH. Marry, Sirrah Ned, thou shalt put on my cap and my
coat and my dagger, and I will put on thy clothes and　　30
thy sword; and so thou shalt be my fool.

PRINCE EDWARD. And what of this?

RALPH. Why, so thou shalt beguile Love; for Love is such a

---

[1] Lately.　　[2] Outstripped.　　[3] Hounds.　　[4] Coarse woolen cloth.
[5] Downcast.

proud scab, that he will never meddle with fools nor children.
Is not Ralph's counsel good, Ned?   35

PRINCE EDWARD. Tell me, Ned Lacy, didst thou mark the maid,
How lively in her country-weeds she looked?
A bonnier wench all Suffolk cannot yield:
All Suffolk? Nay, all England holds none such.

RALPH. Sirrah Will Ermsby, Ned is deceived.   40

ERMSBY. Why, Ralph?

RALPH. He says all England hath no such, and I say, and I'll
stand to it, there is one better in Warwickshire.

WARREN. How provest thou that, Ralph?

RALPH. Why, is not the abbot a learned man, and hath   45
read many books, and thinkest thou he hath not more learning
than thou to choose a bonny wench? Yes, I warrant thee, by
his whole grammar.

ERMSBY. A good reason, Ralph.

PRINCE EDWARD. I tell thee, Lacy, that her sparkling eyes   50
Do lighten forth sweet love's alluring fire;
And in her tresses she doth fold the looks
Of such as gaze upon her golden hair;
Her bashful white, mixed with the morning's red,
Luna doth boast upon her lovely cheeks;   55
Her front is beauty's table, where she paints
The glories of her gorgeous excellence;
Her teeth are shelves of precious marguerites,[1]
Richly enclosed with ruddy coral cliffs.
Tush, Lacy, she is beauty's over-match,   60
If thou survey'st her curious imagery.[2]

LACY. I grant, my lord, the damsel is as fair
As simple Suffolk's homely towns can yield;
But in the court be quainter[3] dames than she,

---

[1] Pearls.   [2] Rare appearance.   [3] Rarer.

Whose faces are enriched with honor's tint, 65
Whose beauties stand upon the stage of fame,
And vaunt their trophies in the courts of love.

PRINCE EDWARD. Ned, but hadst thou watched her as myself,
And seen the secret beauties of the maid,
Their courtly coyness were but foolery. 70

ERMSBY. Why, how watched you her, my lord?

PRINCE EDWARD. Whenas she swept like Venus through the
    house,
And in her shape fast folded up my thoughts,
into the milk-house went I with the maid, 75
And there amongst the cream-bowls she did shine
As Pallas 'mongst her princely huswifery.
She turned her smock over her lily arms,
And dived them into milk to run her cheese;
But whiter than the milk her crystal skin, 80
Checked with lines of azure, made her blush
That[1] art or nature durst bring for compare.
Ermsby, if thou hadst seen, as I did note it well,
How beauty played the huswife, how this girl,
Like Lucrece, laid her fingers to the work, 85
Thou wouldst, with Tarquin, hazard Rome and all
To win the lovely maid of Fressingfield.

RALPH. Sirrah Ned, would'st fain have her?

PRINCE EDWARD. Ay, Ralph.

RALPH. Why, Ned, I have laid the plot in my head; 90
thou shalt have her already.

PRINCE EDWARD. I'll give thee a new coat, an learn me that.

RALPH. Why Sirrah Ned, we'll ride to Oxford to Friar Bacon.
O, he is a brave scholar, sirrah; they say he is a brave necromancer,
that he can make women of devils, and he can juggle cats 95
into costermongers.

---

[1] Relative pronoun; antecedent is *her*.

PRINCE EDWARD. And how then, Ralph?

RALPH. Marry, sirrah, thou shalt go to him; and because thy father Harry shall not miss thee, he shall turn me into thee; and I'll to the court, and I'll prince it out; and he shall   100 make thee either a silken purse full of gold, or else a fine wrought smock.

PRINCE EDWARD. But how shall I have the maid?

RALPH. Marry, sirrah, if thou be'st a silken purse full of gold, then on Sundays she'll hang thee by her side, and you   105 must not say a word. Now, sir, when she comes into a great press of people, for fear of the cutpurse, on a sudden she'll swap thee into her plackerd[1]; then, sirrah, being there, you may plead for yourself.

ERMSBY. Excellent policy!   110

PRINCE EDWARD. But how if I be a wrought smock?

RALPH. Then she'll put thee into her chest and lay thee into lavender, and upon some good day she'll put thee on; and at night when you go to bed, then being turned from a smock to a man, you may make up the match.   115

LACY. Wonderfully wisely counseled, Ralph.

PRINCE EDWARD. Ralph shall have a new coat.

RALPH. God thank you when I have it on my back, Ned.

PRINCE EDWARD. Lacy, the Fool hath laid a perfect plot;
For why[2] our country Margaret is so coy,   120
And stands so much upon her honest points,
That marriage or no market with the maid.
Ermsby, it must be necromantic spells
And charms of art that must enchain her love,
Or else shall Edward never win the girl.   125
Therefore, my wags, we'll horse us in the morn,
And post to Oxford to this jolly friar:
Bacon shall by his magic do this deed.

---

[1] Placket; slit in skirt.   [2] Because.

WARREN. Content, my lord; and that's a speedy way
To wean these headstrong puppies from the teat. 130
  PRINCE EDWARD. I am unknown, not taken for the prince;
They only deem us frolic courtiers,
That revel thus among our liege's game;
Therefore I have devised a policy:
Lacy, thou know'st next Friday is Saint James'[1], 135
And then the country flocks to Harleston fair;
Then will the Keeper's daughter frolic there,
And over-shine the troop of all the maids
That come to see and to be seen that day.
Haunt thee disguised among the country-swains, 140
Feign thou'rt a farmer's son, not far from thence,
Espy her loves, and who she liketh best;
Cote[2] him, and court her to control the clown;
Say that the courtier 'tired all in green,
That helped her handsomely to run her cheese, 145
And filled her father's lodge with venison,
Commends him, and sends fairings to herself.
Buy something worthy of her parentage,
Not worth her beauty; for, Lacy, then the fair
Affords no jewel fitting for the maid. 150
And when thou talk'st of me, note if she blush;
O, then she loves; but if her cheeks wax pale,
Disdain it is. Lacy, send how she fares,
And spare no time nor cost to win her loves.
  LACY. I will, my lord, so execute this charge 155
As if that Lacy were in love with her.
  PRINCE EDWARD. Send letters speedily to Oxford of the news.
  RALPH. And, Sirrah Lacy, buy me a thousand thousand
million of fine bells.

---

[1] July 25.   [2] Keep up with.

LACY. What wilt thou do with them, Ralph? 160

RALPH. Marry, every time that Ned sighs for the Keeper's
daughter, I'll tie a bell about him, and so within three or four
days I will send word to his father Harry, that his son and
my master Ned is become Love's morris-dance.

PRINCE EDWARD. Well, Lacy, look with care unto thy charge,
And I will haste to Oxford to the friar, 166
That he by art and thou by secret gifts
Mayst make me lord of merry Fressingfield.

LACY. God send your honor your heart's desire. *Exeunt.*

[Scene II. FRIAR BACON's *Cell at Oxford.*]

Enter FRIAR BACON, *with* MILES, *his poor scholar, with books under
his arm; with them* BURDEN, MASON, CLEMENT, *three* DOCTORS.

BACON. Miles, where are you?

MILES. *Hic sum, doctissime et reverendissime doctor.*

BACON. *Attulisti nos libros meos de necromantia?*

MILES. *Ecce quam bonum et quam jucundum habitare libros in
unum!*[1] 5

BACON. Now, masters of our academic state,
That rule in Oxford, viceroys in your place,
Whose heads contain maps of the liberal arts,
Spending your time in depth of learned skill,
Why flock you thus to Bacon's secret cell, 10
A friar newly stalled in Brazen-nose?
Say what's your mind, that I may make reply.

BURDEN. Bacon, we hear that long we have suspect,
That thou art read in magic's mystery;

---

[1] Here I am, learned and reverend doctor.
   Have you brought us my books on necromancy?
   Behold, how good and pleasant it is for books to dwell in one place.
                                              Cf. *Psalm* 133.

In pyromancy, to divine by flames; 15
To tell, by hydromatic, ebbs and tides;
By aeromancy to discover doubts,
To plain out questions, as Apollo did.

BACON. Well, Master Burden, what of all this?

MILES. Marry, sir, he doth but fulfil, by rehearsing of 20
these names, the fable of the Fox and the Grapes; that which
is above us pertains nothing to us.

BURDEN. I tell thee, Bacon, Oxford makes report,
Nay, England, and the court of Henry says,
Thou'rt making of a brazen head by art, 25
Which shall unfold strange doubts and aphorisms,
And read a lecture in philosophy;
And, by the help of devils and ghastly fiends,
Thou mean'st, ere many years or days be past,
To compass England with a wall of brass. 30

BACON. And what of this?

MILES. What of this, master! Why, he doth speak mystically;
for he knows, if your skill fail to make a brazen head, yet
Mother Waters' strong ale will fit his turn to make him have
a copper nose. 35

CLEMENT. Bacon, we come not grieving at thy skill,
But joying that our academy yields
A man supposed the wonder of the world;
For if thy cunning work these miracles,
England and Europe shall admire thy fame, 40
And Oxford shall in characters of brass,
And statues, such as were built up in Rome,
Eternize Friar Bacon for his art.

MASON. Then, gentle friar, tell us thy intent.

BACON. Seeing you come as friends unto the friar, 45
Resolve you, doctors, Bacon can by books
Make storming Boreas thunder from his cave,

And dim fair Luna to a dark eclipse.
The great arch-ruler, potentate of hell,
Trembles when Bacon bids him or his fiends, 50
Bow to the force of his pentagonon[1].
What art can work, the frolic friar knows;
And therefore will I turn my magic books,
And strain out necromancy to the deep.
I have contrived and framed a head of brass 55
(I made Belcephon hammer out the stuff),
And that by art shall read philosophy;
And I will strengthen England by my skill,
That if ten Caesars lived and reigned in Rome,
With all the legions Europe doth contain, 60
They should not touch a grass of English ground.
The work that Ninus reared at Babylon,
The brazen walls framed by Semiramis,
Carved out like to the portal of the sun,
Shall not be such as rings the English strand 65
From Dover to the market-place of Rye.
  BURDEN. Is this possible?
  MILES. I'll bring ye two or three witnesses.
  BURDEN. What be those?
  MILES. Marry, sir, three or four as honest devils and 70
good companions as any be in hell.
  MASON. No doubt but magic may do much in this;
For he that reads but mathematic rules
Shall find conclusions that avail to work
Wonders that pass the common sense of men. 75
  BURDEN. But Bacon roves a bow[2] beyond his reach,
And tells of more than magic can perform,
Thinking to get a fame by fooleries.

---

[1] Pentagram, the five-rayed star used as a magical defense against demons.   [2] Ventures a bowshot.

Have I not passed as far in state of schools,
And read of many secrets? Yet to think   80
That heads of brass can utter any voice,
Or more, to tell of deep philosophy,
This is a fable Æsop had forgot.

BACON. Burden, thou wrong'st me in detracting thus;
Bacon loves not to stuff himself with lies.   85
But tell me 'fore these doctors, if thou dare,
Of certain questions I shall move to thee.

BURDEN. I will; ask what thou can.

MILES. Marry, sir, he'll straight be on your pick-pack,[1] to
know whether the feminine or the masculine gender be   90
most worthy.

BACON. Were you not yesterday, Master Burden, at Henly
upon the Thames?

BURDEN. I was; what then?

BACON. What book studied you thereon all night?   95

BURDEN. I! None at all; I read not there a line.

BACON. Then, doctors, Friar Bacon's art knows naught.

CLEMENT. What say you to this, Master Burden? Doth he
not touch you?   100

BURDEN. I pass not of[2] his frivolous speeches.

MILES. Nay, Master Burden, my master, ere he hath done
with you, will turn you from a doctor to a dunce, and shake
you so small, that he will leave no more learning in you than
is in Balaam's ass.   105

BACON. Master, for that learned Burden's skill is deep,
And sore he doubts of Bacon's cabalism,
I'll show you why he haunts to Henley oft:
Not, doctors, for to taste the fragrant air,
But there to spend the night in alchemy,   110

----

[1] Pick-a-back; shoulders.   [2] Am indifferent to.

To multiply with secret spells of art;
Thus private steals he learning from us all.
To prove my sayings true, I'll show you straight
The book he keeps at Henley for himself.

MILES. Nay, now my master goes to conjuration, take
heed.   115

BACON. Masters, stand still, fear not, I'll show you but his
book.   *Here he conjures.*
Per omnes deos infernales, Belcephon[1]!

Enter a woman with a shoulder of mutton on a spit, and a DEVIL.

MILES. O, master, cease your conjuration, or you spoil all; for
here's a she-devil come with a shoulder of mutton on   120
a spit. You have marred the devil's supper; but no doubt he
thinks our college fare is slender, and so hath sent you his cook
with a shoulder of mutton, to make it exceed.

HOSTESS. O, where am I, or what's become of me?

BACON. What art thou?   125

HOSTESS. Hostess at Henley, mistress of the Bell.

BACON. How camest thou here?

HOSTESS. As I was in the kitchen 'mongst the maids,
Spitting the meat 'gainst supper for my guests,
A motion[2] moved me to look forth of door: 130
No sooner had I pried into the yard,
But straight a whirlwind hoisted me from thence,
And mounted me aloft unto the clouds.
As in a trance I thought nor feared naught,
Nor know I where or whither I was ta'en,   135
Nor where I am nor what these persons be.

BACON. No? Know you not Master Burden?

HOSTESS. O, yes, good sir, he is my daily guest.—

---

[1] By all infernal gods, Belcephon.   [2] Impulse.

What, Master Burden! 'twas but yesternight
That you and I at Henley played at cards.   140

  BURDEN. I know not what we did.—A pox of all conjuring
    friars!

  CLEMENT. Now, jolly friar, tell us, is this the book
That Burden is so careful to look on?

  BACON. It is.— But, Burden, tell me now,
Think'st thou that Bacon's necromantic skill   145
Cannot perform his head and wall of brass,
When he can fetch thine hostess in such post?

  MILES. I'll warrant you, master, if Master Burden could
conjure as well as you, he would have his book every night
from Henley to study on at Oxford.   150

  MASON. Burden, what, are you mated[1] by this frolic friar?—
Look how he droops; his guilty conscience
Drives him to 'bash[2], and makes his hostess blush.

  BACON. Well, mistress, for I will not have you missed,
You shall to Henley to cheer up your guests   155
'Fore supper 'gin.—Burden, bid her adieu;
Say farewell to your hostess 'fore she goes.—
Sirrah, away, and set her safe at home.

  HOSTESS. Master Burden, when shall we see you at Henley?

  BURDEN. The devil take thee and Henley too.   160

           Exeunt HOSTESS *and* DEVIL.

  MILES. Master, shall I make a good motion?

  BACON. What's that?

  MILES. Marry, sir, now that my hostess is gone to provide
supper, conjure up another spirit, and send Doctor Burden
flying after.   165

  BACON. Thus, rulers of our academic state,

---

[1] Checkmated.   [2] Be abashed.

You have seen the friar frame his art by proof;
And as the college called Brazen-nose
Is under him, and he the master there,
So surely shall this head of brass be framed,   170
And yield forth strange and uncouth aphorisms;
And hell and Hecate shall fail the friar,
But I will circle England round with brass.

MILES. So be it *et nunc et semper*; amen.   *Exeunt.*

[Scene III. *Harleston Fair.*]

Enter MARGARET, *the fair maid of Fressingfield, and* JOAN; THOMAS,
[RICHARD,] *and other* CLOWNS; *and* LACY *disguised in country
apparel.*

THOMAS. By my troth, Margaret, here's a weather is able to
make a man call his father "whoreson"; if this weather hold,
we shall have hay good cheap, and butter and cheese at   5
Harleston will bear no price.

MARGARET. Thomas, maids when they come to see the fair
Count not to make a cope[1] for dearth of hay;
When we have turned our butter to the salt,
And set our cheese safely upon the racks,
Then let our fathers price it as they please.
We country sluts of merry Fressingfield   10
Come to buy needless naughts to make us fine,
And look that young men should be frank this **day,**
And court us with such fairings[2] as they can.
Phoebus is blithe, and frolic looks from heaven,
As when he courted lovely Semele,   15
Swearing the pedlars shall have empty packs,
If that fair weather may make chapmen buy.

LACY. But, lovely Peggy, Semele is dead,
And therefore Phoebus from his palace pries.

---

[1] Bargain.   [2] Presents, from a fair.

And, seeing such a sweet and seemly saint,   20
Shows all his glories for to court yourself.

MARGARET. This is a fairing, gentle sir, indeed,
To soothe me up with such smooth flattery;
But learn of me, your scoff's too broad before[1]—
Well, Joan, our beauties must abide theirs jests;   25
We serve the turn in jolly Fressingfield.

JOAN. Margaret, a farmer's daughter for a farmer's son;
I warrant you, the meanest of us both
Shall have a mate to lead us from the church.
But, Thomas, what's the news? What, in a dump?   30
Give me your hand, we are near a pedlar's shop;
Out with your purse, we must have fairings now.

THOMAS. Faith, Joan, and shall. I'll bestow a fairing on you,
and then we will to the tavern, and snap off a pint of wine
or two.   35

All this while LACY *whispers* MARGARET *in the ear.*

MARGARET. Whence are you, sir? Of Suffolk? For your terms
Are finer than the common sort of men.

LACY. Faith, lovely girl, I am of Beccles by,
Your neighbor, not above six miles from hence,
A farmer's son, that never was so quaint[2]   40
But that he could do courtesy to such dames.
But trust me, Margaret, I am sent in charge
From him that reveled in your father's house,
And filled his lodge with cheer and venison,
'Tired in green. He sent you this rich purse,   45
His token that he helped you run your cheese,
And in the milkhouse chatted with yourself.

MARGARET. To me? You forget yourself.

---

[1] On the face of it.   [2] Nice; i. e., here, "stuck up."

LACY. Women are often weak in memory.

MARGARET. O, pardon, sir, I call to mind the man.   50
'Twere little manners to refuse his gift,
And yet I hope he sends it not for love;
For we have little leisure to debate of that.

JOAN. What, Margaret! Blush not; maids must have their loves.

THOMAS. Nay, by the mass, she looks pale as if she were
angry.   55

RICHARD. Sirrah, are you of Beccles? I pray, how doth Good-
man Cob? My father bought a horse of him:—I'll tell you,
Margaret, 'a were good to be a gentleman's jade, for of all
things the foul hilding[1] could not abide a dung-cart.   60

MARGARET. [*Aside*]. How different is this farmer from the rest
That erst as yet have pleased my wandering sight!
His words are witty, quickened with a smile,
His courtesy gentle, smelling of the court;
Facile and debonair in all his deeds;   65
Proportioned as was Paris, when, in gray,
He courted Œnon in the vale by Troy.
Great lords have come and pleaded for my love;
Who but the Keeper's lass of Fressingfield?
And yet methinks this farmer's jolly son   70
Passeth the proudest that hath pleased mine eye.
But, Peg, disclose not that thou art in love,
And show as yet no sign of love to him,
Although thou well wouldst wish him for thy love;
Keep that to thee till time doth serve thy turn,   75
To show the grief wherein thy heart doth burn.—
Come, Joan and Thomas, shall we to the fair?—
You, Beccles man, will not forsake us now?

LACY. Not whilst I may have such quaint girls as you.

---

[1] Wretch.

MARGARET. Well, if you chance to come by Fressingfield, 80
Make but a step into the Keeper's lodge,
And such poor fare as woodmen can afford,
Butter and cheese, cream and fat venison,
You shall have store, and welcome therewithal.
  LACY. Gramercies, Peggy; look for me ere long.

Exeunt omnes.

[Scene IV. *Hampton Court.*]

Enter KING HENRY THE THIRD, *the* EMPEROR, *the* KING OF CASTILE,
  ELINOR, *his daughter, and* VANDERMAST, *a German.*

  KING HENRY. Great men of Europe, monarchs of the west,
Ringed with the walls of old Oceanus,
Whose lofty surge is like the battlements
That compassed high-built Babel in with towers,
Welcome, my lords, welcome, brave western kings, 5
To England's shore, whose promontory cliffs
Show Albion is another little world;
Welcome, says English Henry to you all;
Chiefly unto the lovely Elinor,
Who dared for Edward's sake cut through the seas, 10
And venture as Agenor's damsel through the deep,
To get the love of Henry's wanton son.
  KING OF CASTILE. England's rich monarch, brave Plantagenet,
The Pyren Mounts swelling above the clouds,
That ward the wealthy Castile in with walls, 15
Could not detain the beauteous Elinor;
But, hearing of the fame of Edward's youth,
She dared to brook Neptunus' haughty pride,
And bide the brunt of froward Æolus.
Then may fair England welcome her the more. 20
  ELINOR. After that English Henry by his lords

Had sent Prince Edward's lovely counterfeit,
A present to the Castile Elinor,
The comely portrait of so brave a man,
The virtuous fame discoursed of his deeds,   25
Edward's courageous resolution,
Done at the Holy Land 'fore Damas' walls,
Led both mine eye and thoughts in equal links
To like so of the English monarch's son,
That I attempted perils for his sake.   30
  EMPEROR. Where is the prince, my lord?
  KING HENRY. He posted down, not long since, from the court,
To Suffolk side, to merry Framlingham,
To sport himself amongst my fallow deer;
From thence, by packets sent to Hampton-house,   35
We hear the prince is ridden with his lords,
To Oxford, in the academy there
To hear dispute amongst the learned men.
But we will send forth letters for my son,
To will him come from Oxford to the court.   40
  EMPEROR. Nay, rather, Henry, let us, as we be,
Ride for to visit Oxford with our train.
Fain would I see your universities,
And what learned men your academy yields.
From Hapsburg have I brought a learned clerk   45
To hold dispute with English orators.
This doctor, surnamed Jaques Vandermast,
A German born, passed into Padua,
To Florence and to fair Bologna,
To Paris, Rheims, and stately Orleans,   50
And, talking there with men of art, put down
The chiefest of them all in aphorisms,
In magic, and the mathematic rules.
Now let us, Henry, try him in your schools.

KING HENRY. He shall, my lord; this motion likes me well. 55
We'll progress straight to Oxford with our trains,
And see what men our academy brings:—
And, wonder Vandermast, welcome to me.
In Oxford shalt thou find a jolly friar,
Called Friar Bacon, England's only flower; 60
Set him but nonplus in his magic spells,
And make him yield in mathematic rules,
And for thy glory I will bind thy brows,
Not with a poet's garland made of bays,
But with a coronet of choicest gold. 65
Whilst then we set to Oxford with our troops,
Let's in and banquet in our English court. *Exeunt.*

[Scene V. *Oxford.*]

Enter RALPH SIMNELL, *in* PRINCE EDWARD'S *apparel; and* EDWARD,
WARREN, *and* ERMSBY, *disguised.*

RALPH. Where be these vagabond knaves, that they attend no
better on their master?

PRINCE EDWARD. If it please your honor, we are all ready at an
inch[1].

RALPH. Sirrah Ned, I'll have no more post-horse to 5
ride on. I'll have another fetch[2].

ERMSBY. I pray you, how is that, my lord?

RALPH. Marry, sir, I'll send to the Isle of Ely for four or five
dozen of geese, and I'll have them tied six and six together with
whip-cord. Now upon their backs will I have a fair 10
field-bed with a canopy; and so, when it is my pleasure, I'll flee
into what place I please. This will be easy.

WARREN. Your honor hath said well; but shall we to Brazen-
nose College before we pull off our boots?

---

[1] At a moment's notice.   [2] Trick.

ERMSBY. Warren, well motioned; we will to the friar   15
Before we revel it within the town.
Ralph, see you keep your countenance like a prince.

RALPH. Wherefore have I such a company of cutting[1] knaves
to wait upon me, but to keep and defend my countenance
against all mine enemies? Have you not good swords and
bucklers?   20

ERMSBY. Stay, who comes here?

Enter [FRIAR] BACON *and* MILES.

WARREN. Some scholar; and we'll ask him where Friar
Bacon is.

BACON. Why, thou arrant dunce, shall I never make   25
thee a good scholar? Doth not all the town cry out and say,
Friar Bacon's subsizer[2] is the greatest blockhead in all Oxford?
Why, thou canst not speak one word of true Latin.

MILES. No, sir? Yes, what is this else? *Ego sum tuus homo,*
"I am your man"; I warrant you, sir, as good Tully's   30
phrase as any is in Oxford.

BACON. Come on, sirrah; what part of speech is *Ego?*

MILES. *Ego,* that is "I"; marry, *nomen substantivo.*

BACON. How prove you that?

MILES. Why, sir, let him prove himself an 'a will; I   35
can be heard, felt, and understood.

BACON. O gross dunce!   *Here beats him.*

PRINCE EDWARD. Come, let us break off this dispute between
    these two.—
Sirrah, where is Brazen-nose College?

MILES. Not far from Coppersmith's Hall.

PRINCE EDWARD. What, dost thou mock me?   40

MILES. Not I, sir; but what would you at Brazen-nose?

---

[1] Swaggering.   [2] Student who worked for board and tuition.

ERMSBY. Marry, we would speak with Friar Bacon.

MILES. Whose men be you?

ERMSBY. Marry, scholar, here's our master.

RALPH. Sirrah, I am the master of these good fellows; 45
mayst thou not know me to be a lord by my reparrel?

MILES. Then here's good game for the hawk; for here's the
master-fool and a covey of coxcombs. One wise man, I think,
would spring you all.

PRINCE EDWARD. Gog's wounds! Warren, kill him. 50

WARREN. Why, Ned, I think the devil be in my sheath; I cannot get out my dagger.

ERMSBY. Nor I mine. 'Swounds, Ned, I think I am bewitched.

MILES. A company of scabs! The proudest of you 55
all draw your weapon, if he can.—[*Aside.*] See how boldly I
speak, now my master is by.

PRINCE EDWARD. I strive in vain; but if my sword be shut
And conjured fast by magic in my sheath,
Villain, here is my fist.   *Strikes* MILES *a box on the ear.* 60

MILES. O, I beseech you conjure his hands too, that he may
not lift his arms to his head, for he is light-fingered!

RALPH. Ned, strike him; I'll warrant thee by mine honor.

BACON. What means the English prince to wrong my man?

PRINCE EDWARD. To whom speak'st thou? 65

BACON. To thee.

PRINCE EDWARD. Who art thou?

BACON. Could you not judge when all your swords grew
    fast,
That Friar Bacon was not far from hence?
Edward, King Henry's son and Prince of Wales, 70
Thy fool disguised cannot conceal thyself.
I know both Ermsby and the Sussex Earl,
Else Friar Bacon had but little skill.

Thou com'st in post from merry Fressingfield,
Fast-fancied[1] to the Keeper's bonny lass,   75
To crave some succor of the jolly friar;
And Lacy, Earl of Lincoln, hast thou left
To treat[2] fair Margaret to allow thy loves;
But friends are men, and love can baffle lords;
The earl both woos and courts her for himself.   80

WARREN. Ned, this is strange; the friar knoweth all.

ERMSBY. Apollo could not utter more than this.

PRINCE EDWARD. I stand amazed to hear this jolly friar
Tell even the very secrets of my thoughts.—
But, learned Bacon, since thou know'st the cause   85
Why I did post so fast from Fressingfield,
Help, friar, at a pinch, that I may have
The love of lovely Margaret to myself,
And, as I am true Prince of Wales, I'll give
Living and lands to strength thy college state.   90

WARREN. Good friar, help the prince in this.

RALPH. Why, servant Ned, will not the friar do it? Were not
my sword glued to my scabbard by conjuration, I would cut
off his head, and make him do it by force.

MILES. In faith, my lord, your manhood and your sword is   95
all alike; they are so fast conjured that we shall never see them.

ERMSBY. What, doctor, in a dump! Tush, help the prince,
And thou shalt see how liberal he will prove.

BACON. Crave not such actions greater dumps than these?
I will, my lord, strain out my magic spells;   100
For this day comes the earl to Fressingfield,
And 'fore that night shuts in the day with dark,
They'll be betrothed each to other fast.
But come with me; we'll to my study straight,

---

[1] Bound by love.   [2] Entreat.

And in a glass prospective I will show   105
What's done this day in merry Fressingfield.

PRINCE EDWARD. Gramercies, Bacon; I will 'quite thy pain.

BACON. But send your train, my lord, into the town;
My scholar shall go bring them to their inn;
Meanwhile we'll see the knavery of the earl.   110

PRINCE EDWARD. Warren, leave me; and, Ermsby, take the
    fool;
Let him be master, and go revel it,
Till I and Friar Bacon talk awhile.

WARREN. We will, my lord.

RALPH. Faith, Ned, and I'll lord it out till thou comest.   115
I'll be Prince of Wales over all the black-pots[1] in Oxford. *Exeunt.*

[Scene VI. FRIAR BACON'S *Cell.*]

FRIAR BACON *and* PRINCE EDWARD *go into the study.*

BACON. Now, frolic Edward, welcome to my cell;
Here tempers Friar Bacon many toys,
And holds this place his consistory-court,
Wherein the devils plead homage to his words.
Within this glass prospective thou shalt see   5
This day what's done in merry Fressingfield
'Twixt lovely Peggy and the Lincoln Earl.

PRINCE EDWARD. Friar, thou glad'st me. Now shall Edward
    try
How Lacy meaneth to his sovereign Lord.

BACON. Stand there and look directly in the glass.   10

Enter MARGARET *and* FRIAR BUNGAY.

What sees my lord?

PRINCE EDWARD. I see the Keeper's lovely lass appear,

[1] Leather wine jugs.

As brightsome as the paramour of Mars,
Only attended by a jolly friar.

BACON. Sit still, and keep the crystal in your eye.   15

MARGARET. But tell me, Friar Bungay, is it true
That this fair courteous country swain,
Who says his father is a farmer nigh,
Can be Lord Lacy, Earl of Lincolnshire?

BUNGAY. Peggy, 'tis true, 'tis Lacy for my life,   20
Or else mine art and cunning both do fail,
Left by Prince Edward to procure his loves;
For he in green, that holp you run your cheese,
Is son to Henry, and the Prince of Wales.

MARGARET. Be what he will, his lure is but for lust.   25
But did Lord Lacy like poor Margaret,
Or would he deign to wed a country lass,
Friar, I would his humble handmaid be,
And for great wealth 'quite him with courtesy.

BUNGAY. Why, Margaret, dost thou love him?   30

MARGARET. His personage, like the pride of vaunting Troy,
Might well avouch to shadow[1] Helen's scape:
His wit is quick and ready in conceit,
As Greece afforded in her chiefest prime.
Courteous, ah friar, full of pleasing smiles!   35
Trust me, I love too much to tell thee more;
Suffice to me he's England's paramour.

BUNGAY. Hath not each eye that viewed thy pleasing face
Surnamed thee Fair Maid of Fressingfield?

MARGARET. Yes, Bungay; and would God the lovely earl   40
Had that in *esse*[2] that so many sought.

BUNGAY. Fear not, the friar will not be behind
To show his cunning to entangle love.

---

[1] Excuse.   [2] Being, reality.

PRINCE EDWARD. I think the friar courts the bonny wench[1];
Bacon, methinks he is a lusty churl.   45
BACON. Now look, my lord.

Enter LACY.

PRINCE EDWARD. Gog's wounds, Bacon, here comes Lacy!
FRIAR BACON. Sit still, my lord, and mark the comedy.
FRIAR BUNGAY. Here's Lacy, Margaret; step aside awhile.

They withdraw.

LACY. Daphne, the damsel that caught Phoebus fast,   50
And locked him in the brightness of her looks,
Was not so beauteous in Apollo's eyes
As is fair Margaret to the Lincoln Earl.
Recant thee, Lacy, thou art put in trust.
Edward, thy sovereign's son, hath chosen thee,   55
A secret friend, to court her for himself,
And dar'st thou wrong thy prince with treachery?
Lacy, love makes no exception of a friend,
Nor deems it of a prince but as a man.
Honor bids thee control him in his lust;   60
His wooing is not for to wed the girl,
But to entrap her and beguile the lass.
Lacy, thou lov'st, then brook not such abuse,
But wed her, and abide thy prince's frown;
For better die than see her live disgraced.   65
MARGARET. Come, friar, I will shake him from his dumps.—

Comes forward.

How cheer you, sir? A penny for your thought.
You're early up, pray God it be the near[2].

---

[1] Edward does not hear the words between Margaret and Bungay
[2] Nearer; propitious.

What, come from Beccles in a morn so soon?

LACY. Thus watchful are such men as live in love,   70
Whose eyes brook broken slumbers for their sleep.
I tell thee, Peggy, since last Harleston fair
My mind hath felt a heap of passions.

MARGARET. A trusty man, that court it for your friend.
Woo you still for the courtier all in green?   75
I marvel that he sues not for himself. [*Aside*]

LACY. Peggy, I pleaded first to get your grace for him;
But when mine eyes surveyed your beauteous looks,
Love, like a wag, straight dived into my heart,
And there did shrine the idea of yourself.   80
Pity me, though I be a farmer's son,
And measure not my riches, but my love.

MARGARET. You are very hasty; for to garden well,
Seeds must have time to sprout before they spring:
Love ought to creep as doth the dial's shade,   85
For timely[1] ripe is rotten too too soon.

BUNGAY [*Advancing*]. *Deus hic*[2]; room for a merry friar!
What, youth of Beccles, with the Keeper's lass?
'Tis well; but tell me, hear you any news?

LACY. No, friar. What news?   90

FRIAR BUNGAY. Hear you not how the pursuivants do post
With proclamations through each country-town?

LACY. For what, gentle friar? Tell the news,

BUNGAY. Dwell'st thou in Beccles, and hear'st not of these
news?
Lacy, the Earl of Lincoln, is late fled   95
From Windsor court, disguised like a swain,
And lurks about the country here unknown.
Henry suspects him of some treachery,

---

[1] Untimely, too early.   [2] God here.

And therefore doth proclaim in every way,
That who can take the Lincoln Earl shall have,   100
Paid in the Exchequer, twenty thousand crowns.

LACY. The Earl of Lincoln! Friar, thou art mad.
It was some other; thou mistak'st the man.
The Earl of Lincoln! Why, it cannot be.

MARGARET. Yes, very well, my lord, for you are he.   105
The Keeper's daughter took you prisoner.
Lord Lacy, yield, I'll be your jailer once.

PRINCE EDWARD. How familiar they be, Bacon!

BACON. Sit still, and mark the sequel of their loves.

LACY. Then am I double prisoner to thyself.   110
Peggy, I yield. But are these news in jest?

MARGARET. In jest with you, but earnest unto me;
For-why these wrongs do wring me at the heart.
Ah, how these earls and noblemen of birth
Flatter and feign to forge poor women's ill!   115

LACY. Believe me, lass, I am the Lincoln Earl.
I not deny, but, 'tired thus in rags,
I lived disguised to win fair Peggy's love.

MARGARET. What love is there where wedding ends not love?

LACY. I meant, fair girl, to make thee Lacy's wife.   120

MARGARET. I little think that earls will stoop so low.

LACY. Say, shall I make thee countess ere I sleep?

MARGARET. Handmaid unto the earl, so please himself;
A wife in name, but servant in obedience.

LACY. The Lincoln Countess, for it shall be so;   125
I'll plight the bands, and seal it with a kiss.

PRINCE EDWARD. Gog's wounds, Bacon, they kiss! I'll stab
them.

BACON. O, hold your hands, my lord, it is the glass!

PRINCE EDWARD. Choler to see the traitors 'gree so well
Made me think the shadows substances.   130

BACON. 'Twere a long poniard, my lord, to reach between
Oxford and Fressingfield; but sit still and see more.

BUNGAY. Well, Lord of Lincoln, if your loves be knit,
And that your tongues and thoughts do both agree,
To avoid ensuing jars, I'll hamper up the match.   135
I'll take my portace[1] forth and wed you here,
Then go to bed and seal up your desires.

LACY. Friar, content. Peggy, how like you this?

MARGARET. What likes my lord is pleasing unto me.

BUNGAY. Then hand-fast hand, and I will to my book.   140

BACON: What sees my lord now?

PRINCE EDWARD. Bacon, I see the lovers hand in hand,
The friar ready with his portace there
To wed them both; then am I quite undone.
Bacon, help now, if e'er thy magic served;   145
Help, Bacon; stop the marriage now,
If devils or necromancy may suffice,
And I will give thee forty thousand crowns.

BACON. Fear not, my lord, I'll stop the jolly friar
For mumbling up[2] his orisons this day.   150

LACY. Why speak'st not, Bungay? Friar, to thy book.

BUNGAY *is mute, crying* "Hud, hud."

MARGARET. How look'st thou, Friar, as a man distraught?
Reft of thy senses, Bungay? Show by signs,
If thou be dumb, what passion holdeth thee.

LACY. He's dumb indeed. Bacon hath with his devils   155
Enchanted him, or else some strange disease
Or apoplexy hath possessed his lungs.
But, Peggy, what he cannot with his book,
We'll 'twixt us both unite it up in heart.

---

[1] Portable prayer-book.   [2] From completing.

MARGARET. Else let me die, my lord, a miscreant.   160

PRINCE EDWARD. Why stands Friar Bungay so amazed?

BACON. I have struck him dumb, my lord; and, if your
    honor please,

I'll fetch this Bungay straightway from Fressingfield,

And he shall dine with us in Oxford here.   165

PRINCE EDWARD. Bacon, do that, and thou contentest me.

LACY. Of courtesy, Margaret, let us lead the friar

Unto thy father's lodge, to comfort him

With broths, to bring him from this hapless trance.

MARGARET. Or else, my lord, we were passing unkind   170

To leave the friar so in his distress.

      Enter a DEVIL *and carry* BUNGAY *on his back.*

O, help, my lord! A devil, a devil, my lord!

Look how he carries Bungay on his back!

Let's hence, for Bacon's spirits be abroad. *Exit with* LACY.

PRINCE EDWARD. Bacon, I laugh to see the jolly friar   175

Mounted upon the devil, and how the earl

Flees with his bonny lass for fear.

As soon as Bungay is at Brazen-nose,

And I have chatted with the merry friar,

I will in post hie me to Fressingfield,   180

And 'quite these wrongs on Lacy ere 't be long.

BACON. So be it, my lord; but let us to our dinner;

For ere we have taken our repast awhile,

We shall have Bungay brought to Brazen-nose.   *Exeunt.*

    [Scene VII. *The Regent-house at Oxford.*]

   Enter three DOCTORS, BURDEN, MASON, *and* CLEMENT.

MASON. Now that we are gathered in the Regent-house,

It fits us talk about the king's repair[1],

---

[1] Visit.

For he, trooped with all the western kings,
That lie alongst the Dantzic seas by east,
North by the clime of frosty Germany,   5
The Almain monarch, and the Saxon duke,
Castile and lovely Elinor with him,
Have in their jests resolved for Oxford town.

BURDEN. We must lay plots of stately tragedies,
Strange comic shows, such as proud Roscius   10
Vaunted before the Roman emperors,
To welcome all the western potentates.

CLEMENT. But more; the king by letters hath foretold
That Frederick, the Almain emperor,
Hath brought with him a German of esteem,   15
Whose surname is Don Jaques Vandermast,
Skilful in magic and those secret arts.

MASON. Then must we all make suit unto the friar,
To Friar Bacon, that he vouch this task,
And undertake to countervail in skill   20
The German; else there's none in Oxford can
Match and dispute with learned Vandermast.

BURDEN. Bacon, if he will hold the German play,
Will teach him what an English friar can do.
The devil, I think, dare not dispute with him.   25

CLEMENT. Indeed, Mas' doctor, he displeasured you,
In that he brought your hostess with her spit,
From Henley, posting unto Brazen-nose.

BURDEN. A vengeance on the friar for his pains!
But leaving that, let's hie to Bacon straight,   30
To see if he will take this task in hand.

CLEMENT. Stay, what rumor is this? The town is up in a
    mutiny.
What hurly-burly is this?

Enter a CONSTABLE, *with* RALPH SIMNELL, WARREN, ERMSBY
[*all still disguised*], *and* MILES.

CONSTABLE. Nay, masters, if you were ne'er so good, you
shall before the doctors to answer your misdemeanor.   35

BURDEN. What's the matter, fellow?

CONSTABLE. Marry, sir, here's a company of rufflers, that,
drinking in the tavern, have made a great brawl and almost
killed the vintner.

MILES.   *Salve*[1], Doctor Burden!   40
    This lubberly lurden[2]
    Ill-shaped and ill-faced,
    Disdained and disgraced,
    What he tells unto *vobis*
    Mentitur de nobis[3].   45

BURDEN. Who is the master and chief of this crew?

MILES.   *Ecce asinum mundi*
    Figura rotundi[4],
    Neat, sheat[5], and fine,
    As brisk as a cup of wine.   50

BURDEN. What are you?

RALPH. I am, father doctor, as a man would say, the bell-
wether of this company; these are my lords, and I the Prince
of Wales.

CLEMENT. Are you Edward, the king's son?   55

RALPH. Sirrah Miles, bring hither the tapster that drew the
wine, and, I warrant, when they see how soundly I have broke
his head, they'll say 'twas done by no less man than a prince.

MASON. I cannot believe that this is the Prince of Wales.

WARREN. And why so, sir?   60

MASON. For they say the prince is a brave and a wise gentleman.

[1] Greeting.   [2] Lazy, stupid person.   [3] To you, lies about us.
[4] Behold the ass of the world, round in feature. i. e., Ralph.   [5] Lively.

WARREN. Why, and think'st thou, doctor, that he is not so? 63
Dar'st thou detract and derogate from him,
Being so lovely and so brave a youth? 65

ERMSBY. Whose face, shining with many a sugared smile,
Bewrays that he is bred of princely race.

MILES.   And yet, master doctor,
    To speak like a proctor,
    And tell unto you 70
    What is veriment and true;
    To cease of this quarrel,
    Look but on his apparel;
    Then mark but my talis,
    He is great Prince of Walis, 75
    The chief of our *gregis*[1],
    And *filius regis*[2];
    Then 'ware what is done,
    For he is Henry's white[3] son.

RALPH. Doctors, whose doting night-caps are not capable 80
of my ingenious dignity, know that I am Edward Plantagenet,
whom if you displease will make a ship that shall hold all your
colleges, and so carry away the niniversity with a fair wind to
the Bankside in Southwark. How sayest thou, Ned Warren,
shall I not do it? 85

WARREN. Yes, my good lord; and, if it please your lordship,
I will gather up all your old pantofles, and with the cork[4]
make you a pinnace of five-hundred ton, that shall serve the
turn marvelous well, my lord.

ERMSBY. And I, my lord, will have pioners to undermine 90
the town, that the very gardens and orchards be carried away
for your summer-walks.

MILES. And I, with *scientia*

---

[1] Band.   [2] King's son.   [3] Dear.   [4] From the soles of the pantofles.

　　　　And great *diligentia*,
　　　　Will conjure and charm,　　　　　　　95
　　　　To keep you from harm;
　　　　That *utrum horum mavis*[1],
　　　　Your very great *navis*,
　　　　Like Barclay's ship[2],
　　　　From Oxford do skip　　　　　　　100
　　　　With colleges and schools,
　　　　Full-loaden with fools.
　　　　Quid dicis ad hoc,
　　　　Worshipful *Domine* Dawcock[3]?

CLEMENT. Why, hair-brained courtiers, are you drunk or
　　mad,　　　　　　　　　　　　　105
To taunt us up with such scurrility?
Deem you us men of base and light esteem,
To bring us such a fop for Henry's son? —
Call out the beadles and convey them hence
Straight to Bocardo[4]; let the roisters lie　　　　110
Close clapt in bolts, until their wits be tame.

ERMSBY. Why, shall we to prison, my lord?

RALPH. What sayest, Miles, shall I honor the prison with my
presence?

MILES.　No, no; out with your blades,　　　　115
　　　　And hamper these jades;
　　　　Have a flurt and a crash,
　　　　Now play revel-dash,
　　　　And teach these sacerdos
　　　　That the Bocardos[4],　　　　　　　120
　　　　Like peasants and elves,
　　　　Are meet for themselves.

MASON. To the prison with them, constable.

---

[1] Which of these you prefer.　　[2] I. e., *The Ship of Fooles*.
[3] What do you say to this, Lord Dolt?　　[4] Old prison.

WARREN. Well, doctors, seeing I have sported me
With laughing at these mad and merry wags,   125
Know that Prince Edward is at Brazen-nose,
And this, attired like the Prince of Wales,
Is Ralph, King Henry's only loved fool;
I, Earl of Sussex, and this Ermsby,
One of the privy-chamber to the king;   130
Who, while the prince with Friar Bacon stays,
Have reveled it in Oxford as you see.

MASON. My lord, pardon us, we knew not what you were;
But courtiers may make greater scapes than these.
Wilt please your honor dine with me today?   135

WARREN. I will, Master doctor, and satisfy the vintner for
his hurt; only I must desire you to imagine him[1] all this fore-
noon the Prince of Wales.

MASON. I will, sir.

RALPH. And upon that I will lead the way; only I   140
will have Miles go before me, because I have heard Henry
say that wisdom must go before majesty.   *Exeunt.*

[Scene VIII. *Fressingfield.*]

Enter PRINCE EDWARD *with his poniard in his hand*, LACY,
and MARGARET.

PRINCE EDWARD. Lacy, thou canst not shroud thy traitorous
    thoughts,
Nor cover, as did Cassius, all his wiles;
For Edward hath an eye that looks as far
As Lynceus from the shores of Graecia.
Did not I sit in Oxford by the friar,   5

---

[1] Ralph.

And see thee court the maid of Fressingfield,
Sealing thy flattering fancies with a kiss?
Did not proud Bungay draw his portace forth,
And joining hand in hand had married you,
If Friar Bacon had not struck him dumb,   10
And mounted him upon a spirit's back,
That we might chat at Oxford with the friar?
Traitor, what answer'st? Is not all this true?
  LACY. Truth all, my lord; and thus I make reply:
At Harleston fair, there courting for your grace,   15
Whenas mine eye surveyed her curious shape,
And drew the beauteous glory of her looks
To dive into the center of my heart,
Love taught me that your honor did but jest,
That princes were in fancy but as men;   20
How that the lovely maid of Fressingfield
Was fitter to be Lacy's wedded wife
Than concubine unto the Prince of Wales.
  PRINCE EDWARD. Injurious Lacy, did I love thee more
Than Alexander his Hephæstion?   25
Did I unfold the passions of my love,
And lock them in the closet of thy thoughts?
Wert thou to Edward second to himself,
Sole friend, and partner of his secret loves?
And could a glance of fading beauty break   30
Th' enchained fetters of such private friends?
Base coward, false, and too effeminate
To be corrival¹ with a prince in thoughts!
From Oxford have I posted since I dined,
To 'quite a traitor 'fore that Edward sleep.   35
  MARGARET. 'Twas I, my lord, not Lacy stept awry;

¹ Sharer.

For oft he sued and courted for yourself,
And still wooed for the courtier all in green;
But I, whom fancy made but over-fond,
Pleaded myself with looks as if I loved;   40
I fed mine eye with gazing on his face,
And still bewitched loved Lacy with my looks;
My heart with sighs, mine eyes pleaded with tears,
My face held pity and content at once,
And more I could not cipher-out by signs,   45
But that I loved Lord Lacy with my heart.
Then, worthy Edward, measure with thy mind
If women's favors will not force men fall,
If beauty, and if darts of piercing love,
Are not of force to bury thoughts of friends.   50
    PRINCE EDWARD. I tell thee, Peggy, I will have thy loves;
Edward or none shall conquer Margaret.
In frigates bottomed with rich Sethin[1] planks,
Topt with the lofty firs of Lebanon,
Stemmed and incased with burnished ivory,   55
And over-laid with plates of Persian wealth,
Like Thetis shalt thou wanton on the waves,
And draw the dolphins to thy lovely eyes,
To dance lavoltas[2] in the purple streams;
Sirens, with harps and silver psalteries,   60
Shall wait with music at thy frigate's stem,
And entertain fair Margaret with their lays.
England and England's wealth shall wait on thee;
Britain shall bend unto her prince's love,
And do due homage to thine excellence,   65
If thou wilt be but Edward's Margaret.
    MARGARET. Pardon, my lord; if Jove's great royalty

---

[1] Shittim. Cf. Exodus 25:10.   [2] Round dance.

Sent me such presents as to Danæ;
If Phœbus, 'tired in Latona's webs,
Come courting from the beauty of his lodge;   70
The dulcet tunes of frolic Mercury,
Nor all the wealth heaven's treasury affords,
Should make me leave Lord Lacy or his love.

   PRINCE EDWARD. I have learned at Oxford, then, this point
     of schools,—

Ablata causa, tollitur effectus[1] :   75
Lacy, the cause that Margaret cannot love
Nor fix her liking on the English prince,
Take him away, and then th' effects will fail.
Villain, prepare thyself; for I will bathe
My poniard in the bosom of an earl.   80

   LACY. Rather than live, and miss fair Margaret's love,
Prince Edward, stop not at the fatal doom,
But stab it home; end both my loves and life.

   MARGARET. Brave Prince of Wales, honored for royal deeds,
'Twere sin to stain fair Venus' courts with blood;   85
Love's conquest ends, my lord, in courtesy.
Spare Lacy, gentle Edward; let me die,
For so both you and he do cease your loves.

   PRINCE EDWARD. Lacy shall die as traitor to his lord.

   LACY. I have deserved it, Edward; act it well.   90

   MARGARET. What hopes the prince to gain by Lacy's death?

   PRINCE EDWARD. To end the loves 'twixt him and Margaret.

   MARGARET. Why, thinks King Henry's son that Margaret's
     love
Hangs in th' uncertain balance of proud time?
That death shall make a discord of our thoughts?   95
No, stab the earl, and, 'fore the morning sun

---

[1] The cause removed, the effect is taken away.

Shall vaunt him thrice over the lofty east,
Margaret will meet her Lacy in the heavens.

 LACY. If aught betides to lovely Margaret
That wrongs or wrings her honor from content,   100
Europe's rich wealth nor England's monarchy
Should not allure Lacy to over-live.
Then, Edward, short my life, and end her loves.

 MARGARET. Rid me, and keep a friend worth many loves.

 LACY. Nay, Edward, keep a love worth many friends. 105

 MARGARET. An if thy mind be such as fame hath blazed,
Then, princely Edward, let us both abide
The fatal resolution of thy rage.
Banish thou fancy, and embrace revenge,
And in one tomb knit both our carcasses,   110
Whose hearts were linked in one perfect love.

 PRINCE EDWARD [*Aside*]. Edward, art thou that famous Prince
  of Wales,
Who at Damasco beat the Saracens,
And brought'st home triumph on thy lance's point?
And shall thy plumes be pulled by Venus down? 115
Is't princely to dissever lovers' leagues,
To part such friends as glory in their loves?
Leave, Ned, and make a virtue of this fault,
And further Peg and Lacy in their loves;
So in subduing fancy's passion,   120
Conquering thyself, thou gett'st the richest spoil.
Lacy, rise up. Fair Peggy, here's my hand.
The Prince of Wales hath conquered all his thoughts,
And all his loves he yields unto the earl.
Lacy, enjoy the maid of Fressingfield;   125
Make her thy Lincoln Countess at the church,
And Ned, as he is true Plantagenet,
Will give her to thee frankly for thy wife.

LACY. Humbly I take her of my sovereign,
As if that Edward gave me England's right,　　130
And riched me with the Albion diadem.

MARGARET. And doth the English prince mean true?
Will he vouchsafe to cease his former loves,
And yield the title of a country maid
Unto Lord Lacy?　　135

PRINCE EDWARD. I will, fair Peggy, as I am true lord.

MARGARET. Then, lordly sir, whose conquest is as great,
In conquering love, as Caesar's victories,
Margaret, as mild and humble in her thoughts
As was Aspasia unto Cyrus' self,　　140
Yields thanks, and, next Lord Lacy, doth enshrine
Edward the second secret in her heart.

PRINCE EDWARD. Gramercy, Peggy. Now that vows are past,
And that your loves are not to be revolt[1],
Once, Lacy, friends again. Come, we will post　　145
To Oxford; for this day the king is there,
And brings for Edward Castile Elinor.
Peggy, 1 must go see and view my wife;
I pray God I like her as I loved thee.
Beside, Lord Lincoln, we shall hear dispute　　150
'Twixt Friar Bacon and learned Vandermast.
Peggy, we'll leave you for a week or two.

MARGARET. As it please Lord Lacy; but love's foolish looks
Think footsteps miles and minutes to be hours.

LACY. I'll hasten, Peggy, to make short return.　　155
But please your honor go unto the lodge,
We shall have butter, cheese, and venison;
And yesterday I brought for Margaret
A lusty bottle of neat claret-wine;

[1] Overturned.

Thus can we feast and entertain your grace.   160

PRINCE EDWARD. 'Tis cheer, Lord Lacy, for an emperor,
If he respect the person and the place.
Come, let us in; for I will all this night
Ride post until I come to Bacon's cell.   *Exeunt.*

[Scene IX. *Oxford.*]

Enter KING HENRY, *the* EMPEROR, *the* KING OF CASTILE, ELINOR,
VANDERMAST, *and* BUNGAY.

EMPEROR. Trust me, Plantagenet, these Oxford schools
Are richly seated near the river-side;
The mountains full of fat and fallow deer,
The battling[1] pastures lade with kine and flocks,
The town gorgeous with high-built colleges,   5
And scholars seemly in their grave attire,
Learned in searching principles of art.
What is thy judgment, Jaques Vandermast?

VANDERMAST. That lordly are the buildings of the town,
Spacious the rooms, and full of pleasant walks;   10
But for the doctors, how that they be learned,
It may be meanly, for aught I can hear.

BUNGAY. I tell thee, German, Hapsburg holds none such,
None read so deep as Oxenford contains:
There are within our academic state   15
Men that may lecture it in Germany
To all the doctors of your Belgic schools.

KING HENRY. Stand to him, Bungay, charm this Vandermast,
And I will use thee as a royal king.

VANDERMAST. Wherein dar'st thou dispute with me?   20

BUNGAY. In what a doctor and a friar can.

VANDERMAST. Before rich Europe's worthies put thou forth

---

[1] Fertile.

The doubtful question unto Vandermast.

BUNGAY. Let it be this,—Whether the spirits of pyromancy
or geomancy be most predominant in magic? 25

VANDERMAST. I say, of pyromancy.

BUNGAY. And I, of geomancy.

VANDERMAST. The cabalists that write of magic spells,
As Hermes, Melchie, and Pythagoras,
Affirm that, 'mongst the quadruplicity 30
Of elemental essence, *terra* is but thought
To be a *punctum* squared[1] to the rest;
And that the compass of ascending elements
Exceed in bigness as they do in height;
Judging the concave circle of the sun 35
To hold the rest in his circumference.
If, then, as Hermes says, the fire be greatest,
Purest, and only giveth shape to spirits,
Then must these dæmones that haunt that place
Be every way superior to the rest. 40

BUNGAY. I reason not of elemental shapes,
Nor tell I of the concave latitudes,
Noting their essence nor their quality,
But of the spirits that pyromancy calls,
And of the vigor of the geomantic fiends. 45
I tell thee, German, magic haunts the ground,
And those strange necromantic spells,
That work such shows and wondering in the world,
Are acted by those geomantic spirits
That Hermes calleth *terræ filii*[2]. 50
The fiery spirits are but transparent shades,
That lightly pass as heralds to bear news;
But earthly fiends, closed in the lowest deep,
Dissever mountains, if they be but charged,

---

[1] Compared.   [2] Sons of the earth.

Being more gross and massy in their power.   55
  VANDERMAST. Rather these earthly geomantic spirits
Are dull and like the place where they remain;
For when proud Lucifer fell from the heavens,
The spirits and angels that did sin with him,
Retained their local essence as their faults,   60
All subject under Luna's continent.
They which offended less hung in the fire,
And second faults did rest within the air;
But Lucifer and his proud-hearted fiends
Were thrown into the center of the earth,   65
Having less understanding than the rest,
As having greater sin and lesser grace.
Therefore such gross and earthly spirits do serve
For jugglers, witches, and vile sorcerers;
Whereas the pyromantic genii   70
Are mighty, swift, and of far-reaching power.
But grant that geomancy hath most force;
Bungay, to please these mighty potentates,
Prove by some instance what thy art can do.
  BUNGAY. I will.   75
  EMPEROR. Now, English Harry, here begins the game;
We shall see sport between these learned men.
  VANDERMAST. What wilt thou do?
  BUNGAY. Show thee the tree, leaved with refined gold,
Whereon the fearful dragon held his seat,   80
That watched the garden called Hesperides,
Subdued and won by conquering Hercules.

   Here BUNGAY *conjures, and the tree appears with the dragon
               shooting fire.*

  VANDERMAST. Well done!
  KING HENRY. What say you, royal lordings, to my friar?
Hath he not done a point of cunning skill?   85

VANDERMAST. Each scholar in the necromantic spells
Can do as much as Bungay hath performed.
But as Alcmena's bastard razed this tree,
So will I raise him up as when he lived,
And cause him pull the dragon from his seat,   90
And tear the branches piecemeal from the root.
Hercules! *Prodi, prodi*[1], Hercules!

      HERCULES *appears in his lion's skin.*

HERCULES. *Quis me vult*[2]?
VANDERMAST. Jove's bastard son, thou Libyan Hercules,
Pull off the sprigs from off th' Hesperian tree,   95
As once thou didst to win the golden fruit.
HERCULES. *Fiat*[3].   *Here he begins to break the branches.*
VANDERMAST. Now Bungay, if thou canst by magic charm
The fiend, appearing like great Hercules,
From pulling down the branches of the tree,   100
Then art thou worthy to be counted learned.
BUNGAY. I cannot.
VANDERMAST. Cease, Hercules, until I give thee charge.
Mighty commander of this English isle,
Henry, come from the stout Plantagenets,   105
Bungay is learned enough to be a friar;
But to compare with Jaques Vandermast,
Oxford and Cambridge must go seek their cells
To find a man to match him in his art.
I have given non-plus to the Paduans,   110
To them of Sien, Florence, and Bologna,
Rheims, Louvain, and fair Rotterdam,
Frankfort, Lutetia[4], and Orleans;
And now must Henry, if he do me right,
Crown me with laurel, as they all have done.   115

  [1] Come forth.   [2] Who wants me?   [3] Let it be done.   [4] Paris.

Enter BACON.

BACON. All hail to this royal company,
That sit to hear and see this strange dispute!
Bungay, how stand'st thou as a man amazed?
What, hath the German acted more than thou?

VANDERMAST. What art thou that question'st thus?   120

BACON. Men call me Bacon.

VANDERMAST. Lordly thou look'st, as if that thou were
    learned;
Thy countenance as if science held her seat
Between the circled arches of thy brows.

KING HENRY. Now, monarchs, hath the German found his
    match.   125

EMPEROR. Bestir thee, Jaques, take not now the foil,
Lest thou dost lose what foretime thou didst gain.

VANDERMAST. Bacon, wilt thou dispute?

BACON. No.
Unless he were more learned than Vandermast;   130
For yet, tell me, what hast thou done?

VANDERMAST. Raised Hercules to ruinate that tree
That Bungay mounted by his magic spells.

BACON. Set Hercules to work.

VANDERMAST. Now Hercules, I charge thee to thy task;   135
Pull off the golden branches from the root.

HERCULES. I dare not. See'st thou not great Bacon here,
Whose frown doth act more than my magic can?

VANDERMAST. By all the thrones, and dominations,
Virtues, powers, and mighty hierarchies,   140
I charge thee to obey to Vandermast.

HERCULES. Bacon, that bridles headstrong Belcephon,
And rules Asmenoth, guider of the north,
Binds me from yielding unto Vandermast.

KING HENRY. How now, Vandermast! Have you met with
your match?   145

VANDERMAST. Never before was't known to Vandermast
That men held devils in such obedient awe.
Bacon doth more than art, or else I fail.

EMPEROR. Why, Vandermast, art thou overcome?
Bacon, dispute with him, and try his skill.   150

BACON. I come not, monarchs, for to hold dispute
With such a novice as is Vandermast;
I came to have your royalties to dine
With Friar Bacon here in Brazen-nose;
And, for this German troubles but the place,   155
And holds this audience with a long suspense,
I'll send him to his academy hence.
Thou Hercules, whom Vandermast did raise,
Transport the German unto Hapsburg straight,
That he may learn by travail, 'gainst the spring,   160
More secret dooms and aphorisms of art.
Vanish the tree, and thou away with him!

Exit the spirit [*of* HERCULES] *with* VANDERMAST *and the tree.*

EMPEROR. Why, Bacon, whither dost thou send him?

BACON. To Hapsburg; there your highness at return
Shall find the German in his study safe.   165

KING HENRY. Bacon, thou hast honored England with thy
skill,
And made fair Oxford famous by thine art;
I will be English Henry to thyself.
But tell me, shall we dine with thee today?

BACON. With me, my lord; and while I fit my cheer,   170
See where Prince Edward comes to welcome you,
Gracious as the morning-star of Heaven.   *Exit.*

Enter EDWARD, LACY, WARREN, ERMSBY.

EMPEROR. Is this Prince Edward, Henry's royal son?
How martial is the figure of his face!
Yet lovely and beset with amorets[1].   175
  KING HENRY. Ned, where hast thou been?
  PRINCE EDWARD. At Framlingham, my lord, to try your bucks
If they could 'scape the teasers or the toil.
But hearing of these lordly potentates
Landed, and progressed up to Oxford town,   180
I posted to give entertain to them;
Chief to the Almain monarch; next to him,
And joint with him, Castile and Saxony
Are welcome as they may be to the English court.
Thus for the men: but see, Venus appears,   185
Or one that overmatcheth Venus in her shape!
Sweet Elinor, beauty's high-swelling pride,
Rich nature's glory and her wealth at once,
Fair of all fairs, welcome to Albion;
Welcome to me, and welcome to thine own,   190
If that thou deign'st the welcome from myself.
  ELINOR. Martial Plantagenet, Henry's high-minded son,
The mark that Elinor did count her aim,
I liked thee 'fore I saw thee; now I love,
And so as in so short a time I may;   195
Yet so as time shall never break that so,
And therefore so accept of Elinor.
  KING OF CASTILE. Fear not, my lord, this couple will agree,
If love may creep into their wanton eyes:
And therefore, Edward, I accept thee here,   200
Without suspense, as my adopted son.
  KING HENRY. Let me that joy in these consorting greets,

[1] Love-kindling looks.

And glory in these honors done to Ned,
Yield thanks for all these favors to my son,
And rest a true Plantagenet to all.   205

> *Enter* MILES *with a cloth and trenchers and salt.*

MILES.   *Salvete, omnes reges*[1],
          That govern your *greges*
          In Saxony and Spain,
          In England and in Almain!
          For all this frolic rabble   210
          Must I cover the table
          With trenchers, salt, and cloth;
          And then look for your broth.

EMPEROR.   What pleasant fellow is this?

KING HENRY.   'Tis, my lord, Doctor Bacon's poor scholar.   215

MILES [*Aside*].   My master hath made me sewer[2] of these
great lords; and, God knows, I am as serviceable at a table
as a sow is under an apple-tree. 'Tis no matter; their cheer shall
not be great, and therefore what skills where the salt stand,
before or behind?   [*Exit.*]   220

KING OF CASTILE.   These scholars know more skill in axioms,
How to use quips and sleights of sophistry,
Than for to cover courtly for a king.

> *Re-enter* MILES *with a mess of pottage and broth; and, after him,*
> BACON.

MILES.   Spill, sir? Why, do you think I never carried two-
          penny chop[3] before in my life?
By your leave, *nobile decus*[4],   225
For here comes Doctor Bacon's *pecus*[5],
Being in his full age
To carry a mess of pottage.

---

[1] Greetings, all kings.   [2] Table setter.   [3] Meat dish.   [4] Famous
glory.   [5] Sheep.

BACON. Lordings, admire[1] not if your cheer be this.
For we must keep our academic fare;   230
No riot where philosophy doth reign:
And therefore, Henry, place these potentates,
And bid them fall unto their frugal cates[2].

EMPEROR. Presumptuous friar! What, scoff'st thou at a king?
What, dost thou taunt us with thy peasant's fare,   235
And give us cates fit for country swains?
Henry, proceeds this jest of thy consent,
To twit us with a pittance of such price?
Tell me, and Frederick will not grieve thee long.

KING HENRY. By Henry's honor, and the royal faith   240
The English monarch beareth to his friend,
I knew not of the friar's feeble fare,
Nor am I pleased he entertains you thus.

BACON. Content thee, Frederick, for I showed the cates,
To let thee see how scholars used to feed;   245
How little meat refines our English wits.
Miles, take away, and let it be thy dinner.

MILES. Marry, sir, I will.
This day shall be a festival day with me;
For I shall exceed in the highest degree.   [*Exit* MILES.] 250

BACON. I tell thee, monarch, all the German peers
Could not afford thy entertainment such,
So royal and so full of majesty,
As Bacon will present to Frederick.
The basest waiter that attends thy cups   255
Shall be in honors greater than thyself;
And for thy cates, rich Alexandria drugs[3],
Fetched by carvels[4] from Ægypt's richest straits,
Found in the wealthy strand of Africa,

---

[1] Wonder.   [2] Delicacies.   [3] Spices.   [4] Light, fast ships.

Shall royalize the table of my king;   26c
Wines richer than th' Ægyptian courtesan
Quaffed to Augustus' kingly countermatch,
Shall be caroused in English Henry's feast;
Candy[1] shall yield the richest of her canes;
Persia, down her Volga by canoes,   265
Send down the secrets of her spicery;
The Afric dates, mirabolans[2] of Spain,
Conserves and suckets[3] from Tiberias,
Cates from Judæa, choicer than the lamp[4]
That fired Rome with sparks of gluttony,   270
Shall beautify the board for Frederick:
And therefore grudge not at a friar's feast.   *Exeunt.*

[Scene X. *Fressingfield.*]

Enter two gentlemen, LAMBERT *and* SERLSBY, *with the* KEEPER.

LAMBERT. Come, frolic Keeper of our liege's game,
Whose table spread hath ever venison
And jacks[5] of wine to welcome passengers,
Know I'm in love with jolly Margaret,
That overshines our damsels as the moon   5
Darkeneth the brightest sparkles of the night.
In Laxfield here my land and living lies;
I'll make thy daughter jointer[6] of it all,
So thou consent to give her to my wife;
And I can spend five hundred marks a-year.   10
  SERLSBY. I am the lands-lord, Keeper, of thy holds,
By copy all thy living lies in me;
Laxfield did never see me raise my due;
I will enfeoff fair Margaret in all,
So she will take her to a lusty squire.   15

---

[1] Candia.   [2] Plums.   [3] Sweets.   [4] Lamprey, i. e., eel (?).   [5] Pitchers.
[6] Jointure.

KEEPER. Now, courteous gentles, if the Keeper's girl
Hath pleased the liking fancy of you both,
And with her beauty hath subdued your thoughts,
'Tis doubtful to decide the question.
It joys me that such men of great esteem   20
Should lay their liking on this base estate,
And that her state should grow so fortunate
To be a wife to meaner men than you.
But sith such squires will stoop to keeper's fee[1],
I will, to avoid displeasure of you both,   25
Call Margaret forth, and she shall make her choice.
   LAMBERT. Content, Keeper; send her unto us.   *Exit* KEEPER.
Why, Serlsby, is thy wife so lately dead,
Are all thy loves so lightly passed over,
As thou canst wed before the year be out?   30
   SERLSBY. I live not, Lambert, to content the dead,
Nor was I wedded but for life to her;
The grave ends and begins a married state.

Enter MARGARET.

   LAMBERT. Peggy, the lovely flower of all towns,
Suffolk's fair Helen, and rich England's star,   35
Whose beauty, tempered with her huswifery,
Makes England talk of merry Fressingfield!
   SERLSBY. I cannot trick it up with poesies,
Nor paint my passions with comparisons,
Nor tell a tale of Phœbus and his loves;   40
But this believe me,—Laxfield here is mine,
Of ancient rent seven hundred pounds a-year.
And if thou canst but love a country squire,
I will enfeoff thee, Margaret, in all.
I cannot flatter; try me, if thou please.   45

[1] Estate.

MARGARET. Brave neighboring squires, the stay of Suffolks'
  clime,
A keeper's daughter is too base in 'gree[1]
To match with men accounted of such worth;
But might I not displease, I would reply.
  LAMBERT. Say, Peggy; naught shall make us discontent. 50
  MARGARET. Then, gentles, note that love hath little stay,
Nor can the flames that Venus sets on fire
Be kindled but by fancy's motion.
Then pardon, gentles, if a maid's reply
Be doubtful, while I have debated with myself,   55
Who, or of whom, love shall constrain me like.
  SERLSBY. Let it be me; and trust me, Margaret,
The meads environed with the silver streams,
Whose battling pastures fatten all my flocks,
Yielding forth fleeces stapled with such wool   60
As Lempster[2] cannot yield more finer stuff,
And forty kine with fair and burnished heads,
With strouting[3] dugs that paggle[4] to the ground,
Shall serve thy dairy, if thou wed with me.
  LAMBERT. Let pass the country wealth, as flocks and kine, 65
And lands that wave with Ceres' golden sheaves,
Filling my barns with plenty of the fields;
But, Peggy, if thou wed thyself to me,
Thou shalt have garments of embroidered silk,
Lawns, and rich net-works for thy head-attire.   70
Costly shall be thy fair habiliments,
If thou wilt be but Lambert's loving wife.
  MARGARET. Content you, gentles, you have proffered fair,
And more than fits a country maid's degree;
But give me leave to counsel me a time   75

---

[1] Degree.   [2] Leominster.   [3] Swelling.   [4] Hang loosely.

For fancy blooms not at the first assault;
Give me—but ten days' respite, and I will reply,
Which or to whom myself affectionates.

SERLSBY. Lambert, I tell thee, thou'rt importunate;
Such beauty fits not such a base esquire;   80
It is for Serlsby to have Margaret.

LAMBERT. Think'st thou with wealth to overreach me?
Serlsby, I scorn to brook thy country braves;
I dare thee, coward, to maintain this wrong,
At dint of rapier, single in the field.   85

SERLSBY. I'll answer, Lambert, what I have avouched.
Margaret, farewell; another time shall serve.   *Exit* SERLSBY

LAMBERT. I'll follow.—Peggy, farewell to thyself;
Listen how well I'll answer for thy love.   *Exit* LAMBERT.

MARGARET. How fortune tempers lucky haps with frowns 90
And wrongs me with the sweets of my delight!
Love is my bliss and love is now my bale.
Shall I be Helen in my froward fates,
As I am Helen in my matchless hue,
And set rich Suffolk with my face afire?   95
If lovely Lacy were but with his Peggy,
The cloudy darkness of his bitter frown,
Would check the pride of these aspiring squires.
Before the term of ten days be expired,
Whenas they look for answer of their loves,   100
My lord will come to merry Fressingfield,
And end their fancies and their follies both.
Till when, Peggy, be blithe and of good cheer.

Enter a POST *with a letter and a bag of gold.*

POST. Fair lovely damsel, which way leads this path?
How might I post me unto Fressingfield?   105
Which footpath leadeth to the Keeper's lodge?

MARGARET. Your way is ready, and this path is right;
Myself do dwell hereby in Fressingfield;
And if the Keeper be the man you seek,
I am his daughter. May I know the cause?   110
   POST. Lovely, and once beloved of my lord,—
No marvel if his eye was lodged so low,
When brighter beauty is not in the heavens,—
The Lincoln Earl hath sent you letters here,
And, with them, just an hundred pounds in gold.   115
Sweet, bonny wench, read them, and make reply.
   MARGARET. The scrolls that Jove sent Danaë,
Wrapt in rich closures of fine burnished gold,
Were not more welcome than these lines to me.
Tell me, whilst that I 'do unrip the seals,   120
Lives Lacy well? How fares my lovely lord?
   POST. Well, if that wealth may make men to live well.

Gives the letter, and MARGARET *reads it.*

   MARGARET. *The blooms of the almond-tree grow in a night, and
vanish in a morn; the flies hæmeræ[1], fair Peggy, take life with the
sun, and die with the dew; fancy that slippeth in with a gaze,   125
goeth out with a wink; and too timely loves have ever the shortest
length. I write this as thy grief, and my folly, who at Fressingfield
loved that which time hath taught me to be but mean dainties. Eyes
are dissemblers, and fancy is but queasy; therefore know, Margaret,
I have chosen a Spanish lady to be my wife, chief waiting-   130
woman to the Princess Elinor; a lady fair, and no less fair than thyself,
honorable and wealthy. In that I forsake thee, I leave thee to thine
own liking; and for thy dowry I have sent thee an hundred pounds;
and ever assure thee of my favor, which shall avail thee and thine
much.*   135
   Farewell.   *Not thine, nor his own,*
                                            EDWARD LACY.

[1] Ephemerae.

Fond Ate, doomer of bad-boding fates,
That wrapp'st proud fortune in thy snaky locks,
Didst thou enchant my birthday with such stars   140
As lightened mischief from their infancy?
If heavens had vowed, if stars had made decree,
To show on me their froward influence,
If Lacy had but loved, heavens, hell, and all,
Could not have wronged the patience of my mind.   145

POST. It grieves me, damsel; but the earl is forced
To love the lady by the king's command.

MARGARET. The wealth combined within the English shelves,
Europe's commander, nor the English king,
Should not have moved the love of Peggy from her   150
    lord.

POST. What answer shall I return to my lord?

MARGARET. First, for thou cam'st from Lacy whom I loved,—
Ah, give me leave to sigh at every thought!
Take thou, my friend, the hundred pound he sent;
For Margaret's resolution craves no dower.   155
The world shall be to her as vanity;
Wealth, trash; love, hate; pleasure, despair—
For I will straight to stately Framlingham,
And in the abbey there be shorn a nun,
And yield my loves and liberty to God.   160
Fellow, I give thee this, not for the news,
For those be hateful unto Margaret,
But for thou'rt Lacy's man, once Margaret's love.

POST. What I have heard, what passions I have seen,
I'll make report of them unto the earl.   165

MARGARET. Say that she joys his fancies be at rest,
And prays that his misfortune may be hers.   *Exeunt.*

[Scene XI. FRIAR BACON'C *cell.*]

Enter FRIAR BACON *drawing the curtains with a white stick, a book
     in his hand, and a lamp lighted by him, and the* BRAZEN HEAD,
     and MILES, *with weapons by him.*

BACON. Miles, where are you?

MILES. Here, sir.

BACON. How chance you tarry so long?

MILES. Think you that the watching of the Brazen Head
craves no furniture? I warrant you, sir, I have so armed   5
myself that if all your devils come, I will not fear them an
inch.

BACON. Miles, thou know's that I have dived into hell,
And sought the darkest palaces of fiends;
That with my magic spells great Belcephon   10
Hath left his lodge and kneeled at my cell;
The rafters of the earth rent from the poles,
And three-formed Luna hid her silver looks,
Trembling upon her concave continent,
When Bacon read upon his magic book.   15
With seven years' tossing necromantic charms,
Poring upon dark Hecat's principles,
I have framed out a monstrous head of brass,
That, by the enchanting forces of the devil,
Shall tell out strange and uncouth aphorisms,   20
And girt fair England with a wall of brass.
Bungay and I have watched these threescore days,
And now our vital spirits crave some rest.
If Argus lived, and had his hundred eyes,
They could not over-watch Phobetor's night.   25
Now, Miles, in thee rests Friar Bacon's weal:
The honor and renown of all his life
Hangs in the watching of this Brazen Head;

Therefore I charge thee by the immortal God,
That holds the souls of men within his fist,   30
This night thou watch; for ere the morning-star
Sends out his glorious glister on the north,
The head will speak; then, Miles, upon thy life,
Wake me; for then by magic art I'll work
To end my seven years' task with excellence.   35
If that a wink but shut thy watchful eye,
Then farewell Bacon's glory and his fame!
Draw close the curtains, Miles: now for thy life,
Be watchful, and—   *Here he falleth asleep.*

MILES. So; I thought you would talk yourself asleep   40
anon; and 'tis no marvel, for Bungay on the days, and he on
the nights, have watched just these ten and fifty days; now this
is the night, and 'tis my task, and no more. Now, Jesus bless
me, what a goodly head it is! And a nose! You talk of *nos autem
glorificare*[1]; but here's a nose that I warrant may be called   45
nos autem populare[1] for the people of the parish. Well, I am
furnished with weapons; now, sir, I will set me down by a post,
and make it as good as a watchman to wake me, if I chance to
slumber. I thought, Goodman Head, I would call you out of
your *memento*[2]... Passion o' God, I have almost broke my   50
pate! Up, Miles, to your task; take your brown-bill[3] in your
hand; here's some of your master's hobgoblins abroad.

With this a great noise. THE HEAD *speaks.*

THE BRAZEN HEAD. Time is!

MILES. Time is! Why, Master Brazen-head, have you such a
capital nose, and answer you with syllables, "Time is"?   55
Is this all my master's cunning, to spend seven years' study
about "Time is"? Well, sir, it may be we shall have some better

---

[1] Miles puns on *nose* and *nos* (us). To glorify us, to destroy us.
[2] *Memento mori*: a reminder of death, a death's head.   [3] Pike.

orations of it anon. Well, I'll watch you as narrowly as ever
you were watched, and I'll play with you as the nightingale
with the slow-worm; I'll set a prick against my breast.   60
Now rest there, Miles. Lord have mercy upon me, I have
almost killed myself! Up, Miles; list how they rumble.

THE BRAZEN HEAD. Time was!

MILES. Well, Friar Bacon, you have spent your seven-years'
study well, that can make your head speak but two words   65
at once, "Time was." Yea, marry, time was when my master
was a wise man, but that was before he began to make the
Brazen Head. You shall lie while your arse ache, an your head
speak no better. Well, I will watch, and walk up and down,
and be a peripatetian and a philosopher of Aristotle's   70
stamp. What, a fresh noise? Take thy pistols in hand, Miles.

Here THE HEAD *speaks, and a lightning flashes forth, and a hand
appears that breaks down* THE HEAD *with a hammer.*

THE BRAZEN HEAD. Time is past!

MILES. Master, master, up! Hell's broken loose; your head
speaks; and there's such a thunder and lightning, that I warrant
all Oxford is up in arms. Out of your bed, and take a   75
brown-bill in your hand; the latter day is come.

BACON. Miles, I come. [*Rises and comes forward.*] O, passing
    warily watched!
Bacon will make thee next himself in love.
When spake the head?

MILES. When spake the head! Did not you say that he   80
should tell strange principles of philosophy? Why, sir, it speaks
but two words at a time.

BACON. Why, villain, hath it spoken oft?

MILES. Oft! ay, marry, hath it, thrice; but in all those three
times it hath uttered but seven words.   85

BACON. As how?

MILES. Marry, sir, the first time he said "Time is," as if
Fabius Commentator should have pronounced a sentence; the
second time he said "Time was"; and the third time, with
thunder and lightning, as in great choler, he said, "Time   90
is past."

BACON. 'Tis past indeed. Ah, villain! time is past.
My life, my fame, my glory, all are past.
Bacon, the turrets of thy hope are ruined down,
Thy seven years' study lieth in the dust;   95
Thy Brazen Head lies broken through a slave
That watched, and would not when the head did will.
What said the head first?

MILES. Even, sir, "Time is."

BACON. Villain, if thou hadst called to Bacon then,   100
If thou hadst watched, and waked the sleepy friar,
The Brazen Head had uttered aphorisms,
And England had been circled round with brass;
But proud Asmenoth, ruler of the north,
And Demogorgon, master of the fates,   105
Grudge that a mortal man should work so much.
Hell trembled at my deep-commanding spells,
Fiends frowned to see a man their over-match;
Bacon might boast more than a man might boast.
But now the braves of Bacon have an end,   110
Europe's conceit of Bacon hath an end,
His seven years' practice sorteth to ill end:
And, villain, sith my glory hath an end,
I will appoint thee to some fatal end.
Villain, avoid! Get thee from Bacon's sight!   115
Vagrant, go roam and range about the world,
And perish as a vagabond on earth!

MILES. Why, then, sir, you forbid me your service?

BACON. My service, villain, with a fatal curse,

That direful plagues and mischief fall on thee.   120

MILES. 'Tis no matter, I am against you with the old proverb,—
The more the fox is cursed[1], the better he fares. God be with
you, sir. I'll take but a book in my hand, a wide-sleeved gown
on my back, and a crowned cap on my head, and see if I can
want promotion.   125

BACON. Some fiend or ghost haunt on thy weary steps,
Until they do transport thee quick to hell;
For Bacon shall have never merry day,
To lose the fame and honor of his head.   *Exeunt.*

[Scene XII. *Court.*]

Enter the EMPEROR, *the* KING OF CASTILE, KING HENRY, ELINOR,
   PRINCE EDWARD, LACY, *and* RALPH SIMNELL.

EMPEROR. Now, lovely prince, the prime of Albion's wealth,
How fare the Lady Elinor and you?
What, have you courted and found Castile fit
To answer England in equivalence?
Will't be a match 'twixt bonny Nell and thee?   5

PRINCE EDWARD. Should Paris enter in the courts of Greece,
And not lie fettered in fair Helen's looks?
Or Phœbus 'scape those piercing amorets
That Daphne glanced at his deity?
Can Edward, then, sit by a flame and freeze,   10
Whose heat puts Helen and fair Daphne down?
Now, monarchs, ask the lady if we 'gree.

KING HENRY. What, madam, hath my son found grace or no?

ELINOR. Seeing, my lord, his lovely counterfeit,
And hearing how his mind and shape agreed,   15
I came not, trooped with all this warlike train,
Doubting of love, but so affectionate
As[2] Edward hath in England what he won in Spain.

---

[1] Pun on *coursed*.   [2] That.

KING OF CASTILE. A match, my lord; these wantons needs
    must love;

Men must have wives, and women will be wed.   20

Let's haste the day to honor up the rites.

RALPH. Sirrah Harry, shall Ned marry Nell?

KING HENRY. Ay, Ralph; how then?

RALPH. Marry, Harry, follow my counsel. Send for Friar
Bacon to marry them, for he'll so conjure him and her with   25
his necromancy, that they shall love together like pig and
lamb whilst they live.

KING OF CASTILE. But hearest thou, Ralph, art thou content
    to have Elinor to thy lady?

RALPH. Ay, so she will promise me two things.

KING OF CASTILE. What's that, Ralph?   30

RALPH. That she will never scold with Ned, nor fight with
    me.—

Sirrah Harry, I have put her down with a thing unpossible.

KING HENRY. What's that, Ralph?

RALPH. Why, Harry, didst thou ever see that a woman could
both hold her tongue and her hands? No; but when egg-pies   35
grow on apple-trees, then will thy gray mare prove a bag-piper.

EMPEROR. What say the Lord of Castile and the Earl of Lincoln, that they are in such earnest and secret talk?

KING OF CASTILE. I stand, my lord, amazed at his talk,

How he discourseth of the constancy   40

Of one surnamed, for beauty's excellence,

The Fair Maid of merry Fressingfield.

KING HENRY. 'Tis true, my lord, 'tis wondrous for to hear;

Her beauty passing Mars's paramour,

Her virgin's right as rich as Vesta's was.   45

Lacy and Ned have told me miracles.

KING OF CASTILE. What says Lord Lacy? Shall she be his wife?

LACY. Or else Lord Lacy is unfit to live.

May it please your highness give me leave to post
To Fressingfield, I'll fetch the bonny girl,   50
And prove, in true appearance at the court,
What I have vouched often with my tongue.

KING HENRY. Lacy, go to the 'querry of my stable,
And take such coursers as shall fit thy turn;
Hie thee to Fressingfield, and bring home the lass;   55
And, for her fame flies through the English coast,
If it may please the Lady Elinor,
One day shall match your excellence and her.

ELINOR. We Castile ladies are not very coy;
Your highness may command a greater boon;   60
And glad were I to grace the Lincoln Earl
With being partner of his marriage-day.

PRINCE EDWARD. Gramercy, Nell, for I do love the lord,
As he that's second to thyself in love.

RALPH. You love her?—Madame Nell, never believe him   65
you, though he swears he loves you.

ELINOR. Why, Ralph?

RALPH. Why, his love is like unto a tapster's glass that is
broken with every touch; for he loved the fair maid of Fressingfield once out of all ho[1].—Nay, Ned, never wink upon me;   70
I care not, I.

KING HENRY. Ralph tells all; you shall have a good secretary
of him.

But, Lacy, haste thee post to Fressingfield;
For ere thou hast fitted all things for her state,
The solemn marriage-day will be at hand.   75

LACY. I go, my lord.   *Exit.*

EMPEROR. How shall we pass this day, my lord?

KING HENRY. To horse, my lord; the day is passing fair,

---

[1] Out of cry; greatly.

We'll fly the partridge, or go rouse the deer.
Follow, my lords; you shall not want for sport. *Exeunt.* 80

[Scene XIII. FRIAR BACON'S *cell.*]

Enter FRIAR BACON *with* FRIAR BUNGAY *to his cell.*

BUNGAY. What means the friar that frolicked it of late,
To sit as melancholy in his cell
As if he had neither lost nor won today?
BACON. Ah, Bungay, ... my Brazen Head is spoiled,
My glory gone, my seven years' study lost! 5
The fame of Bacon, bruited through the world,
Shall end and perish with this deep disgrace.
BUNGAY. Bacon hath built foundation of his fame
So surely on the wings of true report,
With acting strange and uncouth miracles, 10
As this cannot infringe what he deserves.
BACON. Bungay, sit down, for by prospective skill
I find this day shall fall out ominous;
Some deadly act shall 'tide me ere I sleep;
But what and wherein little can I guess. 15
BUNGAY. My mind is heavy, whatsoe'er shall hap.

Enter TWO SCHOLARS, *sons to* LAMBERT *and* SERLSBY.

BACON. Who's that knocks?
BUNGAY. Two scholars that desire to speak with you.
BACON. Bid them come in.
Now, my youths, what would you have? 20
FIRST SCHOLAR. Sir, we are Suffolk-men and neighboring
friends;
Our fathers in their countries lusty squires;
Their lands adjoin; in Cratfield mine doth dwell,
And his in Laxfield. We are college-mates,
Sworn brothers, as our fathers live as friends. 25
BACON. To what end is all this?

SECOND SCHOLAR. Hearing your worship kept within your cell
A glass prospective, wherein men might see
Whatso their thoughts or hearts' desire could wish,
We come to know how that our fathers fare.   30
  BACON. My glass is free for every honest man.
Sit down, and you shall see ere long, how
Or in what state your friendly fathers live.
Meanwhile, tell me your names.
  FIRST SCHOLAR. Mine Lambert.   35
  SECOND SCHOLAR. And mine Serlsby.
  BACON. Bungay, I smell there will be a tragedy.

Enter LAMBERT *and* SERLSBY *with rapiers and daggers.*

  LAMBERT. Serlsby, thou hast kept thine hour like a man:
Thou'rt worthy of the title of a squire,
That durst, for proof of thy affection   40
And for thy mistress' favor, prize[1] thy blood.
Thou know'st what words did pass at Fressingfield,
Such shameless braves as manhood cannot brook.
Ay, for I scorn to bear such piercing taunts,
Prepare thee, Serlsby; one of us will die.   45
  SERLSBY. Thou see'st I single meet thee in the field,
And what I spake, I'll maintain with my sword.
Stand on thy guard, I cannot scold it out.
An if thou kill me, think I have a son,
That lives in Oxford in the Broadgates-hall,   50
Who will revenge his father's blood with blood.
  LAMBERT. And, Serlsby, I have there a lusty boy,
That dares at weapon buckle with thy son,
And lives in Broadgates too, as well as thine.
But draw thy rapier, for we'll have a bout.   55
  BACON. Now, lusty younkers, look within the glass,

---

[1] Risk.

And tell me if you can discern your sires.

FIRST SCHOLAR. Serlsby, 'tis hard; thy father offers wrong,
To combat with my father in the field.

SECOND SCHOLAR. Lambert, thou liest, my father's is th'
    abuse,   60
And thou shalt find it, if my father harm.

BUNGAY. How goes it, sirs?

FIRST SCHOLAR. Our fathers are in combat hard by Fressing-
    field.

BACON. Sit still, my friends, and see the event.

LAMBERT. Why stand'st thou, Serlsby? Doubt'st thou of thy
    life?   65
A veney[1], man! Fair Margaret craves so much.

SERLSBY. Then this for her.

FIRST SCHOLAR. Ah, well thrust!

SECOND SCHOLAR. But mark the ward.

    [LAMBERT *and* SERLSBY] *fight and kill each other.*

LAMBERT. O, I am slain!   *Dies.*   70

SERLSBY. And I,—Lord have mercy on me!   *Dies.*

FIRST SCHOLAR. My Father slain!—Serlsby, ward that.

SECOND SCHOLAR. And so is mine!—Lambert, I'll 'quite thee
    well.

    The TWO SCHOLARS *stab one another* [*and die*].

BUNGAY. O strange stratagem!

BACON. See, friar, where the fathers both lie dead!   75
Bacon, thy magic doth effect this massacre.
This glass prospective worketh many woes;
And therefore seeing these brave lusty Brutes[2],
These friendly youths, did perish by thine art,
End all thy magic and thine art at once.   80

---

[1] Venture.   [2] Britons.

The poniard that did end their fatal[1] lives,
Shall break the cause efficient of their woes.
So fade the glass, and end with it the shows
That necromancy did infuse the crystal with.

He breaks the glass.

BUNGAY. What means learned Bacon thus to break his   85
glass?
BACON. I tell thee, Bungay, it repents me sore
That ever Bacon meddled in this art.
The hours I have spent in pyromantic spells,
The fearful tossing in the latest night
Of papers full of necromantic charms,   90
Conjuring and adjuring devils and fiends,
With stole and alb and strong pentagonon;
The wresting of the holy name of God,
As Sother, Eloim, and Adonai,
Alpha, Manoth, and Tetragrammaton,   95
With praying to the five-fold powers of heaven,
Are instances that Bacon must be damned
For using devils to countervail his God.
Yet, Bacon, cheer thee, drown not in despair;
Sins have their salves, repentance can do much.   100
Think Mercy sits where Justice holds her seat,
And from those wounds those bloody Jews did pierce,
Which by thy magic oft did bleed afresh,
From thence for thee the dew of mercy drops,
To wash the wrath of high Jehovah's ire,   105
And make thee as a new-born babe from sin.
Bungay, I'll spend the remnant of my life
In pure devotion, praying to my God
That he would save what Bacon vainly lost.   *Exeunt.*

[1] Fated.

[Scene XIV. *Fressing field.*]

Enter MARGARET *in nun's apparel, the* KEEPER, *her father,*
and their FRIEND.

KEEPER. Margaret, be not so headstrong in these vows;
O, bury not such beauty in a cell,
That England hath held famous for the hue!
Thy father's hair, like to the silver blooms
That beautify the shrubs of Africa,   5
Shall fall before the dated time of death,
Thus to forego his lovely Margaret.
        MARGARET. Ah, father, when the harmony of heaven
Soundeth the measures of a lively faith,
The vain illusions of this flattering world   10
Seem odious to the thoughts of Margaret.
I loved once,—Lord Lacy was my love,
And now I hate myself for that I loved,
And doted more on him than on my God,
For this I scourge myself with sharp repents.   15
But now the touch of such aspiring sins
Tells me all love is lust but love of heavens;
That beauty used for love is vanity.
The world contains naught but alluring baits,
Pride, flattery, and inconstant thoughts.   20
To shun the pricks of death, I leave the world,
And vow to meditate on heavenly bliss,
To live in Framlingham a holy nun,
Holy and pure in conscience and in deed;
And for to wish all maids to learn of me   25
To seek heaven's joy before earth's vanity.
        FRIEND. And will you, then, Margaret, be shorn a nun, and
so leave us all?
        MARGARET. Now farewell world, the engine of all woe!

Farewell to friends and father! Welcome Christ! 30
Adieu to dainty robes! This base attire
Better befits an humble mind to God
Than all the show of rich habiliments.
Farewell, O love! and, with fond love, farewell
Sweet Lacy, whom I loved once so dear! 35
Ever be well, but never in my thoughts,
Lest I offend to think on Lacy's love:
But even to that, as to the rest, farewell!

Enter LACY, WARREN, *and* ERMSBY, *booted and spurred.*

LACY. Come on, my wags, we're near the Keeper's lodge.
Here have I oft walked in the watery meads, 40
And chatted with my lovely Margaret.

WARREN. Sirrah Ned, is not this the Keeper?

LACY. 'Tis the same.

ERMSBY. The old lecher hath gotten holy mutton[1] to him;
a nun, my lord. 45

LACY. Keeper, how far'st thou? Holla, man, what cheer?
How doth Peggy, thy daughter and my love?

KEEPER. Ah, good my lord! O, woe is me for Peggy!
See where she stands clad in her nun's attire,
Ready for to be shorn in Framlingham; 50
She leaves the world because she left your love.
O, good my lord, persuade her if you can!

LACY. Why, how now, Margaret! What, a malcontent?
A nun? What holy father taught you this,
To task yourself to such a tedious life 55
As die a maid? 'Twere injury to me,
To smother up such beauty in a cell.

MARGARET. Lord Lacy, thinking of thy former miss,

---

[1] Lewd woman.

How fond[1] the prime of wanton years were spent
In love (O, fie upon that fond conceit, 60
Whose hap and essence hangeth in the eye!),
I leave both love and love's content at once,
Betaking me to Him that is true love,
And leaving all the world for love of Him.

LACY. Whence, Peggy, comes this metamorphosis? 65
What, shorn a nun, and I have from the court
Posted with coursers to convey thee hence
To Windsor, where our marriage shall be kept!
Thy wedding-robes are in the tailor's hands.
Come, Peggy, leave these peremptory vows. 70

MARGARET. Did not my lord resign his interest,
And make divorce 'twixt Margaret and him?

LACY. 'Twas but to try sweet Peggy's constancy.
But will fair Margaret leave her love and lord?

MARGARET. Is not heaven's joy before earth's fading bliss, 75
And life above sweeter than life in love?

LACY. Why, then, Margaret will be shorn a nun?

MARGARET. Margaret hath made a vow which may not be
revoked.

WARREN. We cannot stay, my lord; an if she be so strict,
Our leisure grants us not to woo afresh. 80

ERMSBY. Choose you, fair damsel; yet the choice is yours:
Either a solemn nunnery or the court,
God or Lord Lacy. Which contents you best,
To be a nun or else Lord Lacy's wife?

LACY. A good motion.—Peggy, your answer must 85
be short.

MARGARET. The flesh is frail; my lord doth know it well
That when he comes with his enchanting face,

---

[1] Foolishly.

Whatsoe'er betide, I cannot say him nay.
Off goes the habit of a maiden's heart,
And, seeing fortune will, fair Framlingham,　　90
And all the show of holy nuns, farewell!
Lacy for me, if he will be my lord.

LACY. Peggy, thy lord, thy love, thy husband.
Trust me, by truth of knighthood, that the king
Stays for to marry matchless Elinor,　　95
Until I bring thee richly to the court,
That one day may both marry her and thee.
How say'st thou, Keeper? Art thou glad of this?

KEEPER. As if the English king had given
The park and deer of Fressingfield to me.　　100

ERMSBY. I pray thee, my Lord of Sussex, why art thou in a
brown study?

WARREN. To see the nature of women; that be they never
so near
God, yet they love to die in a man's arms.

LACY. What have you fit for breakfast? We have hied
And posted all this night to Fressingfield.　　105

MARGARET. Butter and cheese, and umbles[1] of a deer,
Such as poor keepers have within their lodge.

LACY. And not a bottle of wine?

MARGARET. We'll find one for my lord.

LACY. Come, Sussex, let us in; we shall have more,　　110
For she speaks least, to hold her promise sure.　　*Exeunt.*

[Scene XV.　FRIAR BACON's *cell.*]

Enter a DEVIL *to seek* MILES.

DEVIL. How restless are the ghosts of hellish spirits,
When every charmer with his magic spells

---

[1] Numbles: edible entrails.

Calls us from nine-fold-trenched Phlegethon,
To scud and over-scour the earth in post
Upon the speedy wings of swiftest winds!   5
Now Bacon hath raised me from the darkest deep,
To search about the world for Miles his man,
For Miles, and to torment his lazy bones
For careless watching of his Brazen Head.
See where he comes. O, he is mine.   10

Enter MILES *with a gown and a corner-cap.*

MILES. A scholar, quoth you! Marry, sir, I would I had
been a bottle-maker when I was made a scholar; for I can get
neither to be a deacon, reader, nor schoolmaster, no, not the
clerk of a parish. Some call me a dunce; another saith, my head
is as full of Latin as an egg's full of oatmeal. Thus I am   15
tormented, that the devil and Friar Bacon haunt me.—Good
Lord, here's one of my master's devils! I'll go speak to him.—
What, master Plutus, how cheer you?

DEVIL. Dost thou know me?

MILES. Know you, sir! Why, are not you one of my   20
master's devils, that were wont to come to my master, Doctor
Bacon, at Brazen-nose?

DEVIL. Yes, marry, am I.

MILES. Good Lord, Master Plutus, I have seen you a thousand times at my master's, and yet I had never the manners   25
to make you drink. But, sir, I am glad to see how conformable
you are to the statute. I warrant you, he's as yeomanly a man
as you shall see; mark you, masters, here's a plain, honest man,
without welt or guard[1].—But I pray you sir, do you come
lately from hell?   30

DEVIL. Ay, marry; how then?

MILES. Faith, 'tis a place I have desired long to see. Have

[1] Trimmings or facings.

you not good tippling-houses there? May not a man have a
lusty fire there, a pot of good ale, a pair[1] of cards, a swinging
piece of chalk[2], and a brown toast that will clap a white 35
waistcoat[3] on a cup of good drink?

DEVIL. All this you may have there.

MILES. You are for me, friend, and I am for you. But I pray
you, may I not have an office there?

DEVIL. Yes, a thousand. What wouldst thou be?   40

MILES. By my troth, sir, in a place where I may profit myself.
I know hell is a hot place, and men are marvelous dry, and
much drink is spent there; I would be a tapster.

DEVIL. Thou shalt.

MILES. There's nothing lets me from going with you, 45
but that 'tis a long journey, and I have never a horse.

DEVIL. Thou shalt ride on my back.

MILES. Now surely here's a courteous devil, that, for to
pleasure his friend, will not stick to make a jade of himself.—
But I pray you, goodman friend, let me move a question 50
to you.

DEVIL. What's that?

MILES. I pray you, whether is your pace a trot or an amble?

DEVIL. An amble.

MILES. 'Tis well; but take heed it be not a trot. But 'tis 55
no matter, I'll prevent it.

DEVIL. What dost?

MILES. Marry, friend, I put on my spurs; for if I find your
pace either a trot or else uneasy, I'll put you to a false gallop;
I'll make you feel the benefit of my spurs.   60

DEVIL. Get up upon my back.

---

[1] Deck.   [2] To mark credit for ale.   [3] Foam.

MILES. O Lord, here's even a goodly marvel, when a man
rides to hell on the devil's back!   *Exeunt roaring.*

[Scene XVI.   *The Court.*]

Enter the EMPEROR *with a pointless sword; next the* KING OF CASTILE
carrying a sword with a point; LACY *carrying the Globe;* PRINCE
EDWARD; WARREN *carrying a rod of gold with a dove on it*[1]; ERMSBY
with a crown and scepter; the QUEEN [PRINCESS ELINOR] *with the
fair maid of Fressingfield on her left hand;* KING HENRY; BACON;
with other LORDS *attending.*

PRINCE EDWARD. Great potentates, earth's miracles for state,
Think that Prince Edward humbles at your feet,
And, for these favors, on his martial sword
He vows perpetual homage to yourselves,
Yielding these honors unto Elinor.   5

KING HENRY. Gramercies, lordings; old Plantagenet,
That rules and sways the Albion diadem,
With tears discovers these conceived joys,
And vows requital, if his men-at-arms,
The wealth of England, or due honors done   10
To Elinor, may 'quite his favorites.
But all this while what say you to the dames
That shine like to the crystal lamps of heaven?

EMPEROR. If but a third were added to these two,
They did surpass those gorgeous images   15
That gloried Ida with rich beauty's wealth.

MARGARET. 'Tis I, my lords, who humbly on my knee
Must yield her orisons to mighty Jove
For lifting up his handmaid to this state;

----

[1] Pointless sword, mercy; pointed sword, justice; rod of gold, equity.

Brought from her homely cottage to the court,   20
And graced with kings, princes, and emperors,
To whom (next to the noble Lincoln Earl)
I vow obedience, and such humble love
As may a handmaid to such mighty men.

  PRINCESS ELINOR. Thou martial man that wears the Almain
    crown,   25
And you the western potentates of might,
The Albion princess, English Edward's wife,
Proud that the lovely star of Fressingfield,
Fair Margaret, Countess to the Lincoln Earl,
Attends on Elinor,—gramercies, lord, for her,—   30
'Tis I give thanks for Margaret to you all,
And rest for her due bounden to yourselves.

  KING HENRY. Seeing the marriage is solemnized,
Let's march in triumph to the royal feast.—
But why stands Friar Bacon here so mute?   35

  BACON. Repentant for the follies of my youth,
That magic's secret mysteries misled,
And joyful that this royal marriage
Portends such bliss unto this matchless realm.

  KING HENRY. Why, Bacon,   40
What strange event shall happen to this land?
Or what shall grow from Edward and his queen?

  BACON. I find by deep prescience of mine art,
Which once I tempered in my secret cell,
That here where Brute did build his Troynovant[1],   45
From forth the royal garden of a king
Shall flourish out so rich and fair a bud[2],

---

[1] London.   [2] Elizabeth.

Whose brightness shall deface proud Phœbus' flower,
And over-shadow Albion with her leaves.
Till then Mars shall be master of the field,   50
But then the stormy threats of wars shall cease;
The horse shall stamp as careless of the pike,
Drums shall be turned to timbrels of delight;
With wealthy favors plenty shall enrich
The strand that gladded wandering Brute to see,   55
And peace from heaven shall harbor in these leaves
That gorgeous beautify this matchless flower;
Apollo's heliotropion[1] then shall stoop,
And Venus' hyacinth shall vail[2] her top;
Juno shall shut her gilliflowers up,   60
And Pallas' bay shall 'bash her brightest green;
Ceres' carnation, in consort with those,
Shall stoop and wonder at Diana's rose.
    KING HENRY. This prophecy is mystical.
But, glorious commanders of Europa's love,   65
That make fair England like that wealthy isle
Circled with Gihon and swift Euphrates,
In royalizing Henry's Albion
With presence of your princely mightiness,
Let's march: the tables all are spread,   30
And viands, such as England's wealth affords,
Are ready set to furnish out the boards.
You shall have welcome, mighty potentates;
It rests to furnish up this royal feast,
Only your hearts be frolic; for the time   35
Craves that we taste of naught but jouissance.

---

[1] Astronomical instrument.   [2] Lower.

Thus glories England over all the west.   *Exeunt omnes*

Omne tulit punctum qui miscuit utile dulci[1].

---

[1] "He has won every vote who has mingled profit with pleasure." — Horace.

THE SPANISH TRAGEDY*

OR

HIERONIMO IS MAD AGAIN

❧

THOMAS KYD

DRAMATIS PERSONÆ

GHOST OF ANDREA, *a Spanish courtier*, } *Chorus*
REVENGE,
KING OF SPAIN
DON CYPRIAN, DUKE OF CASTILE, *his brother*
LORENZO, *the Duke's son*
BEL-IMPERIA, *Lorenzo's sister*
VICEROY OF PORTUGAL
BALTHAZAR, *his son*
DON PEDRO, *the Viceroy's brother*
HIERONIMO, *Marshal of Spain*
ISABELLA, *his wife*
HORATIO, *their son*
SPANISH GENERAL
DEPUTY
DON BAZULTO, *an old man*
THREE CITIZENS
PORTUGUESE AMBASSADOR
ALEXANDRO, VILLUPPO, } *Portuguese Noblemen*
TWO PORTUGUESE
PEDRINGANO, *Bel-imperia's servant*
CHRISTOPHIL, *Bel-imperia's custodian*

LORENZO'S PAGE
SERBERINE, *Balthazar's servant*
ISABELLA'S MAID
MESSENGER
HANGMAN
SOLIMAN, *Sultan of Turkey (Balthazar)*
ERASTUS. *Knight of Rhodes (Lorenzo)*
THE BASHAW (Hieronimo) } *In Hieronimo's Play*
PERSEDA (Bel-imperia)
THREE KINGS *and* THREE KNIGHTS *in the first Dumb-show*
HYMEN *and two torch-bearers in the second*
BAZARDO, *a Painter*
PEDRO *and* JACQUES, *Hieronimo's servants*, } *In the additions to the play*
ARMY, ROYAL SUITES, NOBLEMEN, HALBERDIERS, OFFICERS, THREE WATCHMEN, SERVANTS, ETC.

[Scene: *Spain and Portugal*.]

* C. 1586.

ACT I

[Chorus]

Enter the GHOST OF ANDREA, *and with him* REVENGE.

GHOST. When this eternal substance of my soul
Did live imprisoned in my wanton flesh,
Each in their function serving other's need,
I was a courtier in the Spanish court.
My name was Don Andrea; my descent, 5
Though not ignoble, yet inferior far
To gracious fortunes of my tender youth,
For there in prime and pride of all my years,
By duteous service and deserving love,
In secret I possessed a worthy dame, 10
Which hight sweet Bel-imperia by name.
But in the harvest of my summer joys
Death's winter nipped the blossoms of my bliss,
Forcing divorce betwixt my love and me.
For in the late conflict with Portingale 15
My valor drew me into danger's mouth
Till life to death made passage through my wounds.
When I was slain, my soul descended straight
To pass the flowing stream of Acheron;
But churlish Charon, only boatman there, 20
Said that, my rites of burial not performed,
I might not sit amongst his passengers.
Ere Sol had slept three nights in Thetis' lap,
And slaked his smoking chariot in her flood,
By Don Horatio, our knight marshal's son, 25
My funerals and obsequies were done.
Then was the ferryman of hell content
To pass me over to the slimy strond,
That leads to fell Avernus' ugly waves

There, pleasing Cerberus with honeyed speech,   30
I passed the perils of the foremost porch.
Not far from hence, amidst ten thousand souls,
Sat Minos, Aeacus, and Rhadamanth;
To whom no sooner 'gan I make approach,
To crave a passport for my wandering ghost,   35
But Minos, in graven leaves of lottery,
Drew forth the manner of my life and death.
"This knight," quoth he, "both lived and died in love;
And for his love tried fortune of the wars;
And by war's fortune lost both love and life."   40
"Why then," said Aeacus, "convey him hence,
To walk with lovers in our fields of love,
And spend the course of everlasting time
Under green myrtle-trees and cypress shades."
"No, no," said Rhadamanth, "it were not well,   45
With loving souls to place a martialist.
He died in war and must to martial fields,
Where wounded Hector lives in lasting pain,
And Achilles' Myrmidons do scour the plain."
Then Minos, mildest censor of the three,   50
Made this device to end the difference:
"Send him," quoth he, "to our infernal king,
To doom him as best seems his Majesty."
To this effect my passport straight was drawn.
In keeping on my way to Pluto's court   55
Through dreadful shades of ever-glooming night,
I saw more sights than thousand tongues can tell,
Or pens can write, or mortal hearts can think.
Three ways there were: that on the right-hand side
Was ready way unto the 'foresaid fields,   60
Where lovers live and bloody martialists;
But either sort contained within his bounds.

The left-hand path, declining fearfully,
Was ready downfall to the deepest hell,
Where bloody Furies shakes their whips of steel,　　65
And poor Ixion turns an endless wheel;
Where usurers are choked with melting gold,
And wantons are embraced with ugly snakes,
And murderers groan with never-killing wounds,
And perjured wights scalded in boiling lead,　　70
And all foul sins with torments overwhelmed.
'Twixt these two ways I trod the middle path,
Which brought me to the fair Elysian green,
In midst whereof there stands a stately tower,
The walls of brass, the gates of adamant.　　75
Here finding Pluto with his Proserpine,
I showed my passport, humbled on my knee;
Whereat fair Proserpine began to smile,
And begged that only she might give my doom.
Pluto was pleased, and sealed it with a kiss.　　80
Forthwith, Revenge, she rounded[1] thee in th' ear,
And bade thee lead me through the gates of horn,
Where dreams have passage in the silent night.
No sooner had she spoke, but we were here—
I wot not how—in twinkling of an eye.　　85
　REVENGE. Then know, Andrea, that thou art arrived
Where thou shalt see the author of thy death,
Don Balthazar, the prince of Portingale,
Deprived of life by Bel-imperia.
Here sit we down to see the mystery,　　90
And serve for Chorus in this tragedy.

---

[1] Whispered.

[Scene I. *The Spanish Court.*]

Enter SPANISH KING, GENERAL, CASTILE, *and* HIERONIMO.

KING. Now say, lord General, how fares our camp?
GENERAL. All well, my sovereign liege, except some few
That are deceased by fortune of the war.
KING. But what portends thy cheerful countenance,
And posting to our presence thus in haste?   5
Speak, man, hath fortune given us victory?
GENERAL. Victory, my liege, and that with little loss.
KING. Our Portingals will pay us tribute then?
GENERAL. Tribute and wonted homage therewithal.
KING. Then blessed be heaven and guider of the heavens,   10
From whose fair influence such justice flows.
CASTILE. *O multum dilecte Deo, tibi militat aether,*
Et conjuratae curvato poplite gentes
Succumbunt: recti soror est victoria juris.[1]
KING. Thanks to my loving brother of Castile.   15
But, General, unfold in brief discourse
Your form of battle and your war's success,
That, adding all the pleasure of thy news
Unto the height of former happiness,
With deeper wage and greater dignity   20
We may reward thy blissful chivalry.
GENERAL. Where Spain and Portingale do jointly knit
Their frontiers, leaning on each other's bound,
There met our armies in their proud array;
Both furnished well, both full of hope and fear,   25
Both menacing alike with daring shows,
Both vaunting sundry colors of device[2],
Both cheerly sounding trumpets, drums, and fifes,

[1] O much loved of God, heaven fights for you, and on bended knee the conspiring nations fall; victory is the sister of just law.
[2] Heraldic design.

Both raising dreadful clamors to the sky,
That valleys, hills, and rivers made rebound,   30
And heaven itself was frighted with the sound.
Our battles both were pitched in squadron form,
Each corner strongly fenced with wings of shot;
But ere we joined and came to push of pike,
I brought a squadron of our readiest shot   35
From out our rearward to begin the fight:
They brought another wing t' encounter us.
Meanwhile, our ordnance played on either side,
And captains strove to have their valors tried.
Don Pedro, their chief horsemen's colonel,   40
Did with his cornet[1] bravely make attempt
To break the order of our battle ranks;
But Don Rogero, worthy man of war,
Marched forth against him with our musketeers,
And stopped the malice of his fell approach.   45
While they maintain hot skirmish to and fro,
Both battles join, and fall to handy-blows,
Their violent shot resembling th'ocean's rage,
When, roaring loud, and with a swelling tide,
It beats upon the rampires of huge rocks,   50
And gapes to swallow neighbor-bounding lands.
Now, while Bellona rageth here and there,
Thick storms of bullets rain like winter's hail,
And shivered lances dark the troubled air.
Pede pes et cuspide cuspis;   55
Arma sonant armis, vir petiturque viro[2].
On every side drop captains to the ground,
And soldiers, some ill-maimed, some slain outright;
Here falls a body sundered from his head,

[1] Cavalry troop.   [2] Foot for foot and point for point; arms resound against arms, and man is attacked by man.

There legs and arms lie bleeding on the grass,   60
Mingled with weapons and unbowelled steeds,
That scattering overspread the purple plain.
In all this turmoil, three long hours and more,
The victory to neither part inclined;
Till Don Andrea, with his brave lanciers,   65
In their main battle made so great a breach,
That, half dismayed, the multitude retired;
But Balthazar, the Portingals' young prince,
Brought rescue and encouraged them to stay.
Here-hence the fight was eagerly renewed,   70
And in that conflict was Andrea slain—
Brave man at arms, but weak to Balthazar.
Yet while the prince, insulting over him,
Breathed out proud vaunts, sounding to our reproach,
Friendship and hardy valor joined in one   75
Pricked forth Horatio, our knight marshal's son,
To challenge forth that prince in single fight.
Not long between these twain the fight endured,
But straight the prince was beaten from his horse,
And forced to yield him prisoner to his foe.   80
When he was taken, all the rest they fled,
And our carbines pursued them to the death,
Till, Phoebus waving[1] to the western deep,
Our trumpeters were charged to sound retreat.

    KING. Thanks, good lord General, for these good news;   85
And for some argument of more to come,
Take this and wear it for thy sovereign's sake.

Gives him his chain.

But tell me now, hast thou confirmed a peace?
    GENERAL. No peace, my liege, but peace conditional,

---

[1] Setting.

That if with homage tribute be well paid, 90
The fury of your forces will be stayed;
And to this peace their viceroy hath subscribed,

Gives the KING *a paper.*

And made a solemm vow that, during life,
His tribute shall be truly paid to Spain.

KING. These words, these deeds, become thy person well. 95
But now, knight marshal, frolic with thy king,
For 'tis thy son that wins this battle's prize.

HIERONIMO. Long may he live to serve my sovereign liege,
And soon decay, unless he serve my liege.

KING. Nor thou, nor he, shall die without reward. 100

A tucket[1] afar off.

What means this warning of this trumpet's sound?
GENERAL. This tells me that your Grace's men of war,
Such as war's fortune hath reserved from death,
Come marching on towards your royal seat,
To show themselves before your majesty; 105
For so I gave in charge at my depart.
Whereby by demonstration shall appear
That all, except three hundred or few more,
Are safe returned, and by their foes enriched.

The ARMY *enters;* BALTHAZAR, *between* LORENZO *and* HORATIO,
captive.

KING. A gladsome sight! I long to see them here. 110

They enter and pass by.

Was that the warlike prince of Portingale,
That by our nephew was in triumph led?
GENERAL. It was, my liege, the prince of Portingale.

[1] Flourish of trumpets.

KING. But what was he that on the other side
Held him by th' arm, as partner of the prize?   115
  HIERONIMO. That was my son, my gracious sovereign;
Of whom though from his tender infancy
My loving thoughts did never hope but well,
He never pleased his father's eyes till now,
Nor filled my heart with over-cloying joys.   120
  KING. Go, let them march once more about these walls,
That, staying them, we may confer and talk
With our brave prisoner and his double guard.   *Exit a messenger.*
Hieronimo, it greatly pleaseth us
That in our victory thou have a share,   125
By virtue of thy worthy son's exploit.

Enter again.

Bring hither the young prince of Portingale.
The rest march on: but, ere they be dismissed,
We will bestow on every soldier
Two ducats and on every leader ten,   130
That they may know our largess welcomes them.

Exeunt all but BALTHAZAR, LORENZO *and* HORATIO.

Welcome, Don Balthazar! Welcome, nephew!
And thou, Horatio, thou art welcome too.
Young Prince, although thy father's hard misdeeds,
In keeping back the tribute that he owes,   135
Deserve but evil measure at our hands,
Yet shalt thou know that Spain is honorable.
  BALTHAZAR. The trespass that my father made in peace
Is now controlled by fortune of the wars;
And cards once dealt, it boots not ask why so.   140
His men are slain, a weakening to his realm;
His colors seized, a blot unto his name;

His son distressed, a corsive[1] to his heart:
These punishments may clear his late offence.

 KING. Ay, Balthazar, if he observe this truce,   145
Our peace will grow the stronger for these wars.
Meanwhile live thou, though not in liberty,
Yet free from bearing any servile yoke;
For in our hearing thy deserts were great,
And in our sight thyself art gracious.   150

 BALTHAZAR. And I shall study to deserve this grace.

 KING. But tell me—for their holding makes me doubt—
To which of these twain art thou prisoner?

 LORENZO. To me, my liege.

 HORATIO.   To me, my sovereign.

 LORENZO. This hand first took his courser by the reins. 155

 HORATIO. But first my lance did put him from his horse.

 LORENZO. I seized his weapon, and enjoyed it first.

 HORATIO. But first I forced him lay his weapons down.

 KING. Let go his arm, upon our privilege. *They let him go.*
Say, worthy Prince, to whether[2] did'st thou yield? 160

 BALTHAZAR. To him in courtesy, to this perforce.
He spake me fair, this other gave me strokes:
He promised life, this other threatened death;
He won my love, this other conquered me,
And, truth to say, I yield myself to both.   165

 HIERONIMO. But that I know your grace for just and wise,
And might seem partial in this difference,
Enforced by nature and by law of arms
My tongue should plead for young Horatio's right.
He hunted well that was a lion's death,   170
Not he that in a garment wore his skin;
So hares may pull dead lions by the beard.

----

[1] Corrosive.   [2] Which one.

KING. Content thee, marshal, thou shalt have no wrong;
And, for thy sake, thy son shall want no right.
Will both abide the censure of my doom?   175
  LORENZO. I crave no better than your grace awards.
  HORATIO. Nor I, although I sit beside my right.
  KING. Then by my judgment, thus your strife shall end:
You both deserve, and both shall have reward.
Nephew, thou tookst his weapon and his horse: 180
His weapons and his horse are thy reward.
Horatio, thou didst force him first to yield:
His ransom therefore is thy valor's fee;
Appoint the sum, as you shall both agree.
But, nephew, thou shalt have the prince in guard,   185
For thine estate best fitteth such a guest;
Horatio's house were small for all his train.
Yet, in regard thy substance passeth his,
And that just guerdon may befall desert,
To him we yield the armor of the prince.   190
How likes Don Balthazar of this device?
  BALTHAZAR. Right well, my liege, if this proviso were,
That Don Horatio bear us company,
Whom I admire and love for chivalry.
  KING. Horatio, leave him not that loves thee so.   195
Now let us hence to see our soldiers paid,
And feast our prisoner as our friendly guest.   *Exeunt.*

[Scene II. *Portugal: the* VICEROY's *Palace.*]
Enter VICEROY, ALEXANDRO, VILLUPPO.

VICEROY. Is our ambassador despatched for Spain?
ALEXANDRO. Two days, my liege, are past since his depart.
VICEROY. And tribute-payment gone along with him?
ALEXANDRO. Ay, my good lord.
VICEROY. Then rest we here awhile in our unrest,   5

And feed our sorrows with some inward sighs,
For deepest cares break never into tears.
But wherefore sit I in a regal throne?
This better fits a wretch's endless moan.
Yet this is higher than my fortunes reach,   10
And therefore better than my state deserves,

Falls to the ground.

Ay, ay, this earth, image of melancholy,
Seeks him whom fates adjudge to misery.
Here let me lie; now am I at the lowest.

> *Qui jacet in terra, non habet unde cadat.*   15
> *In me consumpsit vires fortuna nocendo;*
> *Nil superest ut jam possit obesse magis.*[1]

Yes, Fortune may bereave me of my crown:
Here, take it now; let Fortune do her worst,
She will not rob me of this sable weed.   20
O no, she envies none but pleasant things.
Such is the folly of despiteful chance!
Fortune is blind, and sees not my deserts;
So is she deaf, and hears not my laments;
And could she hear, yet is she wilful-mad,   25
And therefore will not pity my distress.
Suppose that she could pity me, what then?
What help can be expected at her hands
Whose foot [is] standing on a rolling stone,
And mind more mutable than fickle winds?   30
Why wail I, then, where's hope of no redress?
O yes, complaining makes my grief seem less.
My late ambition hath distained[2] my faith;

---

[1] He who lies on the ground has not whence he may fall. Fortune has consumed her powers to harm me. Nothing remains that can me hurt any more.   [2] Tarnished.

My breach of faith occasioned bloody wars;
Those bloody wars have spent my treasure;   35
And with my treasure my people's blood;
And with their blood, my joy and best beloved,
My best beloved, my sweet and only son.
O, wherefore went I not to war myself?
The cause was mine; I might have died for both.   40
My years were mellow, his but young and green,
My death were natural, but his was forced.

ALEXANDRO. No doubt, my liege, but still the prince survives.
VICEROY. Survives! Ay, where?
ALEXANDRO. In Spain, a prisoner by mischance of war.   45
VICEROY. Then they have slain him for his father's fault.
ALEXANDRO. That were a breach to common law of arms.
VICEROY. They reck no laws that meditate revenge.
ALEXANDRO. His ransom's worth will stay from foul revenge.
VICEROY. No; if he lived, the news would soon be here.   50
ALEXANDRO. Nay, evil news fly faster still than good.
VICEROY. Tell me no more of news, for he is dead.
VILLUPPO. My sovereign, pardon the author of ill news,
And I'll bewray[1] the fortune of thy son.

VICEROY. Speak on, I'll guerdon thee, whate'er it be.   55
Mine ear is ready to receive ill news;
My heart grown hard 'gainst mischief's battery.
Stand up, I say, and tell thy tale at large.

VILLUPPO. Then hear that truth which these mine eyes have
    seen.

When both the armies were in battle joined,   60
Don Balthazar, amidst the thickest troops,
To win renown did wondrous feats of arms.
Amongst the rest, I saw him, hand to hand,

---

[1] Reveal.

In single fight with their lord-general;
Till Alexandro, that here counterfeits   65
Under the color of a duteous friend,
Discharged his pistol at the prince's back
As though he would have slain their general;
But therewithal Don Balthazar fell down;
And when he fell, then we began to fly: 70
But, had he lived, the day had sure been ours.

ALEXANDRO. O wicked forgery! O traitorous miscreant!
VICEROY. Hold thou thy peace! But now, Villuppo, say,
Where then became[1] the carcass of my son?

VILLUPPO. I saw them drag it to the Spanish tents.   75
VICEROY. Ay, ay, my nightly dreams have told me this.—
Thou false, unkind, unthankful, traitorous beast,
Wherein had Balthazar offended thee,
That thou shouldst thus betray him to our foes?
Was't Spanish gold that bleared so thine eyes   80
That thou couldst see no part of our deserts?
Perchance, because thou art Terceira's lord,
Thou hadst some hope to wear this diadem,
If first my son and then myself were slain;
But thy ambitious thought shall break thy neck.   85
Ay, this was it that made thee spill his blood;

Takes the crown and puts it on again.

But I'll now wear it till thy blood be spilt.
ALEXANDRO. Vouchsafe, dread sovereign, to hear me speak.
VICEROY. Away with him! His sight is second hell.
Keep him till we determine of his death: 90
If Balthazar be dead, he shall not live.
Villuppo, follow us for thy reward.   *Exit* VICEROY.

---

[1] What became of.

VILLUPPO Thus have I with an envious, forged tale
Deceived the king, betrayed mine enemy,
And hope for guerdon of my villany.   *Exit.*   95

[Scene III. *Spain : the Palace.*]

Enter HORATIO *and* BEL-IMPERIA

BEL-IMPERIA. Signior Horatio, this is the place and hour.
Wherein I must entreat thee to relate
The circumstance of Don Andrea's death,
Who, living, was my garland's sweetest flower,
And in his death hath buried my delights.   5
HORATIO. For love of him and service to yourself,
I nill[1] refuse this heavy doleful charge;
Yet tears and sighs, I fear, will hinder me.
When both our armies were enjoined in fight,
Your worthy chevalier amidst the thickest,   10
For glorious cause still aiming at the fairest,
Was at the last by young Don Balthazar
Encountered hand to hand. Their fight was long,
Their hearts were great, their clamors menacing,
Their strength alike, their strokes both dangerous.   15
But wrathful Nemesis, that wicked power,
Envying at Andrea's praise and worth,
Cut short his life, to end his praise and worth.
She, she herself, disguised in armor's mask,
As Pallas was before proud Pergamus,   20
Brought in a fresh supply of halberdiers,
Which paunched[2] his horse, and dinged[3] him to the ground.
Then young Don Balthazar with ruthless rage,
Taking advantage of his foe's distress,
Did finish what his halberdiers begun,   25

---

[1] Will not.   [2] Disembowelled.   [3] Knocked.

And left not, till Andrea's life was done.
Then, though too late, incensed with just remorse,
I with my band set forth against the prince,
And brought him prisoner from his halberdiers.

BEL-IMPERIA. Would thou hadst slain him that so slew 30
my love!
But then was Don Andrea's carcass lost?

HORATIO. No, that was it for which I chiefly strove,
Nor stepped I back till I recovered him.
I took him up, and wound him in mine arms;
And wielding him unto my private tent, 35
There laid him down, and dewed him with my tears,
And sighed and sorrowed as became a friend.
But neither friendly sorrow, sighs, nor tears
Could win pale Death from his usurped right.
Yet this I did, and less I could not do: 40
I saw him honored with due funeral.
This scarf I plucked from off his lifeless arm,
And wear it in remembrance of my friend.

BEL-IMPERIA. I know the scarf; would he had kept it still!
For had he lived, he would have kept it still, 45
And worn it for his Bel-imperia's sake;
For 't was my favor at his last depart.
But now wear thou it both for him and me;
For after him thou hast deserved it best.
But for thy kindness in his life and death, 50
Be sure, while Bel-imperia's life endures,
She will be Don Horatio's thankful friend.

HORATIO. And, madam, Don Horatio will not slack
Humbly to serve fair Bel-imperia.
But now, if your good liking stand thereto, 55
I'll crave your pardon to go seek the prince;
For so the duke, your father, gave me charge.

BEL-IMPERIA. Ay, go, Horatio, leave me here alone;
For solitude best fits my cheerless mood.

Exit HORATIO.

Yet what avails to wail Andrea's death,   60
From whence Horatio proves my second love?
Had he not loved Andrea as he did,
He could not sit in Bel-imperia's thoughts.
But how can love find harbor in my breast
Till I revenge the death of my beloved?   65
Yes, second love shall further my revenge!
I'll love Horatio, my Andrea's friend,
The more to spite the prince that wrought his end;
And where Don Balthazar, that slew my love,
Himself now pleads for favor at my hands,   70
He shall, in rigor of my just disdain,
Reap long repentance for his murderous deed.
For what was't else but murderous cowardice,
So many to oppress one valiant knight,
Without respect of honor in the fight?   75
And here he comes that murdered my delight.

Enter LORENZO *and* BALTHAZAR.

LORENZO. Sister, what means this melancholy walk?
BEL-IMPERIA. That for a while I wish no company.
LORENZO. But here the prince is come to visit you.
BEL-IMPERIA. That argues that he lives in liberty.   80
BALTHAZAR. No, madam, but in pleasing servitude.
BEL-IMPERIA. Your prison then, belike, is your conceit.[1]
BALTHAZAR. Ay, by conceit my freedom is enthralled.
BEL-IMPERIA. Then with conceit enlarge yourself again.
BALTHAZAR. What, if conceit have laid my heart to gage?   85

---

[1] Imagination.

BEL-IMPERIA. Pay that you borrowed, and recover it.

BALTHAZAR. I die, if it return from whence it lies.

BEL-IMPERIA. A heartless man, and live? A miracle!

BALTHAZAR. Ay, lady, love can work such miracles.

LORENZO. Tush, tush, my lord! Let go these ambages[1], 90
And in plain terms acquaint her with your love.

BEL-IMPERIA. What boots complaint, when there's no remedy?

BALTHAZAR. Yes, to your gracious self must I complain,
In whose fair answer lies my remedy,
On whose perfection all my thoughts attend,   95
On whose aspect mine eyes find beauty's bower,
In whose translucent breast my heart is lodged.

BEL-IMPERIA. Alas, my lord, these are but words of course[2],
And but devised to drive me from this place.

She, in going in, lets fall her glove, which HORATIO, *coming out,
takes up.*

HORATIO. Madam, your glove.   100

BEL-IMPERIA. Thanks, good Horatio; take it for thy pains.

BALTHAZAR. Signior Horatio stooped in happy time!

HORATIO. I reaped more grace than I deserved or hoped.

LORENZO. My lord, be not dismayed for what is past:
You know that women oft are humorous[3].   105
These clouds will overblow with little wind;
Let me alone, I'll scatter them myself.
Meanwhile, let us devise to spend the time
In some delightful sports and revelling.

HORATIO. The king, my lords, is coming hither straight,   110
To feast the Portingal ambassador;
Things were in readiness before I came.

BALTHAZAR. Then here it fits us to attend the king,

---

[1] Circumlocutions.   [2] Conventional phrases.   [3] Erratic.

To welcome hither our ambassador,
And learn my father and my country's health.   115

Enter the Banquet, Trumpets, the KING, *and* AMBASSADOR.

KING. See, Lord Ambassador, how Spain entreats.
Their prisoner Balthazar, thy viceroy's son.
We pleasure more in kindness than in wars.
   AMBASSADOR. Sad is our king, and Portingale laments,
Supposing that Don Balthazar is slain.   120
   BALTHAZAR. So am I, slain by beauty's tyranny!
You see, my Lord, how Balthazar is slain:
I frolic with the Duke of Castile's son,
Wrapped every hour in pleasures of the court,
And graced with favors of his majesty.   125
   KING. Put off your greetings, till our feast be done;
Now come and sit with us, and taste our cheer.

Sit to the banquet.

Sit down, young prince, you are our second guest;
Brother, sit down; and, nephew, take your place.
Signior Horatio, wait thou upon our cup,   130
For well thou hast deserved to be honored.
Now, lordings, fall to; Spain is Portugal,
And Portugal is Spain; we both are friends;
Tribute is paid, and we enjoy our right.
But where is old Hieronimo, our marshal?   135
He promised us, in honor of our guest,
To grace our banquet with some pompous[1] jest.

Enter HIERONIMO, *with a drum, three knights, each his scutcheon;
then he fetches three kings; they take their crowns and them captive.*

Hieronimo, this masque contents mine eye,
Although I sound not well the mystery.

[1] Formal, ceremonial.

HIERONIMO. The first armed knight, that hung his scutcheon
up,　　　　　　　　　　　　　　　　　　　　　140

He takes the scutcheon and gives it to the KING.

Was English Robert, Earl of Gloucester,
Who, when King Stephen bore sway in Albion,
Arrived with five and twenty thousand men
In Portingale, and by success of war
Enforced the king, then but a Saracen,　　　　145
To bear the yoke of the English monarchy.

KING. My lord of Portingale, by this you see
That which may comfort both your king and you,
And make your late discomfort seem the less.
But say, Hieronimo, what was the next?　　　150

HIERONIMO. The second knight, that hung his scutcheon up,

He doth as he did before.

Was Edmund Earl of Kent in Albion,
When English Richard wore the diadem.
He came likewise, and razed Lisbon walls,
And took the King of Portingale in fight;　　　155
For which and other such-like service done
He after was created Duke of York.

KING. This is another special argument,
That Portingale may deign to bear our yoke
When it by little England hath been yoked.　　160
But now, Hieronimo, what were the last?

HIERONIMO. The third and last, not least, in our account,

Doing as before.

Was, as the rest, a valiant Englishman,
Brave John of Gaunt, the Duke of Lancaster,
As by his scutcheon plainly may appear.　　　165
He with a puissant army came to Spain,
And took our King of Castile prisoner.

AMBASSADOR. This is an argument for our viceroy
That Spain may not insult for her success,
Since English warriors likewise conquered Spain,   170
And made them bow their kneess to Albion.
    KING. Hieronimo, I drink to thee for this device,
Which hath pleased both the ambassador and me:
Pledge me, Hieronimo, if thou love the king.

            Takes the cup of HORATIO.

My Lord, I fear we sit but over-long,   175
Unless our dainties were more delicate;
But welcome are you to the best we have.
Now let us in, that you may be despatched;
I think our council is already set.

                                            Exeunt omnes.

            [Chorus.]

    ANDREA. Come we for this from depth of underground,   180
To see him feast that gave me my death's wound?
These pleasant sights are sorrow to my soul:
Nothing but league, and love, and banqueting?
    REVENGE. Be still, Andrea; ere we go from hence,
I'll turn their friendship into fell despite,   185
Their love to mortal hate, their day to night,
Their hope into despair, their peace to war,
Their joys to pain, their bliss to misery.

            ACT II

    [Scene I. *The* DUKE'S *Castle*.]

    Enter LORENZO *and* BALTHAZAR.

    LORENZO. My lord, though Bel-imperia seem thus coy.
Let reason hold you in your wonted joy,
In time the savage bull sustains the yoke,

In time all haggard[1] hawks will stoop to lure[2],
In time small wedges cleave the hardest oak,   5
In time the flint is pierced with softest shower,
And she in time will fall from her disdain,
And rue the sufferance of your friendly pain.
   BALTHAZAR. No, she is wilder, and more hard withal,
Than beast, or bird, or tree, or stony wall.   10
But wherefore blot I Bel-imperia's name?
It is my fault, not she, that merits blame.
My feature is not to content her sight,
My words are rude and work her no delight.
The lines I send her are but harsh and ill,   15
Such as do drop from Pan and Marsyas' quill.
My presents are not of sufficient cost,
And being worthless, all my labor's lost.
Yet might she love me for my valiancy:
Ay, but that's slandered by captivity.   20
Yet might she love me to content her sire:
Ay, but her reason masters his desire.
Yet might she love me as her brother's friend:
Ay, but her hopes aim at some other end.
Yet might she love me to uprear her state: 25
Ay, but perhaps she hopes some nobler mate.
Yet might she love me as her beauty's thrall:
Ay, but I fear she cannot love at all.
   LORENZO. My lord, for my sake leave these ecstasies,
And doubt not but we'll find some remedy.   30
Some cause there is that lets you not be loved;
First that must needs be known, and then removed.
What, if my sister love some other knight?
   BALTHAZAR. My summer's day will turn to winter's night.

---

[1] Intractable.   [2] Decoy for recalling hawks.

LORENZO. I have already found a stratagem   35
To sound the bottom of this doubtful theme.
My lord, for once you shall be ruled by me;
Hinder me not, whate'er you hear or see.
By force or fair means will I cast about
To find the truth of all this question out.   40
Ho, Pedringano!
PEDRINGANO.   *Signior!*
LORENZO.   *Vien qui presto*[1].

Enter PEDRINGANO.

PEDRINGANO. Hath your lordship any service to command me?
LORENZO. Ay, Pedringano, service of import;
And, not to spend the time in trifling words,
Thus stands the case: it is not long, thou knowst,   45
Since I did shield thee from my father's wrath,
For thy conveyance[2] in Andrea's love,
For which thou wert adjudged to punishment.
I stood betwixt thee and thy punishment,
And since, thou knowst how I have favored thee.   50
Now to these favors will I add reward,
Not with fair words, but store of golden coin,
And lands and living joined with dignities,
If thou but satisfy my just demand.
Tell truth, and have me for thy lasting friend.   55
PEDRINGANO. Whate'er it be your lordship shall demand,
My bounden duty bids me tell the truth,
If[3] case it lie in me to tell the truth.
LORENZO. Then, Pedringano, this is my demand:
Whom loves my sister Bel-imperia?   60
For she reposeth all her trust in thee.
Speak, man, and gain both friendship and reward.

---

[1] Come here quickly.   [2] Acting as go-between.   [3] In.

I mean, whom loves she in Andrea's place?

PEDRINGANO. Alas, my lord, since Don Andrea's death
I have no credit with her as before,   65
And therefore know not, if she love or no.

LORENZO. Nay, if thou dally, then I am thy foe,

Draws his sword.

And fear shall force what friendship cannot win.
Thy death shall bury what thy life conceals;
Thou diest for more esteeming her than me.   70

PEDRINGANO. O, stay, my lord!

LORENZO. Yet speak the truth, and I will guerdon thee,
And shield thee from whatever can ensue,
And will conceal whate'er proceeds from thee.
But if thou dally once again, thou diest.   75

PEDRINGANO. If madam Bel-imperia be in love—

LORENZO. What, villain! If's and and's? *Offers to kill him.*

PEDRINGANO. O, stay, my lord! She loves Horatio.

BALTHAZAR *starts back.*

LORENZO. What, Don Horatio, our knight marshal's son?

PEDRINGANO. Even him, my lord.   80

LORENZO. Now say but how know'st thou he is her love,
And thou shalt find me kind and liberal.
Stand up, I say, and fearless tell the truth.

PEDRINGANO. She sent him letters, which myself perused,
Full-fraught with lines and arguments of love,   85
Preferring him before Prince Balthazar.

LORENZO. Swear on this cross[1] that what thou sayst is true,
And that thou wilt conceal what thou hast told.

PEDRINGANO. I swear to both, by him that made us all.

LORENZO. In hope thine oath is true, here's thy reward;   90

[1] Sword hilt.

But if I prove thee perjured and unjust,
This very sword whereon thou tookst thine oath
Shall be the worker of thy tragedy.

   PEDRINGANO. What I have said is true, and shall—for me—
Be still concealed from Bel-imperia.   95
Besides, your honor's liberality
Deserves my duteous service, even till death.

   LORENZO. Let this be all that thou shalt do for me:
Be watchful when and where these lovers meet,
And give me notice in some secret sort.   100

   PEDRINGANO. I will, my lord.

   LORENZO. Then shalt thou find that I am liberal.
Thou knowst that I can more advance thy state
Than she; be therefore wise, and fail me not.
Go and attend her, as thy custom is,   105
Lest absence make her think thou dost amiss. *Exit* PEDRINGANO.
Why so, *tam armis quam ingenio*:
Where words prevail not, violence prevails;
But gold doth more than either of them both.
How likes Prince Balthazar this stratagem?   110

   BALTHAZAR Both well and ill; it makes me glad and sad:
Glad, that I know the hinderer of my love;
Sad, that I fear she hates me whom I love;
Glad, that I know on whom to be revenged;
Sad, that she'll fly me, if I take revenge.   115
Yet must I take revenge, or die myself,
For love resisted grows impatient.
I think Horatio be my destined plague:
First, in his hand he brandished a sword,
And with that sword he fiercely waged war,   120
And in that war he gave me dangerous wounds,
And by those wounds he forced me to yield,
And by my yielding I became his slave.

Now in his mouth he carries pleasing words,
Which pleasing words do harbor sweet conceits,   125
Which sweet conceits are limed with sly deceits,
Which sly deceits smooth Bel Imperia's ears,
And through her ears dive down into her heart,
And in her heart set him, where I should stand.
Thus hath he ta'en my body by his force,   130
And now by sleight would captivate my soul;
But in his fall I'll tempt the destinies,
And either lose my life, or win my love.

LORENZO. Let's go, my lord; your staying stays revenge.
Do you but follow me, and gain your love: 135
Her favor must be won by his remove.   *Exeunt.*

[Scene II. *The* DUKE'S *Castle.*]

Enter HORATIO *and* BEL-IMPERIA.

HORATIO. Now, madam, since by favor of your love
Our hidden smoke is turned to open flame,
And that with looks and words we feed our thought
(Two chief contents, where more cannot be had);
Thus, in the midst of love's fair blandishments,   5
Why show you sign of inward languishments.

PEDRINGANO *showeth all to the* PRINCE *and* LORENZO, *placing them in secret.*

BEL-IMPERIA. My heart, sweet friend, is like a ship at sea:
She wisheth port, where, riding all at ease,
She may repair what stormy times have worn,
And leaning on the shore, may sing with joy   10
That pleasure follows pain, and bliss annoy.
Possession of thy love is the only port,
Wherein my heart, with fears and hopes long tossed,
Each hour doth wish and long to make resort,

There to repair the joys that it hath lost,   15
And, sitting safe, to sing in Cupid's choir
That sweetest bliss is crown of love's desire.

BALTHAZAR *and* LORENZO *above.*

BALTHAZAR. O sleep, mine eyes, see not my love profaned;
Be deaf, my ears, hear not my discontent;
Die, heart; another joys what thou deserv'st.   20
LORENZO. Watch still, mine eyes, to see this love disjoined;
Hear still, mine ears, to hear them both lament;
Live, heart, to joy at fond Horatio's fall.
BEL-IMPERIA. Why stands Horatio speechless all this while?
HORATIO. The less I speak, the more I meditate.   25
BEL-IMPERIA. But whereon dost thou chiefly meditate?
HORATIO. On dangers past, and pleasures to ensue.
BALTHAZAR. On pleasures past, and dangers to ensue.
BEL-IMPERIA. What dangers and what pleasures dost thou
    mean?
HORATIO. Dangers of war, and pleasures of our love.   30
LORENZO. Dangers of death, but pleasures none at all.
BEL-IMPERIA. Let dangers go, thy war shall be with me:
But such a war as breaks no bond of peace.
Speak thou fair words, I'll cross them with fair words;
Send thou sweet looks, I'll meet them with sweet looks;   35
Write loving lines, I'll answer loving lines;
Give me a kiss, I'll countercheck thy kiss:
Be this our warring peace, or peaceful war.
HORATIO. But, gracious madam, then appoint the field,
Where trial of this war shall first be made.   40
BALTHAZAR. Ambitious villain, how his boldness grows!
BEL-IMPERIA. Then be thy father's pleasant bower the field.
Where first we vowed a mutual amity:
The court were dangerous, that place is safe.

Our hour shall be, when Vesper 'gins to rise,   45
That summons home distressful travellers.
There none shall hear us but the harmless birds;
Haply the gentle nightingale
Shall carol us asleep, ere we be ware,
And, singing with the prickle at her breast,   50
Tell our delight and mirthful dalliance.
Till then each hour will seem a year and more.
  HORATIO. But, honey-sweet and honorable love,
Return we now into your father's sight;
Dangerous suspicion waits on our delight.   55
  LORENZO. Ay, danger mixed with jealous despite
Shall send thy soul into eternal night.   *Exeunt.*

[Scene III. *The Spanish Court.*]

Enter KING OF SPAIN, PORTINGALE AMBASSADOR, DON CYPRIAN, *etc.*

  KING. Brother of Castile, to the prince's love
What says your daughter Bel-imperia?
  CYPRIAN. Although she coy it, as becomes her kind,
And yet dissemble that she loves the prince,
I doubt not, I, but she will stoop in time.   5
And were she froward, which she will not be,
Yet herein shall she follow my advice,
Which is to love him, or forgo my love.
  KING. Then, Lord Ambassador of Portingale,
Advise thy king to make this marriage up,   10
For strengthening of our late-confirmed league;
I know no better means to make us friends.
Her dowry shall be large and liberal:
Besides that she is daughter and half-heir
Unto our brother here, Don Cyprian,   15
And shall enjoy the moiety of his land,
I'll grace her marriage with an uncle's gift,

And this it is, in case the match go forward:
The tribute which you pay, shall be released;
And if by Balthazar she have a son,   20
He shall enjoy the kingdom after us.

AMBASSADOR. I'll make the motion to my sovereign liege,
And work it, if my counsel may prevail.

KING. Do so, my lord, and if he give consent,
I hope his presence here will honor us,   25
In celebration of the nuptial day;
And let himself determine of the time.

AMBASSADOR. Will 't please your grace command me aught
   beside?

KING. Commend me to the king, and so farewell.
But where's Prince Balthazar to take his leave?   30

AMBASSADOR. That is performed already, my good lord.

KING. Amongst the rest of what you have in charge,
The prince's ransom must not be forgot:
That's none of mine, but his that took him prisoner;
And well his forwardness deserves reward.   35
It was Horatio, our knight marshal's son.

AMBASSADOR. Between us there's a price already pitched,
And shall be sent with all convenient speed.

KING. Then once again farewell, my Lord.

AMBASSADOR. Farewell, my Lord of Castile, and the rest. 40

Exit.

KING. Now, brother, you must take some little pains
To win fair Bel-imperia from her will.
Young virgins must be ruled by their friends.
The prince is amiable, and loves her well;
If she neglect him and forgo his love,   45
She both will wrong her own estate and ours.
Therefore, whiles I do entertain the prince
With greatest pleasure that our court affords,

Endeavor you to win your daughter's thought:
If she give back[1], all this will come to naught.   *Exeunt.* 50

[Scene IV. HIERONIMO'S *garden*.]

Enter HORATIO, BEL-IMPERIA, *and* PEDRINGANO.

HORATIO. Now that the night begins with sable wings
To overcloud the brightness of the sun,
And that in darkness pleasures may be done:
Come, Bel-imperia, let us to the bower,
And there in safety pass a pleasant hour.   5
BEL-IMPERIA. I follow thee, my love, and will not back,
Although my fainting heart controls my soul.
HORATIO. Why, make you doubt of Pedringano's faith?
BEL-IMPERIA. No, he is as trusty as my second self.—
Go, Pedringano, watch without the gate,   10
And let us know if any make approach.
PEDRINGANO [*Aside*]. Instead of watching, I'll deserve more
     gold
By fetching Don Lorenzo to this match.   *Exit* PEDRINGANO.
HORATIO. What means thy love?
BEL-IMPERIA.   I know not what myself;
And yet my heart foretells me some mischance.   15
HORATIO. Sweet, say not so; fair fortune is our friend,
And heavens have shut up day to pleasure us.
The stars, thou seest, hold back their twinkling shine,
And Luna hides herself to pleasure us.
BEL-IMPERIA. Thou hast prevailed; I'll conquer my mis-   20
     doubt,
And in thy love and counsel drown my fear.
I fear no more; love now is all my thoughts.
Why sit we not? for pleasure asketh ease.

----

[1] Refuse.

HORATIO. The more thou sitt'st within these leafy bowers,
The more will Flora deck it with her flowers.   25

BEL-IMPERIA. Ay, but if Flora spy Horatio here,
Her jealous eye will think I sit too near.

HORATIO. Hark, madam, how the birds record[1] by night,
For joy that Bel-imperia sits in sight.

BEL-IMPERIA. No, Cupid counterfeits the nightingale,   30
To frame sweet music to Horatio's tale.

HORATIO. If Cupid sing, then Venus is not far;
Ay, thou art Venus, or some fairer star.

BEL-IMPERIA. If I be Venus, thou must needs be Mars;
And where Mars reigneth, there must needs be wars.   35

HORATIO. Then thus begin our wars: put forth thy hand,
That it may combat with my ruder hand.

BEL-IMPERIA. Set forth thy foot to try the push of mine.

HORATIO. But first my looks shall combat against thine.

BEL-IMPERIA. Then ward thyself: I dart this kiss at thee. 40

HORATIO. Thus I retort the dart thou threw'st at me.

BEL-IMPERIA. Nay, then to gain the glory of the field,
My twining arms shall yoke and make thee yield.

HORATIO. Nay, then my arms are large and strong withal:
Thus elms by vines are compassed, till they fall.   45

BEL-IMPERIA. O, let me go; for in my troubled eyes
Now mayst thou read that life in passion dies.

HORATIO. O, stay a while, and I will die with thee;
So shalt thou yield, and yet have conquered me.

BEL-IMPERIA. Who's there? Pedringano? We are betrayed! 50

Enter LORENZO, BALTHAZAR, SERBERINE, PEDRINGANO, *disguised.*

LORENZO. My lord, away with her, take her aside.—
O, sir, forbear; your valor is already tried.
Quickly despatch, my masters.   *They hang him in the arbor.*

[1] Sing.

HORATIO.　　　　　　　　What, will you murder me?

LORENZO. Ay, thus, and thus: these are the fruits of love.

They stab him.

BEL-IMPERIA. O, save his life, and let me die for him!　55
O, save him, brother; save him, Balthazar:
I loved Horatio; but he loved not me.

BALTHAZAR. But Balthazar loves Bel-imperia.

LORENZO. Although his life were still ambitious, proud,
Yet is he at the highest now he is dead.　　　　　　60

BEL-IMPERIA. Murder! Murder! Help, Hieronimo, help!

LORENZO. Come, stop her mouth; away with her. *Exeunt.*

Enter HIERONIMO *in his shirt, etc.*

HIERONIMO. What outcries pluck me from my naked bed,
And chill my throbbing heart with trembling fear,
Which never danger yet could daunt before?　　　65
Who calls Hieronimo? Speak, here I am.
I did not slumber; therefore 'twas no dream.
No, no, it was some woman cried for help,
And here within this garden did she cry,
And in this garden must I rescue her.　　　　　70
But stay, what murd'rous spectacle is this?
A man hanged up and all the murderers gone!
And in my bower, to lay the guilt on me!
This place was made for pleasure, not for death.

He cuts him down.

Those garments that he wears I oft have seen—　75
Alas, it is Horatio, my sweet son!
O no, but he that whilom was my son!
O, was it thou that calledst me from my bed?
O speak, if any spark of life remain!

I am thy father; who hath slain my son?   80
What savage monster, not of human kind,
Hath here been glutted with thy harmless blood,
And left thy bloody corpse dishonored here,
For me, amidst these dark and deathful shades,
To drown thee with an ocean of my tears?   85
O heavens, why made you night to cover sin?
By day this deed of darkness had not been.
O earth, why didst thou not in time devour
The vile profaner of this sacred bower?
O poor Horatio, what hadst thou misdone,   90
To lose thy life, ere life was new begun?
O wicked butcher, whatsoe'er thou wert,
How could thou strangle virtue and desert?
Ay me most wretched, that have lost my joy.
In leesing my Horatio, my sweet boy!   95

Enter ISABELLA.

ISABELLA. My husband's absence makes my heart to throb!—
Hieronimo!
HIERONIMO. Here, Isabella, help me to lament;
For sighs are stopped, and all my tears are spent.
ISABELLA. What world of grief! My son Horatio!   100
O, where's the author of this endless woe?
HIERONIMO. To know the author were some ease of grief.
For in revenge my heart would find relief.
ISABELLA. Then is he gone? And is my son gone too?
O, gush out, tears, fountains and floods of tears;   105
Blow, sighs, and raise an everlasting storm;
For outrage fits our cursed wretchedness.
¹[*Ay me, Hieronimo, sweet husband, speak!*

The italic lines are the first of a series of additions which appeared in
the edition of 1602. These additions have been attributed to Ben Jonson.

HIERONIMO. *He supped with us to-night, frolic and merry,*
And said he would go visit Balthazar　　　110
At the duke's palace; there the prince doth lodge.
He had no custom to stay out so late:
He may be in his chamber; some go see.
Roderigo, ho!

Enter PEDRO *and* JAQUES.

ISABELLA. *Ay me, he raves! Sweet Hieronimo!*　　　115
HIERONIMO. *True, all Spain takes note of it.*
Besides, he is so generally beloved;
His majesty the other day did grace him
With waiting on his cup; these be favors,
Which do assure me he cannot be short-lived.　　　120
ISABELLA. *Sweet Hieronimo!*
HIERONIMO. *I wonder how this fellow got his clothes!*
Sirrah, sirrah, I'll know the truth of all.
Jaques, run to the Duke of Castile's presently,
And bid my son Horatio to come home:　　　125
I and his mother have had strange dreams to-night.
Do ye hear me, sir?
JAQUES.　　　*Ay, sir.*
HIERONIMO　　　*Well, sir, be gone.*
Pedro, come hither; know'st thou who this is?
PEDRO. *Too well, sir.*
HIERONIMO. *Too well! Who, who is it? Peace, Isabella!*　　　130
Nay, blush not, man.
PEDRO.　　　*It is my lord Horatio.*
HIERONIMO. *Ha, ha, St. James! But this doth make me laugh,*
That there are more deluded than myself.
PEDRO. *Deluded?*
HIERONIMO.　　　*Ay!*
I would have sworn myself, within this hour,　　　135

That this had been my son Horatio:
His garments are so like.
Ha! are they not great persuasions?

ISABELLA. O, would to God it were not so!

HIERONIMO. Were not, Isabella? Dost thou dream it is?   140
Can thy soft bosom entertain a thought
That such a black deed of mischief should be done
On one so pure and spotless as our son?
Away, I am ashamed.

ISABELLA.   Dear Hieronimo,
Cast a more serious eye upon thy grief;   145
Weak apprehension gives but weak belief.

HIERONIMO. It was a man, sure, that was hanged up here;
A youth, as I remember; I cut him down.
If it should prove my son now after all—
Say you? say you?—Light! lend me a taper;   150
Let me look again.—O God!
Confusion, mischief, torment, death and hell,
Drop all your stings at once in my cold bosom,
That now is stiff with horror; kill me quickly!
Be gracious to me, thou infectious night,   155
And drop this deed of murder down on me;
Gird in my waste of grief with thy large darkness,
And let me not survive to see the light
May put me in the mind I had a son.

ISABELLA. O sweet Horatio! O my dearest son!   160

HIERONIMO. How strangely had I lost my way to grief!]
Sweet, lovely rose, ill-pluckt before thy time.
Fair, worthy son, not conquered, but betrayed,
I'll kiss thee now, for words with tears are stayed.

ISABELLA. And I'll close up the glasses of his sight,   165
For once these eyes were only my delight.

HIERONIMO. Seest thou this handkercher besmeared with blood?

It shall not from me, till I take revenge.
Seest thou those wounds that yet are bleeding fresh?
I'll not entomb them, till I have revenged.   170
Then will I joy amidst my discontent;
Till then my sorrow never shall be spent.

   ISABELLA. The heavens are just; murder cannot be hid:
Time is the author both of truth and right,
And time will bring this treachery to light.   175

   HIERONIMO. Meanwhile, good Isabella, cease thy plaints,
Or, at the least, dissemble them awhile;
So shall we sooner find the practice[1] out,
And learn by whom all this was brought about.
Come, Isabel, now let us take him up,   *They take him up.* 180
And bear him in from out this cursed place.
I'll say his dirge; singing fits not this case.

O aliquis mihi quas pulchrum ver educat herbas,
      HIERONIMO sets his breast unto his sword.
Misceat, et nostro detur medicina dolori;
Aut, si qui faciunt annorum oblivia, succos   185
Praebeat; ipse metam magnum quaecunque per orbem
Gramina Sol pulchras effert in luminis oras;
Ipse bibam quicquid meditatur saga veneni,
Quicquid et herbarum vi caeca nenia nectit:
Omnia perpetiar, lethum quoque, dum semel omnis   190
Noster in extincto moriatur pectore sensus.
Ergo tuos oculos nunquam, mea vita, videbo,
Et tua perpetuus sepelivit lumina somnus?
Emoriar tecum: sic, juvat ire sub umbras.
At tamen absistam properato cedere letho,   195
Ne mortem vindicta tuam tam nulla sequatur[2].

---

[1] Treachery.
[2] O let somebody mix for me the herbs which beautiful spring brings

Here he throws it from him and
bears the body away.

[Chorus.]

ANDREA. Broughtst thou me hither to increase my pain?
I looked that Balthazar should have been slain;
But 'tis my friend Horatio that is slain,
And they abuse fair Bel-imperia,   200
On whom I doted more than all the world,
Because she loved me more than all the world.

REVENGE. Thou talkst of harvest, when the corn is green:
The end is crown of every work well done;
The sickle comes not, till the corn be ripe.   205
Be still; and ere I lead thee from this place,
I'll show thee Balthazar in heavy case.

ACT III

[Scene I. *The Portuguese Court.*]

Enter VICEROY OF PORTINGALE, NOBLES, VILLUPPO.

VICEROY. Infortunate condition of kings,
Seated amidst so many helpless doubts!
First we are placed upon extremest height,
And oft supplanted with exceeding hate,

forth, and let medicine be given to our sorrow; or let him offer potions, if
there be any which cause forgetfulness of the years. May I myself reap
throughout the great earth whatever plants the sun brings forth to the
lovely regions of light. May I drink whatever poison the soothsayer de-
vises, and whatever herbs her incantation joins together with secret power.
May I endure all things, even death, provided all my feeling may die once
for all in a heart that is dead. Shall I then never again, my life, see your
eyes? And has eternal sleep buried your light? May I die along with you;
thus it would be pleasing to go under the shadows. But yet I shall refrain
from yielding to a hurried death, lest then no revenge follow your death.

But ever subject to the wheel of chance;   5
And at our highest never joy we so
As we both doubt and dread our overthrow.
So striveth not the waves with sundry winds
As Fortune toileth in the affairs of kings,
That would be feared, yet fear to be beloved,   10
Sith fear or love to kings is flattery.
For instance, lordings, look upon your king,
By hate deprived of his dearest son,
The only hope of our successive line.

NOBLEMAN. I had not thought that Alexandro's heart   15
Had been envenomed with such extreme hate;
But now I see that words have several works,
And there's no credit in the countenance.

VILLUPPO. No; for, my lord, had you beheld the train[1]
That feigned love had colored in his looks,   20
When he in camp consorted[2] Balthazar,
Far more inconstant had you thought the sun,
That hourly coasts[3] the center of the earth,
Than Alexandro's purpose to the prince.

VICEROY. No more, Villuppo, thou hast said enough,   25
And with thy words thou slayst our wounded thoughts.
Nor shall I longer dally with the world.
Procrastinating Alexandro's death.
Go some of you, and fetch the traitor forth,
That, as he is condemned, he may die.   30

Enter ALEXANDRO *with a* NOBLEMAN *and halberts.*

NOBLEMAN. In such extremes will nought but patience serve.
ALEXANDRO. But in extremes what patience shall I use?
Nor discontents it me to leave the world,

---

[1] Guile.   [2] Accompanied.   [3] Travels around.

With whom there nothing can prevail but wrong.

NOBLEMAN. Yet hope the best.

ALEXANDRO.   'Tis heaven is my hope.   35
As for the earth, it is too much infect
To yield me hope of any of her mold.

VICEROY. Why linger ye? Bring forth that daring fiend,
And let him die for his accursed deed.

ALEXANDRO. Not that I fear the extremity of death   40
(For nobles cannot stoop to servile fear)
Do I, O King, thus discontented live.
But this, O this, torments my laboring soul,
That thus I die suspected of a sin
Whereof, as heavens have known my secret thoughts,   45
So am I free from this suggestion.

VICEROY. No more, I say! To the tortures! When?
Bind him, and burn his body in those flames,

They bind him to a stake.

That shall prefigure those unquenched fires
Of Phlegethon, prepared for his soul.   50

ALEXANDRO. My guiltless death will be avenged on thee,
On thee, Villuppo, that hath maliced[1] thus,
Or for thy meed hast falsely me accused.

VILLUPPO. Nay, Alexandro, if thou menace me,
I'll lend a hand to send thee to the lake   55
Where those thy words shall perish with thy works,
Injurious traitor! monstrous homicide!

Enter AMBASSADOR.

AMBASSADOR. Stay, hold a while;
And here—with pardon of his majesty—
Lay hands upon Villuppo.

[1] Done evil.

VICEROY.   Ambassador,   60
What news hath urged this sudden entrance?
  AMBASSADOR. Know, sovereign lord, that Balthazar doth live.
  VICEROY. What sayst thou? Liveth Balthazar our son?
  AMBASSADOR. Your highness' son, Lord Balthazar, doth live;
And, well entreated in the court of Spain,   65
Humbly commends him to your majesty.
These eyes beheld; and these my followers,
With these, the letters of the king's commends,
                Gives him letters.
Are happy witnesses of his highness' health.

        The KING *looks on the letters, and proceeds.*

  VICEROY. "Thy son doth live, your tribute is received;   70
Thy peace is made, and we are satisfied.
The rest resolve upon as things proposed
For both our honors and thy benefit."
  AMBASSADOR. These are his highness' farther articles.
                He gives him more letters.
  VICEROY. Accursed wretch, to intimate these ills   75
Against the life and reputation
Of noble Alexandro! Come, my lord, unbind him.
Let him unbind thee, that is bound to death,
To make a quital for thy discontent.   *They unbind him.*
  ALEXANDRO. Dread lord, in kindness[1] you could do no less   80
Upon report of such a damned fact;
But thus we see our innocence hath saved
The hopeless life which thou, Villuppo, sought
By thy suggestions to have massacred.
  VICEROY. Say, false Villuppo, wherefore didst thou thus   85
Falsely betray Lord Alexandro's life?

---

[1] Nature.

Him whom thou know'st that no unkindness else
But even the slaughter of our dearest son
Could once have moved us to have misconceived.

ALEXANDRO. Say, treacherous Villuppo, tell the king:
Wherein hath Alexandro used thee ill?   90

VILLUPPO. Rent with remembrance of so foul a deed,
My guilty soul submits me to thy doom;
For not for Alexandro's injuries,
But for reward and hope to be preferred,   95
Thus have I shamelessly hazarded his life.

VICEROY. Which, villain, shall be ransomed with thy death;
And not so mean[1] a torment as we here
Devised for him who, thou saidst, slew our son,
But with the bitt'rest torments and extremes   100
That may be yet invented for thine end.

ALEXANDRO *seems to entreat.*

Entreat me not; go, take the traitor hence: *Exit* VILLUPPO.
And, Alexandro, let us honor thee
With public notice of thy loyalty.
To end those things articulated here   105
By our great lord, the mighty King of Spain,
We with our council will deliberate.
Come, Alexandro, keep us company.   *Exeunt.*

[Scene II. *Spain: Near the* DUKE'S *Castle.*]

Enter HIERONIMO.

HIERONIMO. O eyes! no eyes, but fountains fraught with tears;
O life! no life, but lively form of death;
O world! no world, but mass of public wrongs,
Confused and filled with murder and misdeeds!

[1] Mild.

O sacred heavens! If this unhallowed deed,   5
If this inhuman and barbarous attempt,
If this incomparable murder thus
Of mine, but now no more my son,
Shall unrevealed and unrevenged pass,
How should we term your dealings to be just,   10
If you unjustly deal with those that in your justice trust?
The night, sad secretary to my moans,
With direful visions wake my vexed soul,
And with the wounds of my distressful son
Solicit me for notice of his death.   15
The ugly fiends do sally forth of hell,
And frame my steps to unfrequented paths,
And fear my heart with fierce inflamed thoughts.
The cloudy day my discontents records,
Early begins to register my dreams,   20
And drive me forth to seek the murderer.
Eyes, life, world, heavens, hell, night, and day,
See, search, shew, send some man, some mean, that may—

A letter falleth.

What's here? A letter? Tush! it is not so!—
A letter written to Hieronimo!   *Red ink.*   25
"For want of ink, receive this bloody writ.
Me hath my hapless brother hid from thee;
Revenge thyself on Balthazar and him:
For these were they that murdered thy son.
Hieronimo, revenge Horatio's death,   30
And better fare than Bel-imperia doth."
What means this unexpected miracle?
My son slain by Lorenzo and the prince!
What cause had they Horatio to malign[1]?

---

[1] Treat evilly.

Or what might move thee, Bel-imperia, 35
To accuse thy brother, had he been the mean?
Hieronimo, beware! Thou art betrayed,
And to entrap thy life this train¹ is laid.
Advise thee therefore, be not credulous;
This is devised to endanger thee, 40
That thou, by this, Lorenzo shouldst accuse:
And he, for thy dishonor done, should draw
Thy life in question and thy name in hate.
Dear was the life of my beloved son,
And of his death behoves me be revenged 45
Then hazard not thine own, Hieronimo,
But live t' effect thy resolution.
I therefore will by circumstances² try,
What I can gather to confirm this writ;
And, heark'ning near the Duke of Castile's house, 50
Close, if I can, with Bel-imperia,
To listen more, but nothing to bewray.

Enter PEDRINGANO.

Now, Pedringano!
PEDRINGANO.   Now, Hieronimo!
HIERONIMO. Where's thy lady?
PEDRINGANO.   I know not; here's my lord.

Enter LORENZO.

LORENZO. How now, who's this? Hieronimo?
HIERONIMO.   My lord. 55
PEDRINGANO. He asketh for my lady Bel-imperia.
LORENZO. What to do, Hieronimo? The duke, my father, hath
Upon some disgrace awhile removed her hence;

---

¹ Plot.   ² Roundabout methods.

But, if it be aught I may inform her of,
Tell me, Hieronimo, and I'll let her know it.   60
  HIERONIMO. Nay, nay, my lord, I thank you; it shall
    not need.
I had a suit unto her, but too late,
And her disgrace makes me unfortunate.
  LORENZO. Why so, Hieronimo? Use me.
  HIERONIMO. O no, lord, I dare not; it must not be.   65
I humbly thank your lordship.
  [1][HIERONIMO.   *Who? You, my lord?*
I reserve your favor for a greater honor;
This is a very toy, my lord, a toy[2].
  LORENZO. *All's one, Hieronimo, acquaint me with it.*
  HIERONIMO. *I' faith, my lord, it is an idle thing;*   70
I must confess I ha' been too slack, too tardy,
Too remiss unto your honor.
  LORENZO.   *How now, Hieronimo?*
  HIERONIMO. *In troth, my lord, it is a thing of nothing:*
The murder of a son, or so—
A thing of nothing, my lord!]
  LORENZO.   Why then, farewell.   75
  HIERONIMO. My grief no heart, my thoughts no tongue can
    tell.   *Exit.*
  LORENZO. Come hither, Pedringano, see'st thou this?
  PEDRINGANO. My lord, I see it, and suspect it too.
  LORENZO. This is that damned villain Serberine
That hath, I fear, revealed Horatio's death.   80
  PEDRINGANO. My lord, he could not, 'twas so lately done;
And since he hath not left my company.
  LORENZO. Admit he have not, his condition's such,
As fear of flattering words may make him false.

---

[1] Italic lines are the second passage of additions, a substitute for lines
65-66.   [2] Small matter.

I know his humor, and therewith repent   85
That e'er I used him in this enterprise.
But, Pedringano, to prevent the worst,
And 'cause I know thee secret as my soul,
Here, for thy further satisfaction, take thou this,
                    Gives him more gold.

And hearken to me, thus it is devised: 90
This night thou must (and, prithee, so resolve),
Meet Serberine at Saint Luigi's Park—
Thou knowst 'tis here hard by behind the house—
There take thy stand, and see thou strike him sure,
For die he must, if we do mean to live.   95

  PEDRINGANO. But how shall Serberine be there, my lord?
  LORENZO. Let me alone; I'll send to him to meet
The prince and me, where thou must do this deed.

  PEDRINGANO. It shall be done, my lord, it shall be done;
And I'll go arm myself to meet him there.   100

  LORENZO. When things shall alter, as I hope they will,
Then shalt thou mount for this; thou knowst my mind.
                    Exit PEDRINGANO.

Che le Ieron![1]
                    Enter PAGE.

  PAGE.   My lord?
  LORENZO.   Go, sirrah,
To Serberine, and bid him forthwith meet
The prince and me at Saint Luigi's Park,   105
Behind the house; this evening, boy!

  PAGE.   I go, my lord.

  LORENZO. But, sirrah, let the hour be eight o'clock:
Bid him not fail.

  PAGE.   I fly, my lord.   *Exit.*

----

[1] Unintelligible. Perhaps a call to the Page.

LORENZO. Now to confirm the complot thou hast cast
Of all these practices[1], I'll spread the watch,   110
Upon precise commandment from the king
Strongly to guard the place where Pedringano
This night shall murder hapless Serberine.
Thus must we work that will avoid distrust;
Thus must we practise to prevent mishap,   115
And thus one ill another must expulse.
This sly enquiry of Hieronimo
For Bel-imperia breeds suspicion,
And this suspicion bodes a further ill.
As for myself, I know my secret fault,   120
And so do they; but I have dealt for them.
They that for coin their souls endangered,
To save my life, for coin shall venture theirs;
And better it's that base companions die
Than by their life to hazard our good haps.   125
Nor shall they live, for me to fear their faith:
I'll trust myself, myself shall be my friend;
For die they shall,—
Slaves are ordained to no other end.   *Exit.*

[Scene III. SAINT LUIGI's *Park.*]

Enter PEDRINGANO, *with a pistol.*

PEDRINGANO. Now, Pedringano, bid thy pistol hold,
And hold on, Fortune! Once more favor me;
Give but success to mine attempting spirit,
And let me shift for taking of mine aim.
Here is the gold: this is the gold proposed;
It is no dream that I adventure for,

[1]Stratagems.

But Pedringano is possessed thereof.
And he that would not strain his conscience
For him that thus his liberal purse hath stretched,
Unworthy such a favor, may he fail,　　　　　　　　　10
And, wishing, want when such as I prevail.
As for the fear of apprehension,
I know, if need should be, my noble lord
Will stand between me and ensuing harms;
Besides, this place is free from all suspect.　　　　15
Here therefore will I stay and take my stand.

Enter the WATCH.

FIRST WATCH. I wonder much to what intent it is
That we are thus expressly charged to watch.
　SECOND WATCH. 'Tis by commandment in the king's own
　　name.
　THIRD WATCH. But we were never wont to watch and ward
So near the duke his brother's house before.　　　　21
　SECOND WATCH. Content yourself, stand close, there's some-
　　what in 't.

Enter SERBERINE.

SERBERINE. Here, Serberine, attend and stay thy pace;
For here did Don Lorenzo's page appoint
That thou by his command shouldst meet with him.　　25
How fit a place—if one were so disposed—
Methinks this corner is to close with[1] one.
　PEDRINGANO. Here comes the bird that I must seize upon.
Now, Pedringano, or never, play the man!
　SERBERINE. I wonder that his lordship stays so long,　　30
Or wherefore should he send for me so late?

---

[1] Agree, engage, grapple.

PEDRINGANO. For this, Serberine! And thou shalt ha't.

Shoots the dag[1].

So, there he lies; my promise is performed.

The WATCH.

FIRST WATCH. Hark, gentlemen, this is a pistol shot.

SECOND WATCH. And here's one slain; stay the murderer. 35

PEDRINGANO. Now by the sorrows of the souls in hell,

He strives with the WATCH.

Who first lays hand on me, I'll be his priest[2].

THIRD WATCH. Sirrah, confess, and therein play the priest,

Why hast thou thus unkindly killed the man?

PEDRINGANO. Why? Because he walked abroad so late. 40

THIRD WATCH. Come, sir, you had been better kept your bed,

Than have committed this misdeed so late.

SECOND WATCH. Come, to the marshal's with the murderer!

FIRST WATCH. On to Hieronimo's! Help me here

To bring the murdered body with us too. 45

PEDRINGANO. Hieronimo? Carry me before whom you will.

Whate'er he be, I'll answer him and you;

And do your worst, for I defy you all. *Exeunt.*

[Scene IV. *The* DUKE's *Castle*.]

Enter LORENZO *and* BALTHAZAR.

BALTHAZAR. How now, my lord, what makes you rise so
soon?

LORENZO. Fear of preventing our mishaps too late.

BALTHAZAR. What mischief is it that we not mistrust?

LORENZO. Our greatest ills we least mistrust, my Lord,

And inexpected harms do hurt us most.

---

[1] Pistol.   [2] Attend at his death.

BALTHAZAR. Why, tell me, Don Lorenzo, tell me, man,
If aught concerns our honor and your own.

LORENZO. Nor you, nor me, my lord, but both in one;
For I suspect—and the presumption's great—
That by those base confederates in our fault   10
Touching the death of Don Horatio,
We are betrayed to old Hieronimo.

BALTHAZAR. Betrayed, Lorenzo? Tush, it cannot be.

LORENZO. A guilty conscience, urged with the thought
Of former evils, easily cannot err.   15
I am persuaded—and dissuade me not—
That all's revealed to Hieronimo.
And therefore know that I have cast it thus—

Enter PAGE.

But here's the page. How now? What news with thee?   19
PAGE. My lord, Serberine is slain.

BALTHAZAR.   Who? Serberine, my man?
PAGE. Your highness' man, my lord.

LORENZO.   Speak, page, who murdered him?
PAGE. He that is apprehended for the fact.

LORENZO. Who?
PAGE.   Pedringano.

BALTHAZAR. Is Serberine slain, that loved his lord so well?
Injurious villain, murderer of his friend!   25

LORENZO. Hath Pedringano murdered Serberine?
My lord, let me entreat you to take the pains
To exasperate and hasten his revenge
With your complaints unto my lord the king.
This their dissension breeds a greater doubt.   30

BALTHAZAR. Assure thee, Don Lorenzo, he shall die,
Or else his highness hardly shall deny[1].

---

[1] Refuse me with difficulty.

Meanwhile I'll haste the marshal-sessions,
For die he shall for this his damned deed. *Exit* BALTHAZAR.

LORENZO. Why so, this fits our former policy,   35
And thus experience bids the wise to deal.
I lay the plot; he prosecutes the point.
I set the trap; he breaks the worthless twigs,
And sees not that wherewith the bird was limed[1].
Thus hopeful men, that mean to hold their own,   40
Must look like fowlers to their dearest friends.
He runs to kill whom I have holp to catch,
And no man knows it was my reaching fetch[2].
'Tis hard to trust unto a multitude,
Or any one, in mine opinion,   45
When men themselves their secrets will reveal.

Enter a MESSENGER *with a letter*.
Boy!
PAGE. My lord.
LORENZO. What's he?
MESSENGER.   I have a letter to your lordship.
LORENZO. From whence?
MESSENGER.   From Pedringano that's imprisoned.
LORENZO. So he is in prison then?
MESSENGER.   Ay, my good lord.   50
LORENZO. What would he with us?—He writes us here,
To stand good lord, and help him in distress.—
Tell him I have his letters, know his mind;
And what we may, let him assure him of.
Fellow, begone; my boy shall follow thee.   55

Exit MESSENGER.

This works like wax; yet once more try thy wits.

---

[1] Trapped.   [2] Far-reaching plan.

Boy, go, convey this purse to Pedringano;
Thou knowst the prison, closely[1] give it him,
And be advised that none be there about.
Bid him be merry still, but secret;   60
And though the marshal-sessions be to-day,
Bid him not doubt of his delivery.
Tell him his pardon is already signed,
And thereon bid him boldly be resolved:
For, were he ready to be turned off[2]—   65
As 'tis my will the uttermost be tried—
Thou with his pardon shalt attend him still.
Show him this box, tell him his pardon's in 't;
But open 't not, an if thou lovest thy life,
But let him wisely keep his hopes unknown.   70
He shall not want while Don Lorenzo lives.
Away!
   PAGE. I go, my Lord, I run.
   LORENZO. But, sirrah, see that this be cleanly[3] done. *Exit* PAGE.
Now stands our fortune on a tickle point[4],
And now or never ends Lorenzo's doubts.   75
One only thing is uneffected yet,
And that's to see the executioner.
But to what end? I list not trust the air
With utterance of our pretence[5] therein,
For fear the privy whisp'ring of the wind   80
Convey our words amongst unfriendly ears,
That lie too open to advantages.
E quel che voglio io, nessun lo sa;
Intendo io: quel mi basterà.[6]   *Exit.*

---

[1] Secretly.   [2] Hanged.   [3] Neatly, smoothly.   [4] "Ticklish" situation.
[5] Intention.   [6] And what I wish, no one knows; I understand: which
satisfies me.

[Scene V. *A Street.*]

Enter BOY *with the box.*

BOY. My master hath forbidden me to look in this box; and, by my troth, 'tis likely, if he had not warned me, I should not have had so much idle time; for we men's-kind in our minority are like women in their uncertainty: that they are most forbidden, they will soonest attempt; so I now.— By my bare 5 honesty, here's nothing but the bare empty box! Were it not sin against secrecy, I would say it were a piece of gentlemanlike knavery. I must go to Pedringano, and tell him his pardon is in this box; nay, I would have sworn it, had I not seen the contrary. I cannot choose but smile to think how the villain 10 will flout the gallows, scorn the audience, and descant on the hangman, and all presuming of his pardon from hence. Will 't not be an odd jest for me to stand and grace every jest he makes, pointing my finger at this box, as who would say, "Mock on, here's thy warrant." Is 't not a scurvy jest that a man 15 should jest himself to death? Alas! poor Pedringano, I am in a sort sorry for thee; but if I should be hanged with thee, I cannot weep. *Exit.*

[Scene VI. *The Court of Justice.*]

Enter HIERONIMO *and the* DEPUTY.

HIERONIMO. Thus must we toil in other men's extremes,
That know not how to remedy our own;
And do them justice, when unjustly we,
For all our wrongs, can compass no redress.
But shall I never live to see the day, 5
That I may come, by justice of the heavens,
To know the cause that may my cares allay?
This toils my body, this consumeth age,

That only I to all men just must be,
And neither gods nor men be just to me.   10
  DEPUTY. Worthy Hieronimo, your office asks
A care to punish such as do transgress.
  HIERONIMO. So is 't my duty to regard his death
Who, when he lived, deserved my dearest blood.
But come, for that we came for. Let's begin,   15
For here lies that which bids me to be gone.

Enter OFFICERS, BOY, *and* PEDRINGANO, *with a letter in his hand,*
bound.

  DEPUTY. Bring forth the prisoner, for the court is set.
  PEDRINGANO. Gramercy, boy, but it was time to come;
For I had written to my lord anew
A nearer matter that concerneth him,   20
For fear his lordship had forgotten me.
But sith he hath rememb'red me so well—
Come, come, come on, when shall we to this gear?
  HIERONIMO. Stand forth, thou monster, murderer of men,
And here, for satisfaction of the world,   25
Confess thy folly, and repent thy fault;
For there's thy place of execution.
  PEDRINGANO. This is short work. Well, to your marshalship
First I confess—nor fear I death therefore—
I am the man, 'twas I slew Serberine.   30
But, sir, then you think this shall be the place,
Where we shall satisfy you for this gear?
  DEPUTY. Ay, Pedringano.
  PEDRINGANO.   Now I think not so.
  HIERONIMO. Peace, impudent; for thou shalt find it so;
For blood with blood shall, while I sit as judge,   35
Be satisfied, and the law discharged.
And though myself cannot receive the like,

Yet will I see that others have their right.
Despatch; the fault's approved[1] and confessed,
And by our law he is condemned to die.   40

[*Enter* HANGMAN.]

HANGMAN. Come on, sir, are you ready?

PEDRINGANO. To do what, my fine, officious knave?

HANGMAN. To go to this gear.

PEDRINGANO. O sir, you are too forward: thou wouldst fain
furnish me with a halter, to disfurnish me of my habit[2]. So   45
I should go out of this gear, my raiment, into that gear, the
rope. But, hangman, now I spy your knavery, I'll not change
without boot[3], that's flat.

HANGMAN. Come, sir.

PEDRINGANO. So, then, I must up?   50

HANGMAN. No remedy.

PEDRINGANO. Yes, but there shall be for my coming down.

HANGMAN. Indeed, here's a remedy for that.

PEDRINGANO. How? Be turned off?

HANGMAN. Ay, truly. Come, are you ready? I pray, sir,
despatch; the day goes away.   55

PEDRINGANO. What, do you hang by the hour? If you do,
I may chance to break your old custom.

HANGMAN. Faith, you have reason; for I am like to break
your young neck.

PEDRINGANO. Dost thou mock me, hangman? Pray God,   60
I be not preserved to break your knave's pate for this.

HANGMAN. Alas, sir! You are a foot too low to reach it, and
I hope you will never grow so high while I am in the office.

PEDRINGANO. Sirrah, dost see yonder boy with the box in
his hand?   65

---

[1] Proved.   [2] The hangman received the clothes of the criminals ex-
ecuted.   [3] Cf. "to boot"; extra payment.

HANGMAN. What, he that points to it with his finger?

PEDRINGANO. Ay, that companion.

HANGMAN. I know him not; but what of him?

PEDRINGANO. Dost thou think to live till his old doublet
will make thee a new truss? 70

HANGMAN. Ay, and many a fair year after, to truss up many
an honester man than either thou or he.

PEDRINGANO. What hath he in his box, as thou think'st?

HANGMAN. Faith, I cannot tell, nor I care not greatly; methinks
you should rather hearken to your soul's health. 75

PEDRINGANO. Why, sirrah, hangman, I take it that that is
good for the body is likewise good for the soul; and it may be,
in that box is balm for both.

HANGMAN. Well, thou art even the merriest piece of man's
flesh that e'er groaned at my office door! 80

PEDRINGANO. Is your roguery become an office with a knave's
name?

HANGMAN. Ay, and that shall all they witness that see you
seal it with a thief's name.

PEDRINGANO. I prithee, request this good company to 85
pray with me.

HANGMAN. Ay, marry, sir, this is a good motion. My masters,
you see here's a good fellow.

PEDRINGANO. Nay, nay, now I remember me, let them alone
till some other time; for now I have no great need. 90

HIERONIMO. I have not seen a wretch so impudent.
O monstrous times, where murder's set so light,
And where the soul, that should be shrined in heaven,
Solely delights in interdicted things,
Still wand'ring in the thorny passages, 95
That intercepts itself of[1] happiness.

---

[1] Cuts itself off from

Murder! O bloody monster! God forbid
A fault so foul should 'scape unpunished.
Despatch, and see this execution done!
This makes me to remember thee, my son.　　　100

Exit HIERONIMO.

PEDRINGANO. Nay, soft, no haste.
DEPUTY. Why, wherefore stay you? Have you hope of life?
PEDRINGANO. Why, ay!
HANGMAN.　　　　　　　As how?
PEDRINGANO. Why, rascal, by my pardon from the king.　105
HANGMAN. Stand you on that? Then you shall off with this.

He turns him off.

DEPUTY. So, executioner; convey him hence;
But let his body be unburied:
Let not the earth be choked or infect
With that which heaven contemns, and men neglect.　*Exeunt.*

[Scene VII.　HIERONIMO'S *House.*]

Enter HIERONIMO.

HIERONIMO. Where shall I run to breathe abroad my woes,
My woes, whose weight hath wearied the earth?
Or mine exclaims, that have surcharged the air
With ceaseless plaints for my deceased son?
The blust'ring winds, conspiring with my words,　　　5
At my lament have moved the leafless trees,
Disrobed the meadows of their flowered green,
Made mountains marsh with spring-tides of my tears,
And broken through the brazen gates of hell.
Yet still tormented is my tortured soul　　　10
With broken sighs and restless passions,

That, winged, mount; and, hovering in the air,
Beat at the windows of the brightest heavens,
Soliciting for justice and revenge.
But they are placed in those empyreal heights,   15
Where, countermured[1] with walls of diamond,
I find the place impregnable; and they
Resist my woes, and give my words no way.

Enter HANGMAN *with a letter.*

HANGMAN. O lord, sir! God bless you, sir! The man, sir,
Petergade, sir, he that was so full of merry conceits—   20
   HIERONIMO. Well, what of him?
   HANGMAN. O lord, sir, he went the wrong way; the fellow
had a fair commission to the contrary. Sir, here is his passport;
I pray, you, sir, we have done him wrong.
   HIERONIMO. I warrant thee; give it me.   25
   HANGMAN. You will stand between the gallows and me?
   HIERONIMO. Ay, ay.
   HANGMAN. I thank your lord worship.   *Exit* HANGMAN.
   HIERONIMO. And yet, though somewhat nearer me concerns,
I will, to ease the grief that I sustain,   30
Take truce with sorrow while I read on this.
"My lord, I write, as mine extremes required,
That you would labor my delivery:
If you neglect, my life is desperate,
And in my death I shall reveal the troth.   35
You know, my Lord, I slew him for your sake,
And was confed'rate with the prince and you;
Won by rewards and hopeful promises,
I holp to murder Don Horatio too."
Holp he to murder mine Horatio?   40

---

[1] Doubly walled.

And actors in th' accursed tragedy
Wast thou, Lorenzo, Balthazar and thou,
Of whom my son, my son deserved so well?
What have I heard, what have mine eyes beheld?
O sacred heavens, may it come to pass   45
That such a monstrous and detested deed,
So closely smothered, and so long concealed,
Shall thus by this be venged or revealed?
Now see I what I durst not then suspect,
That Bel-imperia's letter was not feigned.   50
Nor feigned she, though falsely they have wronged
Both her, myself, Horatio, and themselves.
Now may I make compare 'twixt hers and this,
Of every accident I ne'er could find
Till now, and now I feelingly perceive   55
They did what heaven unpunished would not leave.
O false Lorenzo! Are these thy flattering looks?
Is this the honor that thou didst my son?
And Balthazar—bane to thy soul and me!—
Was this the ransom he reserved thee for?   60
Woe to the cause of these constrained wars!
Woe to thy baseness and captivity,
Woe to thy birth, thy body, and thy soul,
Thy cursed father, and thy conquered self!
And banned with bitter execrations be   65
The day and place where he did pity thee!
But wherefore waste I mine unfruitful words,
When nought but blood will satisfy my woes?
I will go plain me to my lord the king,
And cry aloud for justice through the court,   70
Wearing the flints with these my withered feet;
And either purchase justice by entreats,
Or tire them all with my revenging threats.   *Exit.*

[Scene VIII. *The Same.*]

Enter ISABELLA *and her* MAID.

ISABELLA. So that you say this herb will purge the eye,
And this, the head?
Ah, but none of them will purge the heart!
No, there's no medicine left for my disease,
Nor any physic to recure[1] the dead.   *She runs lunatic.*   5
Horatio! O, where's Horatio?

MAID. Good madam, affright not thus yourself
With outrage for your son Horatio;
He sleeps in quiet in the Elysian fields.

ISABELLA. Why, did I not give you gowns and goodly
    things,   10
Bought you a whistle and a whipstalk too,
To be revenged on their villainies?

MAID. Madam, these humors do torment my soul.

ISABELLA. My soul—poor soul, thou talkst of things
Thou knowst not what—my soul hath silver wings,   15
That mounts me up unto the highest heavens;
To heaven? Ay, there sits my Horatio,
Backed with a troop of fiery cherubins,
Dancing about his newly healed wounds,
Singing sweet hymns and chanting heavenly notes,   20
Rare harmony to greet his innocence,
That died, ay died, a mirror in our days.
But say, where shall I find the men, the murderers,
That slew Horatio? Whither shall I run
To find them out that murdered my son?   *Exeunt.* 25

___
[1] Recover.

[Scene IX.　*The* DUKE'S *Castle*.]

BEL-IMPERIA *at a window.*

BEL-IMPERIA. What means this outrage that is offered me?
Why am I thus sequestered from the court?
No notice! Shall I not know the cause
Of these my secret and suspicious ills?
Accursed brother, unkind murderer,　　　　　　　　　　5
Why bend'st thou thus thy mind to martyr me?
Hieronimo, why writ I of thy wrongs,
Or why art thou so slack in thy revenge?
Andrea, O Andrea! that thou saw'st
Me for thy friend Horatio handled thus,　　　　　　　10
And him for me thus causeless murdered!—
Well, force perforce, I must constrain myself
To patience, and apply me[1] to the time,
Till heaven, as I have hoped, shall set me free.

Enter CHRISTOPHIL.

CHRISTOPHIL. Come, Madam Bel-imperia, this may not be.

Exeunt.

[Scene X.　*A Room in the Castle*.]

Enter LORENZO, BALTHAZAR, *and the* PAGE.

LORENZO. Boy, talk no further; thus far things go well.
Thou art assured that thou sawest him dead?
PAGE. Or else, my Lord, I live not.
LORENZO.　　　　　　　　　　　　　　That's enough.
As for his resolution in his end,
Leave that to him with whom he sojourns now.　　　5

---

[1] Accept.

Here, take my ring and give it Christophil,
And bid him let my sister be enlarged,
And bring him hither straight.— *Exit* PAGE.
This that I did was for a policy,
To smooth and keep the murder secret, 10
Which, as a nine-days' wonder, being o'erblown,
My gentle sister will I now enlarge.

BALTHAZAR. And time, Lorenzo; for my lord the duke,
You heard, enquired for her yesternight.

LORENZO. Why, and my Lord, I hope you heard me say 15
Sufficient reason why she kept away;
But that's all one. My Lord, you love her?

BALTHAZAR. Ay.

LORENZO. Then in your love beware; deal cunningly:
Salve all suspicions, only soothe me up[1];
And if she hap to stand on terms[2] with us— 20
As for her sweetheart and concealment so—
Jest with her gently; under feigned jest
Are things concealed that else would breed unrest.
But here she comes.

Enter BEL-IMPERIA.

Now, sister,—

BEL-IMPERIA. Sister? No!
Thou art no brother, but an enemy; 25
Else wouldst thou not have used thy sister so:
First, to affright me with thy weapons drawn,
And with extremes abuse my company[3];
And then to hurry me, like whirlwind's rage,
Amidst a crew of thy confederates, 30
And clap me up where none might come at me,

---

[1] Support my story.   [2] Bargain.   [3] Companion.

Nor I at any to reveal my wrongs.
What madding fury did possess thy wits?
Or wherein is 't that I offended thee?
 LORENZO. Advise you better, Bel-imperia,   35
For I have done you no disparagement;
Unless, by more discretion than deserved,
I sought to save your honor and mine own.
 BEL-IMPERIA. Mine honor? Why, Lorenzo, wherein is 't
That I neglect my reputation so,   40
As you, or any, need to rescue it?
 LORENZO. His highness and my father were resolved
To come confer with old Hieronimo
Concerning certain matters of estate
That by the viceroy was determined.   45
 BEL-IMPERIA. And wherein was mine honor touched in that?
 BALTHAZAR. Have patience, Bel-imperia; hear the rest.
 LORENZO. Me, next in sight, as messenger they sent
To give him notice that they were so nigh:
Now when I came, consorted with the prince,   50
And unexpected in an arbor there
Found Bel-imperia with Horatio—
 BEL-IMPERIA. How then?
 LORENZO. Why, then, remembering that old disgrace,
Which you for Don Andrea had endured,   55
And now were likely longer to sustain,
By being found so meanly accompanied,
Thought rather—for I knew no readier mean—
To thrust Horatio forth my father's way.
 BALTHAZAR. And carry you obscurely somewhere else, 60
Lest that his highness should have found you there.
 BEL-IMPERIA. Even so, my lord? And you are witness
That this is true which he entreateth of?
You, gentle brother, forged this for my sake,

And you, my Lord, were made his instrument?   65
A work of worth, worthy the noting too!
But what's the cause that you concealed me since?
  LORENZO. Your melancholy, sister, since the news
Of your first favorite Don Andrea's death,
My father's old wrath hath exasperate.   70
  BALTHAZAR. And better was 't for you, being in disgrace,
To absent yourself, and give his fury place.
  BEL-IMPERIA. But why had I no notice of his ire?
  LORENZO. That were to add more fuel to your fire,
Who burnt like Aetna for Andrea's loss.   75
  BEL-IMPERIA. Hath not my father then enquired for me?
  LORENZO. Sister, he hath, and thus excused I thee.

He whispereth in her ear.

But Bel-imperia, see the gentle prince;
Look on thy love, behold young Balthazar,
Whose passions by thy presence are increased;   80
And in whose melancholy thou mayst see
Thy hate, his love; thy flight, his following thee.
  BEL-IMPERIA. Brother, you are become an orator—
I know not, I, by what experience—
Too politic for me, past all compare,   85
Since last I saw you; but content yourself:
The prince is meditating higher things.
  BALTHAZAR. 'Tis of thy beauty, then, that conquers kings;
Of those thy tresses, Ariadne's twines,
Wherewith my liberty thou hast surprised;   90
Of that thine ivory front, my sorrow's map,
Wherein I see no haven to rest my hope.
  BEL-IMPERIA. To love and fear, and both at once, my lord,
In my conceit, are things of more import
Than women's wits are to be busied with.   95

BALTHAZAR. 'Tis I that love.

BEL-IMPERIA. Whom?

BALTHAZAR. Bel-imperia.

BEL-IMPERIA. But I that fear.

BALTHAZAR. Whom?

BEL-IMPERIA. Bel-imperia.

LORENZO. Fear yourself?

BEL-IMPERIA. Ay, brother.

LORENZO. How?

BEL-IMPERIA. As those
That what they love are loath and fear to lose.

BALTHAZAR. Then, fair, let Balthazar your keeper be. 100

BEL-IMPERIA. No, Balthazar doth fear as well as we:
Et tremulo metui pavidum iunxere timorem—
Est vanum stolidae proditionis opus[1].

LORENZO. Nay, and you argue things so cunningly,
We'll go continue this discourse at court. 105

BALTHAZAR. Led by the loadstar of her heavenly looks,
Wends poor oppressed Balthazar,
As o'er the mountains walks the wanderer,
Incertain to effect his pilgrimage. *Exeunt.*

[Scene XI. *A Street.*]

Enter TWO PORTINGALES, *and* HIERONIMO *meets them.*

FIRST PORTINGALE. By your leave, sir.

HIERONIMO[2]. [*'Tis neither as you think, nor as you think,*
Nor as you think; you're wide all.
These slippers are not mine, they were my son Horatio's.
My son? And what's a son? A thing begot 5
Within a pair of minutes—thereabout;

---

[1] And I feared to add terrible anxiety to a quaking man; fruitless is the work of stupid treachery.   [2] Third passage of additions.

A lump bred up in darkness, and doth serve
To ballace[1] *these light creatures we call women;*
And, at nine months' end, creeps forth to light.
What is there yet in a son,   10
To make a father dote, rave, or run mad?
Being born, it pouts, cries, and breeds teeth.
What is there yet in a son? He must be fed,
Be taught to go, and speak. Ay, or yet
Why might not a man love a calf as well?   15
Or melt in passion o'er a frisking kid,
As for a son? Methinks, a young bacon,
Or a fine little smooth horse colt,
Should move a man as much as doth a son.
For one of these, in very little time,   20
Will grow to some good use; whereas a son,
The more he grows in stature and in years,
The more unsquared, unbevelled, he appears,
Reckons his parents among the rank of fools,
Strikes care upon their heads with his mad riots,   25
Makes them look old before they meet with age.
This is a son! And what a loss were this,
Considered truly?—O, but my Horatio
Grew out of reach of these insatiate humors:
He loved his loving parents;   30
He was my comfort, and his mother's joy,
The very arm that did hold up our house:
Our hopes were stored up in him,
None but a damned murderer could hate him.
He had not seen the back of nineteen year,   35
When his strong arm unhorsed
The proud Prince Balthazar, and his great mind,

---

[1] Ballast.

Too full of honor, took him unto mercy,
That valiant but ignoble Portingale!
Well, heaven is heaven still! 40
And there is Nemesis, and Furies,
And things called whips,
And they sometimes do meet with murderers;
They do not always 'scape, that's some comfort.
Ay, ay, ay; and then time steals on, 45
And steals, and steals, till violence leaps forth
Like thunder wrapt in a ball of fire,
And so doth bring confusion to them all.]
Good leave have you; nay, I pray you go,
For I'll leave you, if you can leave me so. 50

SECOND PORTINGALE. Pray you, which is the next way to my
   lord the duke's?
HIERONIMO. The next way from me.
FIRST PORTINGALE.   To his house, we mean.
HIEROMINO. O, hard by: 'tis yon house that you see.
SECOND PORINGALE. You could not tell us if his son were
   there?
HIERONIMO. Who, my Lord Lorenzo?
FIRST PORTINGALE.   Ay, sir.
   He goeth in at one door and comes out at another.
HIERONIMO.   O, forbear! 55
For other talk for us far fitter were.
But if you be importunate to know
The way to him, and where to find him out,
Then list to me, and I'll resolve your doubt.
There is a path upon your left-hand side 60
That leadeth from a guilty conscience
Unto a forest of distrust and fear—
A darksome place, and dangerous to pass.
There shall you meet with melancholy thoughts,

Whose baleful humors if you but uphold, 65
It will conduct you to despair and death;
Whose rocky cliffs when you have once beheld,
Within a hugy dale of lasting night,
That, kindled with the world's iniquities,
Doth cast up filthy and detested fumes: 70
Not far from thence, where murderers have built
A habitation for their cursed souls,
There, in a brazen caldron, fixed by Jove,
In his fell wrath, upon a sulphur flame,
Yourselves shall find Lorenzo bathing him 75
In boiling lead and blood of innocents.

FIRST PORTINGALE. Ha, ha, ha!

HIERONIMO. Ha, ha, ha! Why, ha, ha, ha! Farewell, good ha,
   ha, ha!   *Exit.*

SECOND PORTINGALE. Doubtless this man is passing lunatic,
Or imperfection of his age doth make him dote. 80
Come, let's away to seek my lord the duke. *Exeunt*

[Scene XII. *The Spanish Court.*]

Enter HIERONIMO, *with a poniard in one hand and a rope in the other.*

HIERONIMO. Now, sir, perhaps I come and see the king;
The king sees me, and fain would hear my suit.
Why, is not this a strange and seld-seen thing,
That standers-by with toys should strike me mute?
Go to, I see their shifts, and say no more. 5
Hieronimo, 'tis time for thee to trudge.
Down by the dale that flows with purple gore
Standeth a fiery tower; there sits a judge
Upon a seat of steel and molten brass,
And 'twixt his teeth he holds a fire-brand, 10
That leads unto the lake where hell doth stand.

Away, Hieronimo; to him be gone;
He'll do thee justice for Horatio's death.
Turn down this path; thou shalt be with him straight;
Or this, and then thou needst not take thy breath: 15
This way or that way?—Soft and fair, not so!
For if I hang or kill myself, let's know
Who will revenge Horatio's murder then?
No, no! fie, no! Pardon me, I'll none of that.

> *He flings away the dagger and halter.*

This way I'll take, and this way comes the king: 20

> *He takes them up again.*

And here I'll have a fling at him, that's flat;
And, Balthazar, I'll be with thee to bring[1],
And thee, Lorenzo! Here's the king—nay, stay;
And here, ay here—there goes the hare away[2].

> *Enter* KING, AMBASSADOR, CASTILE, *and* LORENZO.

KING. Now show, ambassador, what our viceroy saith.   25
Hath he received the articles we sent?
HIERONIMO. Justice, O justice to Hieronimo.
LORENZO. Back! Seest thou not the king is busy?
HIERONIMO.   O, is he so?
KING. Who is he that interrupts our business?
HIERONIMO. Not I. [*Aside.*] Hieronimo, beware! Go by, go by!
AMBASSADOR. Renowned King, he hath received and read   31
Thy kingly proffers, and thy promised league;
And, as a man extremely over-joyed
To hear his son so princely entertained,
Whose death he had so solemnly bewailed,   35
This for thy further satisfaction
And kingly love he kindly lets thee know:
First, for the marriage of his princely son

---

[1] A blow, a lesson.   [2] "The hunt begins"(?)

With Bel-imperia, thy beloved niece,
The news are more delightful to his soul,   40
Than myrrh or incense to the offended heavens.
In person, therefore, will he come himself,
To see the marriage rites solemnized,
And, in the presence of the court of Spain,
To knit a sure inexplicable[1] band   45
Of kingly love and everlasting league
Betwixt the crowns of Spain and Portingal.
There will he give his crown to Balthazar,
And make a queen of Bel-imperia.

    KING. Brother, how like you this our viceroy's love?   50
    CASTILE. No doubt, my lord, it is an argument
Of honorable care to keep his friend,
And wondrous zeal to Balthazar his son;
Nor am I least indebted to his grace,
That bends his liking to my daughter thus.   55
    AMBASSADOR. Now last, dread lord, here hath his highness
      sent
    (Although he send not that his son return)
His ransom due to Don Horatio.
    HIERONIMO. Horatio! Who calls Horatio?
    KING. And well remembered; thank his majesty.   60
Here, see it given to Horatio.
    HIERONIMO. Justice, O, justice, justice, gentle king!
    KING. Who is that? Hieronimo?
    HIERONIMO. Justice, O, justice! O my son, my son!
My son, whom naught can ransom or redeem!   65
    LORENZO. Hieronimo, you are not well-advised.
    HIERONIMO. Away, Lorenzo, hinder me no more;
For thou hast made me bankrupt of my bliss.

---

[1] Indissoluble.

Give me my son! You shall not ransom him!
Away! I'll rip the bowels of the earth,   70

He diggeth with his dagger.

And ferry over to th' Elysian plains,
And bring my son to show his deadly wounds.
Stand from about me!
I'll make a pickaxe of my poniard,
And here surrender up my marshalship;   75
For I'll go marshal up the fiends in hell,
To be avenged on you all for this.

   KING. What means this outrage?
Will none of you restrain his fury?

   HIERONIMO. Nay, soft and fair! You shall not need to strive. 80
Needs must he go that the devils drive.   *Exit.*

   KING. What accident hath happed Hieronimo?
I have not seen him to demean him so.

   LORENZO. My gracious lord, he is with extreme pride,
Conceived of young Horatio his son   85
And covetous of having to himself
The ransom of the young prince Balthazar,
Distract, and in a manner lunatic.

   KING. Believe me, nephew, we are sorry for 't;
This is the love that fathers bear their sons.   90
But, gentle brother, go give to him this gold,
The prince's ransom; let him have his due.
For what he hath, Horatio shall not want;
Haply Hieronimo hath need thereof.

   LORENZO. But if he be thus helplessly distract,   95
'Tis requisite his office be resigned,
And given to one of more discretion.

   KING. We shall increase his melancholy so.
'Tis best that we see further in it first,

Till when, ourself will exempt[1] the place.   100
And, brother, now bring in the ambassador,
That he may be a witness of the match
'Twixt Balthazar and Bel-imperia,
And that we may prefix a certain time,
Wherein the marriage shall be solemnized,   105
That we may have thy lord, the viceroy, here.

AMBASSADOR. Therein your highness highly shall content
His majesty, that longs to hear from hence.

KING. On, then, and hear you, lord ambassador— *Exeunt.*

[Scene XIII. HIERONIMO'S *Garden.*]

[2][Enter JAQUES and PEDRO.

JAQUES. *I wonder, Pedro, why our master thus*
At midnight sends us with our torches light,
When man and bird and beast are all at rest,
Save those that watch for rape and bloody murder.

PEDRO. *O Jaques, know thou that our master's mind*   5
Is much distraught, since his Horatio died,
And—now his aged years should sleep in rest,
His heart in quiet—like a desperate man,
Grows lunatic and childish for his son.
Sometimes, as he doth at his table sit,   10
He speaks as if Horatio stood by him;
Then starting in a rage, falls on the earth,
Cries out, "Horatio! Where is my Horatio?"
So that with extreme grief and cutting sorrow
There is not left in him one inch of man.   15
See, where he comes.

---

[1] I. e., from a new appointment.   [2] The following italic lines (1-
160), ending with the entry of Hieronimo on page 317, belong to the
additions.

Enter HIERONIMO.

HIERONIMO. *I pry through every crevice of each wall,*
Look on each tree, and search through every brake,
Beat at the bushes, stamp our grandam earth,
Dive in the water, and stare up to heaven, 20
Yet cannot I behold my son Horatio.
How now, who's there? Spirits, spirits?

PEDRO. *We are your servants that attend you, sir.*

HIERONIMO. *What make you with your torches in the dark?*

PEDRO. *You bid us light them, and attend you here.* 25

HIERONIMO. *No, no, you are deceived!; not I;—you are deceived!*
Was I so mad to bid you light your torches now?
Light me your torches at the mid of noon,
When-as the sun-god rides in all his glory;
Light me your torches then.

PEDRO.   *Then we burn¹ daylight.* 30

HIERONIMO. *Let it be burnt; Night is a murderous slut,*
That would not have her treasons to be seen;
And yonder pale-faced Hecate there, the moon,
Doth give consent to that is done in darkness;
And all those stars that gaze upon her face, 35
Are aglets² on her sleeve, pins on her train;
And those that should be powerful and divine.
Do sleep in darkness when they most should shine.

PEDRO. *Provoke them not, fair sir, with tempting words;*
The heavens are gracious, and your miseries 40
And sorrow makes you speak you know not what.

HIERONIMO. *Villain, thou liest! And thou dost nought*
But tell me I am mad. Thou liest, I am not mad!
I know thee to be Pedro, and he Jaques.
I'll prove it to thee; and were I mad, how could I? 45
Where was she that same night when my Horatio

¹ Waste.   ² Metal ornaments.

Was murdered? She should have shone; search thou the book.
Had the moon shone, in my boy's face there was a kind of grace,
That I know—nay, I do know—had the murderer seen him,
His weapon would have fall'n and cut the earth,　　　　50
Had he been framed of naught but blood and death.
Alack, when mischief doth it knows not what,
What shall we say to mischief?

Enter ISABELLA.

ISABELLA. *Dear Hieronimo, come in a-doors;*
O, seek not means so to increase thy sorrow.　　　　55
　HIERONIMO. *Indeed, Isabella, we do nothing here;*
I do not cry: ask Pedro, and ask Jaques;
Not I indeed; we are very merry, very merry.
　ISABELLA. *How? Be merry here, be merry here?*
Is not this the place, and this the very tree,　　　　60
Where my Horatio died, where he was murdered?
　HIERONIMO. *Was—do not say what: let her weep it out.*
This was the tree; I set it of a kernel;
And when our hot Spain could not let it grow,
But that the infant and the human sap　　　　65
Began to wither, duly twice a morning
Would I be sprinkling it with fountain-water.
At last it grew and grew, and bore and bore,
Till at the length
It grew a gallows, and did bear our son;　　　　70
It bore thy fruit and mine—O wicked, wicked plant!

One knocks within at the door.

See, who knocks there.
　PEDRO.　　　　　　*It is a painter, sir.*
　HIERONIMO. *Bid him come in, and paint some comfort,*
For surely there's none lives but painted comfort.

Let him come in! One knows not what may chance: 75
God's will that I should set this tree!—But even so
Masters ungrateful servants rear from nought,
And then they hate them that did bring them up.

Enter the PAINTER.

PAINTER. God bless you, sir.
HIERONIMO. Wherefore? Why, thou scornful villain? 80
How, where, or by what means should I be blessed?
ISABELLA. What wouldst thou have, good fellow?
PAINTER.   Justice, madam.
HIERONIMO. O ambitious beggar!
Wouldst thou have that that lives not in the world?
Why, all the undelved mines cannot buy 85
An ounce of justice, 'tis a jewel so inestimable.
I tell thee, God hath engrossed all justice in his hands,
And there is none but what comes from him.
PAINTER.   O, then I see
That God must right me for my murdered son. 90
HIERONIMO. How, was thy son murdered?
PAINTER. Ay, sir; no man did hold a son so dear.
HIERONIMO. What, not as thine? That's a lie,
As massy as the earth. I had a son
Whose least unvalued hair did weigh 95
A thousand of thy sons; and he was murdered.
PAINTER. Alas, sir, I had no more but he.
HIERONIMO. Nor I, nor I; but this same one of mine
Was worth a legion. But all is one.
Pedro, Jaques, go in a-doors; Isabella, go, 100
And this good fellow here and I
Will range this hideous orchard up and down,
Like to two lions reaved of their young.
Go in a-doors, I say.

Exeunt. The PAINTER and he sit down.

Come, let's talk wisely now.
Was thy son murdered?

PAINTER. *Ay, sir*

HIERONIMO. *So was mine.* 105
How dost take it? Art thou not sometimes mad?
Is there no tricks[1] that comes before thine eyes?

PAINTER. *O Lord, yes, sir.*

HIERONIMO. *Art a painter? Canst paint me a tear, or a wound,*
a groan, or a sigh? Canst paint me such a tree as this? 110

PAINTER. *Sir, I am sure you have heard of my painting: my name's*
Bazardo.

HIERONIMO. *Bazardo! Afore God, an excellent fellow. Look you,*
sir, do you see? I'd have you paint me [for] my gallery, in your
oil-colors matted[2], and draw me five years younger than I 115
am—do ye see, sir, let five years go; let them go like the marshal of
Spain—my wife Isabella standing by me, with a speaking look to
my son Horatio, which should intend to this or some such-like
purpose: "God bless thee, my sweet son," and my hand leaning upon
his head, thus, sir; do you see? May it be done? 120

PAINTER. *Very well, sir.*

HIERONIMO. *Nay, I pray, mark me, sir. Then, sir, would I have*
you paint me this tree, this very tree. Canst paint a doleful cry?

PAINTER. *Seemingly, sir.*

HIERONIMO. *Nay, it should cry; but all is one. Well, sir,* 125
paint me a youth run through and through with villains' swords,
hanging upon this tree. Canst thou draw a murderer?

PAINTER. *I'll warrant you, sir; I have the pattern of the most*
notorious villains that ever lived in all Spain.

HIERONIMO. *O, let them be worse, worse; stretch thine art, and* 130
let their beards be of Judas his own color; and let their eye-brows jutty

[1] Illusions.　　[2] Laid on heavily.

over: in any case observe that. Then, sir, after some violent noise,
bring me forth in my shirt, and my gown under mine arm, with my
torch in my hand, and my sword reared up, thus—and with these
words: 135
        "What noise is this? Who calls Hieronimo?"
May it be done?

PAINTER. *Yea, sir.*

HIERONIMO. *Well, sir; then bring me forth, bring me through*
alley and alley, still with a distracted countenance going along,   140
and let my hair heave up my night-cap. Let the clouds scowl,
make the moon dark, the stars extinct, the winds blowing, the bells
tolling, the owls shrieking, the toads croaking, the minutes jarring[1],
and the clock striking twelve. And then at last, sir, starting, behold
a man hanging, and tottering and tottering, as you know the wind   145
will wave a man, and I with a trice to cut him down. And looking
upon him by the advantage of my torch, find it to be my son Horatio.
There you may [show] a passion, there you may show a passion!
Draw me like old Priam of Troy, crying, "The house is a-fire,
the house is a-fire, as the torch over my head!" Make me curse,   150
make me rave, make me cry, make me mad, make me well again,
make me curse hell, invocate heaven, and in the end leave me in a
trance—and so forth.

PAINTER. *And is this the end?*

HIERONIMO. *O no, there is no end; the end is death and*   155
madness! As I am never better than when I am mad; then methinks
I am a brave fellow, then I do wonders; but reason abuseth me, and
there's the torment, there's the hell. At the last, sir, bring me to one
of the murderers: were he as strong as Hector, thus would I tear
and drag him up and down.   160

[He beats the PAINTER in, then comes out again, with a book
in his hand.]

---

[1] Ticking.

Enter HIERONIMO, *with a book in his hand.*

HIERONIMO. *Vindicta mihi*[1]!
Ay, heaven will be revenged of every ill;
Nor will they suffer murder unrepaid.
Then stay, Hieronimo, attend their will:
For mortal men may not appoint their time.   165
Per scelus semper tutum est sceleribus iter[2].
Strike, and strike home, where wrong is offered thee;
For evils ills conductors be,
And death's the worst of resolution.
For he that thinks with patience to contend   170
To quiet life, his life shall easily end.
Fata si miseros juvant, habes salutem;
Fata si vitam negant, habes sepulchrum:
"If destiny thy miseries do ease,
Then hast thou health, and happy shalt thou be;   175
If destiny deny thee life, Hieronimo,
Yet shalt thou be assured of a tomb."
If neither, yet let this thy comfort be:
Heaven covereth him that hath no burial.
And to conclude, I will revenge his death!   180
But how? Not as the vulgar wits of men,
With open, but inevitable ills,
As by a secret, yet a certain mean,
Which under kindship[3] will be cloaked best.
Wise men will take their opportunity,   185
Closely and safely fitting things to time.
But in extremes advantage hath no time;
And therefore all times fit not for revenge.
Thus therefore will I rest me in unrest,

---

[1] Vengeance for me.   [2] Through crime is always a safe route to
crimes.   [3] Kindness.

Dissembling quiet in unquietness,   190
Not seeming that I know their villainies,
That my simplicity may make them think
That ignorantly I will let all slip;
For ignorance, I wot, and well they know,
Remedium malorum iners est.[1]   195
Nor ought avails it me to menace them,
Who, as a wintry storm upon a plain,
Will bear me down with their nobility.
No, no, Hieronimo, thou must enjoin
Thine eyes to observation, and thy tongue   200
To milder speeches than thy spirit affords,
Thy heart to patience, and thy hands to rest,
Thy cap to courtesy, and thy knee to bow,
Till to revenge thou know when, where, and how. *A noise within.*
How now, what noise? What coil[2] is that you keep?   205

Enter a SERVANT.

SERVANT. Here are a sort[3] of poor petitioners
That are importunate, and it shall please you, sir,
That you should plead their cases to the king.
HIERONIMO. That I should plead their several actions?
Why, let them enter, and let me see them.   210

Enter THREE CITIZENS *and an* OLD MAN.

FIRST CITIZEN. So, I tell you this: for learning and for law,
There is not any advocate in Spain
That can prevail, or will take half the pain
That he will, in pursuit of equity.
HIERONIMO. Come near, you men, that thus importune me. 215
[*Aside.*] Now must I bear a face of gravity;

---

[1] As a remedy of ills it is worthless.   [2] Disturbance.   [3] Group.

For thus I used, before my marshalship,
To plead in causes as corregidor[1].
Come on, sirs, what's the matter?

SECOND CITIZEN.   Sir, an action.

HIERONIMO. Of battery?

FIRST CITIZEN   Mine of debt.

HIERONIMO.   Give place.   220

SECOND CITIZEN. No, sir, mine is an action of the case.

THIRD CITIZEN. Mine an *ejectione firmae*[2] by a lease.

HIERONIMO. Content you, sirs; are you determined
That I should plead your several actions?

FIRST CITIZEN. Ay, sir, and here's my declaration.   225

SECOND CITIZEN. And here's my band.

THIRD CITIZEN.   And here's my lease.

They give him papers.

HIERONIMO. But wherefore stands yon silly[3] man so mute,
With mournful eyes and hands to heaven upreared?
Come hither, father, let me know thy cause.

SENEX. O worthy sir, my cause, but slightly known,   230
May move the hearts of warlike Myrmidons,
And melt the Corsic rocks with ruthful tears.

HIERONIMO. Say, father, tell me, what's thy suit?

SENEX.   No, sir, could my woes
Give way unto my most distressful words,
Then should I not in paper, as you see,   235
With ink bewray what blood began in me.

HIERONIMO. What's here? "The humble supplication
Of Don Bazulto for his murdered son."

SENEX. Ay, sir.

HIERONIMO.   No, sir, it was my murdered son:

---

[1] Attorney.   [2] Eviction order.   [3] Simple, innocuous.

O my son, my son, O my son Horatio! 240
But mine, or thine, Bazulto, be content.
Here, take my handkercher and wipe thine eyes,
Whiles wretched I in thy mishaps may see
The lively portrait of my dying self.

He draweth out a bloody napkin.

O no, not this; Horatio, this was thine; 245
And when I dyed it in thy dearest blood,
This was a token 'twixt thy soul and me,
That of thy death revenged I should be.
But here, take this, and this—what, my purse?—
Ay, this, and that, and all of them are thine; 250
For all as one are our extremities.
    FIRST CITIZEN. O, see the kindness of Hieronimo!
    SECOND CITIZEN. This gentleness shows him a gentleman.
    HIERONIMO. See, see, O see thy shame, Hieronimo!
See here a loving father to his son! 255
Behold the sorrows and the sad laments,
That he delivereth for his son's decease!
If love's effects so strive in lesser things,
If love enforce such moods in meaner wits,
If love express such power in poor estates, 260
Hieronimo, as when a raging sea,
Tossed with the wind and tide, o'erturneth then
The upper billows, course of waves to keep,
Whilst lesser waters labor in the deep,
Then shamst thou not, Hieronimo, to neglect 265
The sweet revenge of thy Horatio?
Though on this earth justice will not be found,
I'll down to hell, and in this passion
Knock at the dismal gates of Pluto's court,
Getting by force, as once Alcides did, 270

A troop of Furies and tormenting hags
To torture Don Lorenzo and the rest.
Yet lest the triple-headed porter should
Deny my passage to the slimy strand,
The Thracian poet thou shalt counterfeit. 275
Come on, old father, be my Orpheus,
And if thou canst no notes upon the harp,
Then sound the burden of thy sore heart's grief,
Till we do gain that Proserpine may grant
Revenge on them that murdered my son. 280
Then will I rent and tear them, thus and thus,
Shivering their limbs in pieces with my teeth.

Tears the papers.

FIRST CITIZEN.   O sir, my declaration!

Exit HIERONIMO, *and they after.*

SECOND CITIZEN.   Save my bond!

Enter HIERONIMO.

SECOND CITIZEN. Save my bond!
THIRD CITIZEN. Alas, my lease! It cost me ten pound 285
And you, my lord, have torn the same.
HIERONIMO. That cannot be, I gave it never a wound.
Show me one drop of blood fall from the same!
How is it possible I should slay it then?
Tush, no; run after, catch me if you can. 290

Exeunt all but the OLD MAN. BAZULTO *remains till* HIERONIMO
enters again, who, staring him in the face, speaks.

HIERONIMO. And art thou come, Horatio, from the depth,
To ask for justice in this upper earth,

To tell thy father thou art unrevenged,
To wring more tears from Isabella's eyes,
Whose lights are dimmed with over-long laments? 295
Go back, my son, complain to Aeacus,
For here's no justice; gentle boy, begone,
For justice is exiled from earth:
Hieronimo will bear thee company.
The mother cries on righteous Rhadamanth 300
For just revenge against the murderers.
   SENEX. Alas, my lord, whence springs this troubled speech?
   HIERONIMO. But let me look on my Horatio.
Sweet boy, how art thou changed in death's black shade!
Had Proserpine no pity on thy youth, 305
But suffered thy fair crimson-colored spring
With withered winter to be blasted thus?
Horatio, thou art older than thy father.
Ah, ruthless fate, that favor thus transforms!
   BAZULTO. Ah, my good lord, I am not your young son. 310
   HIERONIMO. What, not my son? Thou then a Fury art,
Sent from the empty kingdom of black night
To summon me to make appearance
Before grim Minos and just Rhadamanth,
To plague Hieronimo that is remiss, 315
And seeks not vengeance for Horatio's death.
   BAZULTO. I am a grieved man, and not a ghost,
That came for justice for my murdered son.
   HIERONIMO. Ay, now I know thee, now thou namest thy son.
Thou art the lively image of my grief; 320
Within thy face my sorrows I may see.
Thy eyes are gummed with tears, thy cheeks are wan,
Thy forehead troubled, and thy mutt'ring lips
Murmur sad words abruptly broken off
By force of windy sighs thy spirit breathes; 325

And all this sorrow riseth for thy son:
And selfsame sorrow feel I for my son.
Come in, old man, thou shalt to Isabel.
Lean on my arm; I thee, thou me, shalt stay,
And thou, and I, and she will sing a song,   330
Three parts in one, but all of discords framed—:
Talk not of chords, but let us now be gone,
For with a cord Horatio was slain.   *Exeunt.*

[Scene XIV. *The Spanish Court.*]

Enter KING OF SPAIN, *the* DUKE, VICEROY, *and* LORENZO,
BALTHAZAR, DON PEDRO, *and* BEL-IMPERIA.

KING. Go, brother, it is the Duke of Castile's cause;
Salute the Viceroy in our name.
   CASTILE.   I go.
   VICEROY. Go forth, Don Pedro, for thy nephew's sake,
And greet the Duke of Castile.
   PEDRO.   It shall be so.
   KING. And now to meet these Portuguese: 5
For as we now are, so sometimes were these,
Kings and commanders of the western Indies.
Welcome, brave Viceroy, to the court of Spain,
And welcome all his honorable train!
'Tis not unknown to us for why you come,   10
Or have so kingly crossed the seas.
Sufficeth it, in this we note the troth
And more than common love you lend to us.
So is it that mine honorable niece
(For it beseems us now that it be known)   15
Already is betrothed to Balthazar;
And by appointment and our condescent[1]

---

[1] Consent.

To-morrow are they to be married.
To this intent we entertain thyself,
Thy followers, their pleasure, and our peace.   20
Speak, men of Portingal, shall it be so?
If ay, say so; if not, say flatly no.

VICEROY. Renowned King, I come not, as thou thinkst,
With doubtful followers, unresolved men,
But such as have upon thine articles   25
Confirmed thy motion, and contented me.
Know, sovereign, I come to solemnize
The marriage of thy beloved niece,
Fair Bel-imperia, with my Balthazar,
With thee, my son; whom sith I live to see,   30
Here take my crown, I give it her and thee;
And let me live a solitary life,
In ceaseless prayers,
To think how strangely heaven hath thee preserved.

KING. See, brother, see, how nature strives in him!   35
Come, worthy Viceroy, and accompany
Thy friend with thine extremities;
A place more private fits this princely mood.

VICEROY. Or here, or where your highness thinks it good.

Exeunt all but CASTILE *and* LORENZO.

CASTILE. Nay, stay, Lorenzo, let me talk with you.   40
Seest thou this entertainment of these kings?

LORENZO. I do, my lord, and joy to see the same.

CASTILE. And knowst thou why this meeting is?

LORENZO. For her, my lord, whom Balthazar doth love,
And to confirm their promised marriage.   45

CASTILE. She is thy sister?

LORENZO.   Who, Bel-imperia? Ay,
My gracious lord, and this is the day,

That I have longed so happily to see.

   CASTILE. Thou wouldst be loth that any fault of thine
Should intercept her in her happiness?   50

   LORENZO. Heavens will not let Lorenzo err so much.

   CASTILE. Why then, Lorenzo, listen to my words:
It is suspected, and reported too,
That thou, Lorenzo, wrongst Hieronimo,
And in his suits towards his majesty   55
Still keepst him back, and seekst to cross his suit.

   LORENZO. That I, my lord—?

   CASTILE. I tell thee, son, myself have heard it said,
When (to my sorrow) I have been ashamed
To answer for thee, though thou art my son.   60
Lorenzo, knowst thou not the common love
And kindness that Hieronimo hath won
By his deserts within the court of Spain?
Or seest thou not the king my brother's care
In his behalf, and to procure his health?   65
Lorenzo, shouldst thou thwart his passions,
And he exclaim against thee to the king,
What honor were't in this assembly,
Or what a scandal were't among the kings
To hear Hieronimo exclaim on thee?   70
Tell me—and look thou tell me truly too—
Whence grows the ground of this report in court?

   LORENZO. My lord, it lies not in Lorenzo's power
To stop the vulgar, liberal of their tongues.
A small advantage makes a water-breach,   75
And no man lives that long contenteth all.

   CASTILE. Myself have seen thee busy to keep back
Him and his supplications from the king.

   LORENZO. Yourself, my lord, hath seen his passions,
That ill beseemed the presence of a king;   80

And, for I pitied him in his distress,
I held him thence with kind and courteous words
As free from malice to Hieronimo
As to my soul, my lord.

   CASTILE. Hieronimo, my son, mistakes thee then. 85
   LORENZO. My gracious father, believe me, so he doth.
But what's a silly man, distract in mind
To think upon the murder of his son?
Alas, how easy is it for him to err!
But for his satisfaction and the world's, 90
'Twere good, my lord, that Hieronimo and I
Were reconciled, if he misconster me.

   CASTILE. Lorenzo, thou hast said; it shall be so.
Go one of you, and call Hieronimo.

Enter BALTHAZAR *and* BEL-IMPERIA.

   BALTHAZAR. Come, Bel-imperia, Balthazar's content, 95
My sorrow's ease and sovereign of my bliss;
Sith heaven hath ordained thee to be mine,
Disperse those clouds and melancholy looks,
And clear them up with those thy sun-bright eyes,
Wherein my hope and heaven's fair beauty lies. 100
   BEL-IMPERIA. My looks, my lord, are fitting for my love,
Which, new-begun, can show no brighter yet.
   BALTHAZAR. New-kindled flames should burn as morning sun.
   BEL-IMPERIA. But not too fast, lest heat and all be done.
I see my lord my father. 105
   BALTHAZAR.   Truce, my love;
I will go salute him.
   CASTILE.   Welcome, Balthazar.
Welcome, brave prince, the pledge of Castile's peace!
And welcome, Bel-imperia!—How now, girl?
Why comest thou sadly to salute us thus?

Content thyself, for I am satisfied: 110
It is not now as when Andrea lived;
We have forgotten and forgiven that,
And thou art graced with a happier love.
But, Balthazar, here comes Hieronimo;
I'll have a word with him. 115

Enter HIERONIMO *and a* SERVANT

HIERONIMO. And where's the duke?

SERVANT. Yonder.

HIERONIMO. Even so.—
What new device have they devised, trow[1]?
Pocas palabras![2] Mild as the lamb!
Is 't I will be revenged? No, I am not the man.

CASTILE. Welcome, Hieronimo. 120

LORENZO. Welcome, Hieronimo.

BALTHAZAR. Welcome, Hieronimo.

HIERONIMO. My lords, I thank you for Horatio.

CASTILE. Hieronimo, the reason that I sent
To speak with you, is this.

HIERONIMO. What so short? 125
Then I'll be gone, I thank you for 't.

CASTILE. Nay, stay, Hieronimo! Go call him, son.

LORENZO. Hieronimo, my father craves a word with you.

HIERONIMO. With me, sir? Why, my lord, I thought you
had done.

LORENZO. No. [*aside*] Would he had!

CASTILE. Hieronimo, I hear 130
You find yourself aggrieved at my son,
Because you have not access unto the king;
And say 'tis he that intercepts your suits.

---

[1] Do you think. [2] Few words.

HIERONIMO. Why, is not this a miserable thing, my lord?

CASTILE. Hieronimo, I hope you have no cause,   135
And would be loath that one of your deserts
Should once have reason to suspect my son,
Considering how I think of you myself.

HIERONIMO. Your son Lorenzo! Whom, my noble lord?
The hope of Spain, mine honorable friend?   140
Grant me the combat of them, if they dare; *Draws out his sword.*
I'll met him face to face, to tell me so!
These be the scandalous reports of such
As love not me, and hate my lord too much.
Should I suspect Lorenzo would prevent   145
Or cross my suit, that loved my son so well?
My lord, I am ashamed it should be said.

LORENZO. Hieronimo, I never gave you cause.

HIERONIMO. My good lord, I know you did not.

CASTILE.   There then
          pause;
And for the satisfaction of the world,   150
Hieronimo, frequent my homely house,
The Duke of Castile, Cyprian's ancient seat;
And when thou wilt, use me, my son, and it.
But here, before Prince Balthazar and me,
Embrace each other, and be perfect friends.   155

HIERONIMO. Ay, marry, my lord, and shall.
Friends, quoth he? See, I'll be friends with you all:
Especially with you, my lovely lord;
For divers causes it is fit for us
That we be friends: the world is suspicious,   160
And men may think what we imagine not.

BALTHAZAR. Why, this is friendly done, Hieronimo.

LORENZO. And that I hope old grudges are forgot.

HIERONIMO. What else? It were a shame it should not be so.

CASTILE. Come on, Hieronimo, at my request; 165
Let us entreat your company to-day. *Exeunt.*
   HIERONIMO. Your lordship's to command.— Pah! keep your
      way:
Chi mi fa piú carezze che non suole,
Tradito mi ha, o tradir mi vuole.[1] *Exit.*

[Chorus.]

Enter GHOST *and* REVENGE.

GHOST. Awake, Erichtho! Cerberus, awake! 170
Solicit Pluto, gentle Proserpine!
To combat, Acheron and Erebus!
For ne'er, by Styx and Phlegethon in hell,
O'er ferried Charon to the fiery lakes
Such fearful sights, as poor Andrea sees. 175
Revenge, awake!
   REVENGE.   Awake? For why?
   GHOST. Awake, Revenge; for thou art ill-advised
To sleep away what thou art warned to watch!
   REVENGE. Content thyself, and do not trouble me.
   GHOST. Awake, Revenge, if love—as love hath had— 180
Have yet the power or prevalence in hell!
Hieronimo with Lorenzo is joined in league,
And intercepts our passage to revenge.
Awake, Revenge, or we are woe-begone!
   REVENGE. Thus worldlings ground[2] what they have dreamed
      upon. 185
Content thyself, Andrea; though I sleep,
Yet is my mood soliciting their souls.
Sufficeth thee that poor Hieronimo

---

[1] He who caresses me more than is customary has betrayed me or wishes
to betray me.   [2] Rely upon.

Cannot forget his son Horatio.
Nor dies Revenge, although he sleep awhile;   190
For in unquiet, quietness is feigned,
And slumb'ring is a common worldly wile.
Behold, Andrea, for an instance, how
Revenge hath slept, and then imagine thou,
What 'tis to be subject to destiny.   195

Enter a Dumb-Show.

GHOST. Awake, Revenge; reveal this mystery.
REVENGE. The two first the nuptial torches bore
As brightly burning as the mid-day's sun;
But after them doth Hymen hie as fast,
Clothed in sable and a saffron robe,   200
And blows them out, and quencheth them with blood,
As discontent that things continue so.
GHOST. Sufficeth me; thy meaning's understood,
And thanks to thee and those infernal powers
That will not tolerate a lover's woe.   205
Rest thee, for I will sit to see the rest.
REVENGE. Then argue not, for thou hast thy request.   *Exeunt.*

ACT IV

[Scene I. *The* DUKE's *Castle.*]

Enter BEL-IMPERIA *and* HIERONIMO.

BEL-IMPERIA. Is this the love thou bearst Horatio?
Is this the kindness that thou counterfeits?
Are these the fruits of thine incessant tears?
Hieronimo, are these thy passions,
Thy protestations and thy deep laments,   5
That thou wert wont to weary men withal?
O unkind father! O deceitful world!

With what excuses canst thou show thyself
From this dishonor and the hate of men,
Thus to neglect the loss and life of him   10
Whom both my letters and thine own belief
Assures thee to be causeless slaughtered?
Hieronimo, for shame, Hieronimo,
Be not a history to after-times
Of such ingratitude unto thy son.   15
Unhappy mothers of such children then!
But monstrous fathers to forget so soon
The death of those whom they with care and cost
Have tendered so, thus careless should be lost.
Myself, a stranger in respect of thee,   20
So loved his life, as still I wish their deaths.
Nor shall his death be unrevenged by me,
Although I bear it out for fashion's sake;
For here I swear, in sight of heaven and earth,
Shouldst thou neglect the love thou shouldst retain,   25
And give it over and devise no more,
Myself should send their hateful souls to hell
That wrought his downfall with extremest death.

    HIERONIMO. But may it be that Bel-imperia
Vows such revenge as she hath deigned to say?   30
Why, then I see that heaven applies our drift[1],
And all the saints do sit soliciting
For vengeance on those cursed murderers.
Madam, 'tis true, and now I find it so,
I found a letter, written in your name,   35
And in that letter, how Horatio died.
Pardon, O pardon, Bel-imperia,
My fear and care in not believing it;

---

[1] Sides with our plan.

Nor think I thoughtless think upon a mean
To let his death be unrevenged at full.　　40
And here I vow—so you but give consent,
And will conceal my resolution—
I will ere long determine of their deaths
That causeless thus have murdered my son.

BEL-IMPERIA. Hieronimo, I will consent, conceal,　　45
And ought that may effect for thine avail,
Join with thee to revenge Horatio's death.

HIERONIMO. On, then. Whatsoever I devise,
Let me entreat you, grace my practices,
For why[1] the plot's already in mine head.　　50
Here they are.

Enter BALTHAZAR *and* LORENZO.

BALTHAZAR.　　How now, Hieronimo?
What, courting Bel-imperia?

HIERONIMO.　　Ay, my lord;
Such courting as, I promise you,
She hath my heart, but you, my lord, have hers.

LORENZO. But now, Hieronimo, or never,　　55
We are to entreat your help.

HIERONIMO.　　My help?
Why, my good lords, assure yourselves of me;
For you have given me cause,—ay, by my faith have you!

BALTHAZAR. It pleased you, at the entertainment of the am-
bassador,
To grace the king so much as with a show.　　60
Now, were your study so well furnished,
As, for the passing of the first night's sport,
To entertain my father with the like,

---

[1] Because.

Or any such-like pleasing motion,
Assure yourself, it would content them well.   65
  HIERONIMO. Is this all?
  BALTHAZAR.   Ay, this is all.
  HIERONIMO. Why then, I'll fit you; say no more.
When I was young, I gave my mind
And plied myself to fruitless poetry;
Which though it profit the professor naught,   70
Yet is it passing pleasing to the world.
  LORENZO. And how for that?
  HIERONIMO.   Marry, my good lord, thus:
And yet methinks, you are too quick with us—
When in Toledo there I studied,
It was my chance to write a tragedy,   75
See here, my lords—   *He shows them a book.*
Which, long forgot, I found this other day.
Now would your lordships favor me so much
As but to grace me with your acting it—
I mean each one of you to play a part—   80
Assure you it will prove most passing strange,
And wondrous plausible[1] to that assembly.
  BALTHAZAR. What, would you have us play a tragedy?
  HIERONIMO. Why, Nero thought it no disparagement,
And kings and emperors have ta'en delight   85
To make experience of their wits in plays.
  LORENZO. Nay, be not angry, good Hieronimo;
The prince but asked a question.
  BALTHAZAR. In faith, Hieronimo, an you be in earnest,
I'll make one.
  LORENZO.   And I another.   90
  HIERONIMO. Now, my good lord, could you entreat

---

[1] Pleasing.

Your sister Bel-imperia to make one?
For what's a play without a woman in it?

BEL-IMPERIA. Little entreaty shall serve me, Hieronimo;
For I must needs be employed in your play.   95

HIERONIMO. Why, this is well. I tell you, lordings
It was determined to have been acted
By gentlemen and scholars too,
Such as could tell what to speak.

BALTHAZAR.   And now
It shall be played by princes and courtiers,   100
Such as can tell how to speak:
If, as it is our country manner,
You will but let us know the argument.

HIERONIMO. That shall I roundly. The chronicles of Spain
Record this written of a knight of Rhodes: 105
He was betrothed, and wedded at the length
To one Perseda, an Italian dame,
Whose beauty ravished all that her beheld,
Especially the soul of Soliman,
Who at the marriage was the chiefest guest.   110
By sundry means sought Soliman to win
Perseda's love, and could not gain the same.
Then 'gan he break his passions to a friend,
One of his bashaws[1], whom he held full dear.
Her had this bashaw long solicited,   115
And saw she was not otherwise to be won,
But by her husband's death, this knight of Rhodes,
Whom presently by treachery he slew.
She, stirred with an exceeding hate therefore,
As cause of this slew Soliman,   120
And, to escape the bashaw's tyranny,

---

[1] Pashas.

Did stab herself; and this the tragedy.

   LORENZO. O excellent!

   BEL-IMPERIA.   But say, Hieronimo,

What then became of him that was the bashaw?

   HIERONIMO. Marry, thus: moved with remorse of his mis-
      deeds,   125

Ran to a mountain-top, and hung himself.

   BALTHAZAR. But which of us is to perform that part?

   HIERONIMO. O, that will I, my lords; make no doubt of it:

I'll play the murderer, I warrant you;

For I already have conceited that.   130

   BALTHAZAR. And what shall I?

   HIERONIMO. Great Soliman, the Turkish emperor.

   LORENZO. And I?

   HIERONIMO   Erastus, the knight of Rhodes.

   BEL-IMPERIA. And I?

   HIERONIMO.   Perseda, chaste and resolute.

And here, my lords, are several abstracts drawn,   135

For each of you to note your parts,

And act it, as occasion's offered you.

You must provide a Turkish cap,

A black mustachio and a falchion; *Gives a paper to* BALTHAZAR.

You with a cross, like to a knight of Rhodes;   140

                    Gives another to LORENZO.

And, madam, you must attire yourself

                  He giveth BEL-IMPERIA *another.*

Like Phoebe, Flora, or the huntress [Dian],

Which to your discretion shall seem best.

And as for me, my lords, I'll look to one,

And, with the ransom that the viceroy sent,   145

So furnish and perform this tragedy,

As all the world shall say, Hieronimo

Was liberal in gracing of it so.

BALTHAZAR. Hieronimo, methinks a comedy were better.

HIERONIMO. A comedy? 150
Fie! comedies are fit for common wits;
But to present a kingly troop withal,
Give me a stately-written tragedy;
Tragoedia cothurnata[1], fitting kings,
Containing matter, and not common things. 155
My lords, all this must be performed,
As fitting for the first night's revelling.
The Italian tragedians were so sharp of wit,
That in one hour's meditation
They would perform anything in action. 160

LORENZO. And well it may; for I have seen the like
In Paris 'mongst the French tragedians.

HIERONIMO. In Paris? mass! And well remembered!
There's one thing more that rests for us to do.

BALTHAZAR. What's that, Hieronimo? Forget not anything. 165

HIERONIMO. Each one of us
Must act his part in unknown languages,
That it may breed the more variety:
As you, my lord, in Latin, I in Greek,
You in Italian; and for because I know 170
That Bel-imperia hath practiced the French,
In courtly French shall all her phrases be.

BEL-IMPERIA. You mean to try my cunning then, Hieronimo?

BALTHAZAR. But this will be a mere confusion
And hardly shall we all be understood. 175

HIERONIMO. It must be so; for the conclusion
Shall prove the invention and all was good;
And I myself in an oration,
And with a strange and wondrous show besides,

[1] Dignified, impressive. From *cothurnis*, the high shoe worn by tragic actors.

That I will have there behind a curtain, 180
Assure yourself, shall make the matter known;
And all shall be concluded in one scene,
For there's no pleasure ta'en in tediousness.

BALTHAZAR. How like you this?

LORENZO.   Why, thus my lord:
We must resolve to soothe his humors up. 185

BALTHAZAR. On then, Hieronimo; farewell till soon.

HIERONIMO. You'll ply this gear?

LORENZO.   I warrant you.

Exeunt all but HIERONIMO.

HIERONIMO.   Why so!
Now shall I see the fall of Babylon,
Wrought by the heavens in this confusion.
And if the world like not this tragedy, 190
Hard is the hap of old Hieronimo.   *Exit.*

[Scene II. HIERONIMO's *garden*].

Enter ISABELLA *with a weapon.*

ISABELLA. Tell me no more!—O monstrous homicides!
Since neither piety or pity moves
The king to justice or compassion,
I will revenge myself upon this place,
Where thus they murdered my beloved son.

She cuts down the arbor.

Down with these branches and these loathsome boughs
Of this unfortunate and fatal pine!
Down with them, Isabella; rent them up,
And burn the roots from whence the rest is sprung!
I will not leave a root, a stalk, a tree, 10
A bough, a branch, a blossom, nor a leaf,

No, not an herb within this garden-plot,—
Accursed complot[1] of my misery!
Fruitless for ever may this garden be,
Barren the earth, and blissless whosoever   15
Imagines not to keep it unmanured[2]!
An eastern wind, commixed with noisome airs,
Shall blast the plants and the young saplings;
The earth with serpents shall be pestered,
And passengers, for fear to be infect,   20
Shall stand aloof, and, looking at it, tell:
"There, murdered, died the son of Isabel."
Ay, here he died, and here I him embrace;
See, where his ghost solicits with his wounds
Revenge on her that should revenge his death.   25
Hieronimo, make haste to see thy son:
For sorrow and despair hath cited me
To hear Horatio plead with Rhadamanth.
Make haste, Hieronimo, to hold excused[3]
Thy negligence in pursuit of their deaths   30
Whose hateful wrath bereaved him of his breath.
Ah, nay, thou dost delay their deaths,
Forgives the murderers of thy noble son,
And none but I bestir me—to no end!
And as I curse this tree from further fruit,   35
So shall my womb be cursed for his sake;
And with this weapon will I wound the breast,
The hapless breast, that gave Horatio suck. *She stabs herself*

---

[1] Accomplice.   [2] Untilled.   [3] Find excuse for.

[Scene III. *The* DUKE'S *Castle.*]

Enter HIERONIMO; *he knocks up the curtain. Enter the*
DUKE OF CASTILE.

CASTILE. How now, Hieronimo, where's your fellows,
That you take all this pain?
HIERONIMO. O sir, it is for the author's credit,
To look that all things may go well.
But, good my lord, let me entreat your grace,   5
To give the king the copy of the play:
This is the argument of what we show.
CASTILE. I will, Hieronimo.
HIERONIMO. One thing more, my good lord.
CASTILE. What's that?
HIERONIMO.   Let me entreat your grace   10
That, when the train are passed into the gallery,
You would vouchsafe to throw me down the key.
CASTILE. I will, Hieronimo.   *Exit* CASTILE.
HIERONIMO. What, are you ready, Balthazar?
Bring a chair and a cushion for the king.   15

Enter BALTHAZAR, *with a chair.*

Well done, Balthazar! Hang up the title:
Our scene is Rhodes. What, is your beard on?
BALTHAZAR. Half on; the other is in my hand.
HIERONIMO. Despatch for shame; are you so long?

Exit BALTHAZAR.

Bethink thyself, Hieronimo,   20
Recall thy wits, recount thy former wrongs
Thou hast received by murder of thy son,
And lastly, not least, how Isabel,
Once his mother and thy dearest wife,

All woe-begone for him, hath slain herself. 25
Behoves thee then, Hieronimo, to be revenged!
The plot is laid of dire revenge.
On, then, Hieronimo, pursue revenge.
For nothing wants but acting of revenge! *Exit* HIERONIMO.

Enter Spanish KING, VICEROY, *the* DUKE *of* CASTILE, *and their train*
[*to the gallery*].

KING. Now, Viceroy, shall we see the tragedy 30
Of Soliman, the Turkish emperor,
Performed of pleasure by your son the prince,
My nephew Don Lorenzo, and my niece.
VICEROY. Who? Bel-imperia?
KING.   Ay, and Hieronimo, our marshal,
At whose request they deign to do't themselves. 35
These be our pastimes in the court of Spain.
Here, brother, you shall be the bookkeeper:
This is the argument of that they show. *He giveth him a book.*

Gentlemen, this play of HIERONIMO, *in sundry languages, was
thought good to be set down in English, more largely, for the* 40
easier understanding to every public reader.

Enter BALTHAZAR, BEL-IMPERIA, *and* HIERONIMO.

BALTHAZAR. *Bashaw, that Rhodes is ours, yield heavens the honor,
And holy Mahomet, our sacred prophet!
And be thou graced with every excellence
That Soliman can give, or thou desire.* 45
*But thy desert in conquering Rhodes is less
Than in reserving this fair Christian nymph,
Perseda, blissful lamp of excellence,
Whose eyes compel, like powerful adamant,
The warlike heart of Soliman to wait.* 50

KING. See, Viceroy, that is Balthazar, your son,
That represents the emperor Soliman:
How well he acts his amorous passion!

VICEROY. Ay, Bel-imperia hath taught him that.

CASTILE. That's because his mind runs all on Bel-imperia. 55

HIERONIMO. *Whatever joy earth yields, betide your majesty.*

BALTHAZAR. *Earth yields no joy without Perseda's love.*

HIERONIMO. *Let then Perseda on your grace attend.*

BALTHAZAR. *She shall not wait on me, but I on her:*
Drawn by the influence of her lights[1]*, I yield.* 60
But let my friend, the Rhodian knight, come forth,
Erasto, dearer than my life to me,
That he may see Perseda, my beloved.

Enter ERASTO.

KING. Here comes Lorenzo: look upon the plot,
And tell me, brother, what part plays he? 65

BEL-IMPERIA. *Ah, my Erasto, welcome to Perseda.*

LORENZO. *Thrice happy is Erasto that thou livest;*
Rhodes' loss is nothing to Erasto's joy;
Sith his Perseda lives, his life survives.

BALTHAZAR. *Ah, bashaw, here is love between Erasto* 70
And fair Perseda sovereign of my soul.

HIERONIMO. *Remove Erasto, mighty Soliman,*
And then Perseda will be quickly won.

BALTHAZAR. *Erasto is my friend; and while he lives,*
Perseda never will remove her love. 75

HIERONIMO. *Let not Erasto live to grieve great Soliman.*

BALTHAZAR. *Dear is Erasto in our princely eye.*

HIERONIMO. *But if he be your rival, let him die.*

BALTHAZAR. *Why, let him die—so love commandeth me.*

[1] Eyes.

Yet grieve I that Erasto should so die.   80
  HIERONIMO. *Erasto, Soliman saluteth thee,*
And lets thee wit by me his highness' will,
Which is, thou shouldst be thus employed.   Stabs him.
  BEL–IMPERIA.   *Ay me!*
Erasto! See, Soliman, Erasto's slain!
  BALTHAZAR. *Yet liveth Soliman to comfort thee.*   85
Fair queen of beauty, let not favor die,
But with a gracious eye behold his grief
That with Perseda's beauty is increased,
If by Perseda his grief be not released.
  BEL–IMPERIA. *Tyrant, desist soliciting vain suits;*   90
Relentless are mine ears to thy laments,
As thy butcher is pitiless and base,
Which seized on my Erasto, harmless knight.
Yet by thy power thou thinkest to command,
And to thy power Perseda doth obey;   95
But, were she able, thus she would revenge
Thy treacheries on thee, ignoble prince: Stabs him.
And on herself she would be thus revenged.   Stabs herself.
  KING. Well said!—Old marshal, this was bravely done!
  HIERONIMO. But Bel-imperia plays Perseda well!   100
  VICEROY. Were this in earnest, Bel-imperia,
You would be better to my son than so.
  KING. But now what follows for Hieronimo?
  HIERONIMO. Marry, this follows for Hieronimo:
Here break we off our sundry languages,   105
And thus conclude I in our vulgar tongue.
Haply you think—but bootless are your thoughts—
That this is fabulously counterfeit,
And that we do as all tragedians do,
To die to-day, for fashioning our scene,   110
The death of Ajax or some Roman peer,

And in a minute starting up again,
Revive to please to-morrow's audience.
No, princes; know I am Hieronimo,
The hopeless father of a hapless son,   115
Whose tongue is tuned to tell his latest tale,
Not to excuse gross errors in the play.
I see, your looks urge instance of these words;
Behold the reason urging me to this!   *Shows his dead son.*
See here my show, look on this spectacle!   120
Here lay my hope, and here my hope hath end;
Here lay my heart, and here my heart was slain;
Here lay my treasure, here my treasure lost;
Here lay my bliss, and here my bliss bereft;
But hope, heart, treasure, joy, and bliss,   125
All fled, failed, died, yea, all decayed with this.
From forth these wounds came breath that gave me life;
They murdered me that made these fatal marks.
The cause was love, whence grew this mortal hate;
The hate, Lorenzo and young Balthazar;   130
The love, my son to Bel-imperia.
But night, the coverer of accursed crimes,
With pitchy silence hushed these traitors' harms,
And lent them leave, for they had sorted[1] leisure
To take advantage in my garden-plot   135
Upon my son, my dear Horatio.
There merciless they butchered up my boy,
In black, dark night, to pale, dim, cruel death.
He shrieks; I heard—and yet, methinks, I hear—
His dismal outcry echo in the air.   140
With soonest speed I hasted to the noise,
Where hanging on a tree I found my son,

[1] Chosen.

Through-girt[1] with wounds, and slaught'red as you see.
And grieved I, think you, at this spectacle?
Speak, Portuguese, whose loss resembles mine: 145
If thou canst weep upon thy Balthazar,
'Tis like I wailed for my Horatio.
And you, my lord, whose reconciled son
Marched in a net, and thought himself unseen,
And rated me for brainsick lunacy,   150
With "God amend that mad Hieronimo!"—
How can you brook our play's catastrophe?
And here behold this bloody handkercher,
Which at Horatio's death I weeping dipped
Within the river of his bleeding wounds: 155
It as propitious, see, I have reserved,
And never hath it left my bloody heart,
Soliciting remembrance of my vow
With these, O, these accursed murderers!
Which now performed, my heart is satisfied.   160
And to this end the bashaw I became
That might revenge me on Lorenzo's life,
Who therefore was appointed to the part,
And was to represent the knight of Rhodes,
That I might kill him more conveniently.   165
So, Viceroy, was this Balthazar, thy son,
That Soliman which Bel-imperia,
In person of Perseda, murdered;
Solely appointed to that tragic part
That she might slay him that offended her.   170
Poor Bel-imperia missed her part in this:
For though the story saith she should have died,
Yet I of kindness, and of care to her,

---

[1] Pierced.

Did otherwise determine of her end;
But love of him whom they did hate too much   175
Did urge her resolution to be such.
And, princes, now behold Hieronimo,
Author and actor in this tragedy,
Bearing his latest fortune in his fist;
And will as resolute conclude his part,   180
As any of the actors gone before.
And, gentles, thus I end my play;
Urge no more words; I have no more to say.

He runs to hang himself.

KING. O hearken, Viceroy! Hold, Hieronimo!
Brother, my nephew and thy son are slain!   185
    VICEROY. We are betrayed; my Balthazar is slain!
Break ope the doors; run, save Hieronimo.

They break in and hold HIERONIMO.

Hieronimo, do but inform the king of these events;
Upon mine honor, thou shalt have no harm.
    HIERONIMO. Viceroy, I will not trust thee with my life,   190
Which I this day have offered to my son.
Accursed wretch!
Why stayst thou him that was resolved to die?
    KING. Speak, traitor! Damned, bloody murderer, speak!
For now I have thee, I will make thee speak.   195
Why hast thou done this undeserving deed?
    VICEROY. Why hast thou murdered my Balthazar?
    CASTILE. Why hast thou butchered both my children thus?
    HIERONIMO. O, good words!
As dear to me was my Horatio   200
As yours, or yours, or yours, my lord, to you.
My guiltless son was by Lorenzo slain,

And by Lorenzo and that Balthazar
Am I at last revenged thoroughly,
Upon whose souls may heavens be yet avenged   205
With greater far than these afflictions.

CASTILE. But who were thy confederates in this?

VICEROY. That was thy daughter Bel-imperia;
For by her hand my Balthazar was slain:
I saw her stab him.

KING.   Why speakst thou not?   210

HIERONIMO. What lesser liberty can kings afford
Than harmless silence? Then afford it me.
Sufficeth, I may not, nor I will not tell thee.

KING. Fetch forth the tortures; traitor as thou art,
I'll make thee tell.

HIERONIMO.   Indeed,   215
Thou mayst torment me as his wretched son
Hath done in murd'ring my Horatio;
But never shalt thou force me to reveal
The thing which I have vowed inviolate.
And therefore, in despite of all thy threats,   220
Pleased with their deaths, and eased with their revenge,
First take my tongue, and afterwards my heart.

[1][HIERONIMO. *But are you sure they are dead?*

CASTILE.   *Ay, slave, too sure.*

HIERONIMO. *What, and yours too?*

VICEROY. *Ay, all are dead; not one of them survive.*   225

HIERONIMO. *Nay, then I care not; come, and we shall be friends;*
Let us lay our heads together:
See, here's a goodly noose will hold them all.

VICEROY. *O damned devil, how secure[2] he is!*

---

[1] This is the final passage of additions (italic lines 223-272), replacing
lines 199-222.   [2] Self-assured.

HIERONIMO. *Secure? Why, dost thou wonder at it?*   230
I tell thee, Viceroy, this day I have seen revenge,
And in that sight am grown a prouder monarch,
Than ever sat under the crown of Spain.
Had I as many lives as there be stars,
As many heavens to go to, as those lives,   235
I'd give them all, ay, and my soul to boot,
But I would see thee ride in this red pool.

   CASTILE. *But who were thy confederates in this?*

   VICEROY. *That was thy daughter Bel-imperia;*
For by her hand my Balthazar was slain: 240
I saw her stab him.

   HIERONIMO. *O, good words!*
As dear to me was my Horatio,
As yours, or yours, or yours, my lord, to you.
My guiltless son was by Lorenzo slain,   245
And by Lorenzo and that Balthazar
Am I at last revenged thoroughly,
Upon whose souls may heavens be yet avenged
With greater far than these afflictions.
Methinks, since I grew inward with revenge,   250
I cannot look with scorn enough on death.

   KING. *What, dost thou mock us, slave? Bring tortures forth.*

   HIERONIMO. *Do, do, do; and meantime I'll torture you.*
You had a son, as I take it; and your son
Should ha' been married to your daughter.   255
Ha, was it not so?—You had a son too,
He was my liege's nephew; he was proud
And politic; had he lived, he might ha' come
To wear the crown of Spain, I think 'twas so.
'Twas I that killed him; look you, this same hand.   260
'Twas it that stabbed his heart—do ye see? this hand—

For one Horatio, if you ever knew him: a youth,
One that they hanged up in his father's garden;
One that did force your valiant son to yield,
While your more valiant son did take him prisoner. 265
 VICEROY. *Be deaf, my senses; I can hear no more.*
 KING. *Fall, heaven, and cover us with thy sad ruins.*
 CASTILE. *Roll all the world within thy pitchy cloud.*
 HIERONIMO. *Now do I applaud what I have acted.*
Nunc iners cadat manus![1] 270
Now to express the rupture of my part,—
First take my tongue, and afterward my heart.]

   He bites out his tongue.

 KING. O monstrous resolution of a wretch!
See, Viceroy, he hath bitten forth his tongue,
Rather than to reveal what we required. 275
 CASTILE. Yet can he write.
 KING. And if in this he satisfy us not,
We will devise th' extremest kind of death
That ever was invented for a wretch.

  Then he make signs for a knife to mend his pen.

 CASTILE. O, he would have a knife to mend his pen. 280
Here, and advise thee that thou write the troth.—
Look to my brother! Save Hieronimo!

  He with a knife stabs the DUKE *and himself.*

 KING. What age hath ever heard such monstrous deeds?
My brother, and the whole succeeding hope
That Spain expected after my decease! 285

---

[1] Now may my hand fall idle.

Go, bear his body hence, that we may mourn
The loss of our beloved brother's death,
That he may be entombed whate'er befall.
I am the next, the nearest, last of all.

   VICEROY. And thou, Don Pedro, do the like for us: 290
Take up our hapless son, untimely slain;
Set me with him, and he with woeful me,
Upon the main-mast of a ship unmanned,
And let the wind and tide haul me along
To Scylla's barking and untamed gulf,   295
Or to the loathsome pool of Acheron,
To weep my want for my sweet Balthazar:
Spain hath no refuge for a Portingale.

The trumpets sound a dead march, the KING OF SPAIN *mourning
after his brother's body, and the* KING OF PORTINGAL *bearing
the body of his son.*

[Chorus.]

Enter GHOST *and* REVENGE.

   GHOST. Ay, now my hopes have end in their effects,
When blood and sorrow finish my desires: 300
Horatio murdered in his father's bower;
Vile Serberine by Pedringano slain;
False Pedringano hanged by quaint device;
Fair Isabella by herself misdone;
Prince Balthazar by Bel-imperia stabbed;   305
The Duke of Castile and his wicked son
Both done to death by old Hieronimo;
My Bel-imperia fallen as Dido fell,
And good Hieronimo slain by himself:

Ay, these were spectacles to please my soul! 310
Now will I beg at lovely Proserpine
That, by the virtue of her princely doom,
I may consort my[1] friends in pleasing sort,
And on my foes work just and sharp revenge.
I'll lead my friend Horatio through those fields, 315
Where never-dying wars are still inured[2];
I'll lead fair Isabella to that train,
Where pity weeps, but never feeleth pain;
I'll lead my Bel-imperia to those joys,
That vestal virgins and fair queens possess; 320
I'll lead Hieronimo where Orpheus plays,
Adding sweet pleasure to eternal days.
But say, Revenge, for thou must help, or none,
Against the rest how shall my hate be shown?
    REVENGE. This hand shall hale them down to deepest hell,
Where none but Furies, bugs[3], and tortures dwell. 326
    GHOST. Then, sweet Revenge, do this at my request:
Let me be judge, and doom them to unrest.
Let loose poor Tityus from the vulture's gripe,
And let Don Cyprian supply his room; 330
Place Don Lorenzo on Ixion's wheel,
And let the lover's endless pains surcease
(Juno forgets old wrath, and grants him ease);
Hang Balthazar about Chimaera's neck,
And let him there bewail his bloody love, 335
Repining at our joys that are above;
Let Serberine go roll the fatal stone,
And take from Sisyphus his endless moan;
False Pedringano, for his treachery,
Let him be dragged through boiling Acheron, 340

---

[1] Select.   [2] Carried on.   [3] Bugbears.

And there live, dying still in endless flames,
Blaspheming gods and all their holy names.

    REVENGE. Then haste we down to meet thy friends and foes:
To place thy friends in ease, the rest in woes;
For here though death hath end their misery,   345
I'll there begin their endless tragedy.   *Exeunt.*

THE TRAGICAL HISTORY OF*
DR. FAUSTUS

CHRISTOPHER MARLOWE

DRAMATIS PERSONÆ

THE POPE

CARDINAL OF LORRAIN

EMPEROR OF GERMANY

DUKE OF VANHOLT

FAUSTUS

VALDES *and* CORNELIUS, *Friends to Faustus*

WAGNER, *Servant to Faustus*

CLOWN

ROBIN

RALPH

VINTNER

HORSE-COURSER

KNIGHT

OLD MAN

SCHOLARS, FRIARS, *and* ATTENDANTS

DUCHESS OF VANHOLT

LUCIFER

BELZEBUB

MEPHISTOPHILIS

GOOD ANGEL

EVIL ANGEL

THE SEVEN DEADLY SINS

DEVILS

SPIRITS *in the shape of Alexander the Great, of his Paramour, and of Helen of Troy*

CHORUS

Enter CHORUS

CHORUS. Not marching now in fields of Thrasimene,
Where Mars did mate[1] the Carthaginians;
Nor sporting in the dalliance of love,
In courts of kings where state is overturned;

* C. 1589.
[1] Defeat (?). Possibly, since the Carthaginians won, join with.

Nor in the pomp of proud audacious deeds,   5
Intends our Muse to vaunt his heavenly verse:
Only this, gentlemen—we must perform
The form of Faustus' fortunes, good or bad.
To patient judgments we appeal our plaud[1],
And speak for Faustus in his infancy.   10
Now is he born, his parents base of stock,
In Germany, within a town called Rhodes;
Of riper years to Wittenberg he went,
Whereas his kinsmen chiefly brought him up.
So soon he profits in divinity[2],   15
The fruitful plot of scholarism graced,
That shortly he was graced with doctor's name,
Excelling all whose sweet delight disputes
In heavenly matters of theology;
Till swollen with cunning, of a self-conceit[3],   20
His waxen wings did mount above his reach,
And, melting, Heavens conspired his overthrow;
For, falling to a devilish exercise,
And glutted now with learning's golden gifts,
He surfeits upon cursed necromancy.   25
Nothing so sweet as magic is to him,
Which he prefers before his chiefest bliss.
And this the man that in his study sits!   *Exit.*

[Scene I.]

Enter FAUSTUS *in his study.*

FAUSTUS. Settle my studies, Faustus, and begin
To sound the depth of that thou wilt profess[4];
Having commenced,[5] be a divine in show.

[1] Ask applause.   [2] Theology.   [3] Complacently swollen with knowledge.
[4] Teach.   [5] Taken a degree.

Yet level[1] at the end of every art,
And live and die in Aristotle's works.   5
Sweet Analytics[2], 'tis thou hast ravished me,
Bene disserere est finis logices.
Is to dispute well logic's chiefest end?
Affords this art no greater miracle?
Then read no more, thou hast attained the end;   10
A greater subject fitteth Faustus' wit.
Bid ὂν καὶ μὴ ὂν[3] farewell; Galen come,
Seeing *Ubi desinit philosophus, ibi incipit medicus;*[4]
Be a physician, Faustus, heap up gold,
And be eternized for some wondrous cure.   15
Summum bonum medicinæ sanitas,
"The end of physic is our body's health."
Why, Faustus, hast thou not attained that end?
Is not thy common talk sound Aphorisms[5]?
Are not thy bills[6] hung up as monuments,   20
Whereby whole cities have escaped the plague,
And thousand desperate maladies been eased?
Yet art thou still but Faustus and a man.
Wouldst thou make men to live eternally,
Or, being dead, raise them to life again?   25
Then this profession were to be esteemed.
Physic, farewell. Where is Justinian?   [*Reads.*]
Si una eademque res legatur duobus, alter rem, alter valorem rei, &c.[7]
A pretty case of paltry legacies!   [*Reads.*]
Exhæreditare filium non potest pater nisi, &c.[8]   30
Such is the subject of the Institute

---

[1] Aim.   [2] Logic.   [3] Being and not being.   [4] Where the
philosopher stops, there the physician begins.   [5] Medical rules.
[6] Prescriptions.   [7] If one and the same thing is willed to two people,
one takes the thing, the other the value of it.   [8] The father cannot
disinherit a son, unless, etc.

And universal body of the law.
His[1] study fits a mercenary drudge,
Who aims at nothing but external trash;
Too servile and illiberal for me.   35
When all is done, divinity is best;
Jerome's Bible[2], Faustus, view it well.   [*Reads.*]
Stipendium peccati mors est.[3] Ha! *Stipendium, &c.*
"The reward of sin is death." That's hard.   [*Reads.*]
Si peccasse negamus, fallimur, et nulla est in nobis veritas.[4]   40
"If we say that we have no sin we deceive ourselves, and there's
no truth in us." Why then, belike we must sin and so conse-
quently die.
Ay, we must die an everlasting death.
What doctrine call you this, *Che sera sera,*   45
"What will be shall be?" Divinity, adieu!
These metaphysics of magicians
And necromantic books are heavenly;
Lines, circles, scenes, letters, and characters,
Ay, these are those that Faustus most desires.   50
O what a world of profit and delight,
Of power, of honor, of omnipotence
Is promised to the studious artisan!
All things that move between the quiet poles
Shall be at my command. Emperors and kings   55
Are but obeyed in their several provinces,
Nor can they raise the wind or rend the clouds;
But his dominion that exceeds[5] in this
Stretcheth as far as doth the mind of man.
A sound magician is a mighty god: 60
Here, Faustus, try thy brains to gain a deity.
Wagner!

---

[1] Its.   [2] The Vulgate (Latin translation).   [3] Romans 6:23
[4] I John 1:8.   [5] Excels.

Enter WAGNER.

Commend me to my dearest friends,
The German Valdes and Cornelius;
Request them earnestly to visit me.
　WAGNER. I will, sir.　　　　　　　　　　　　*Exit.* 65
　FAUSTUS. Their conference will be a greater help to me
Than all my labors, plod I ne'er so fast.

Enter GOOD ANGEL *and* EVIL ANGEL.

　GOOD ANGEL. O Faustus! lay that damned book aside,
And gaze not upon it lest it tempt thy soul,
And heap God's heavy wrath upon thy head.　　　　70
Read, read the Scriptures; that is blasphemy.
　EVIL ANGEL. Go forward, Faustus, in that famous art,
Wherein all Nature's treasure is contained;
Be thou on earth as Jove is in the sky,
Lord and commander of these elements. *Exeunt* [ANGELS]. 75
　FAUSTUS. How am I glutted with conceit[1] of this!
Shall I make spirits fetch me what I please,
Resolve me of all ambiguities,
Perform what desperate enterprise I will?
I'll have them fly to India for gold,　　　　　　80
Ransack the ocean for orient pearl,
And search all corners of the new-found world
For pleasant fruits and princely delicates;
I'll have them read me strange philosophy
And tell the secrets of all foreign kings;　　　　85
I'll have them wall all Germany with brass,
And make swift Rhine circle fair Wittenberg;
I'll have them fill the public schools with [silk],
Wherewith the students shall be bravely clad;

---

[1] "This idea."

I'll levy soldiers with the coin they bring,   90
And chase the Prince of Parma from our land,[1]
And reign sole king of all the provinces;
Yea, stranger engines for the brunt of war
Than was the fiery keel[2] at Antwerp's bridge,
I'll make my servile spirits to invent.   95
Come, German Valdes and Cornelius,
And make me blest with your sage conference.

Enter VALDES *and* CORNELIUS.

Valdes, sweet Valdes, and Cornelius,
Know that your words have won me at the last
To practice magic and concealed arts—   100
Yet not your words only, but mine own fantasy,
That will receive no object[3]; for my head
But ruminates on necromantic skill.
Philosophy is odious and obscure,
Both law and physic are for petty wits;   105
Divinity is basest of the three,
Unpleasant, harsh, contemptible, and vile;
'Tis magic, magic, that hath ravished me.
Then, gentle friends, aid me in this attempt;
And I that have with concise syllogisms   110
Gravelled[4] the pastors of the German church,
And made the flow'ring pride of Wittenberg
Swarm to my problems[5], as the infernal spirits
On sweet Musæus, when he came to hell,
Will be as cunning as Agrippa[6] was,   115
Whose shadows[7] made all Europe honor him.

---

[1] The Prince ruled the Netherlands for Spain (1579-1592).   [2] A fire-
ship used by the Dutch (1585).   [3] Stop at nothing else.   [4] Perplexed.
[5] Lectures.   [6] Cornelius Agrippa, 1486-1535, physician, magician, etc.
[7] Shades (raised from the dead).

VALDES. Faustus, these books, thy wit, and our experience
Shall make all nations to canonize us.
As Indian Moors[1] obey their Spanish lords,
So shall the subjects of every element   120
Be always serviceable to us three;
Like lions shall they guard us when we please;
Like Almain rutters[2] with their horsemen's staves,
Or Lapland giants, trotting by our sides;
Sometimes like women or unwedded maids,   125
Shadowing more beauty in their airy brows
Than have the white breasts of the queen of love;
From Venice shall they drag huge argosies,
And from America the golden fleece
That yearly stuffs old Philip's treasury;   130
If learned Faustus will be resolute.

FAUSTUS. Valdes, as resolute am I in this
As thou to live; therefore object it not.

CORNELIUS. The miracles that magic will perform
Will make thee vow to study nothing else.   135
He that is grounded in astrology,
Enriched with tongues, well seen[3] in minerals,
Hath all the principles magic doth require.
Then doubt not, Faustus, but to be renowned,
And more frequented for this mystery   140
Than heretofore the Delphian Oracle.
The spirits tell me they can dry the sea,
And fetch the treasure of all foreign wracks,
Ay, all the wealth that our forefathers hid
Within the massy entrails of the earth;   145
Then tell me, Faustus, what shall we three want?

FAUSTUS. Nothing, Cornelius! O this cheers my soul!

---

[1] American Indians.   [2] German knights.   [3] Skilled.

Come show me some demonstrations magical,
That I may conjure in some lusty grove,
And have these joys in full possession. 150

VALDES. Then haste thee to some solitary grove,
And bear wise Bacon's[1] and Albanus's[2] works,
The Hebrew Psalter and New Testament;
And whatsoever else is requisite
We will inform thee ere our conference cease. 155

CORNELIUS. Valdes, first let him know the words of art;
And then, all other ceremonies learned,
Faustus may try his cunning by himself.

VALDES. First I'll instruct thee in the rudiments,
And then wilt thou be perfecter than I. 160

FAUSTUS. Then come and dine with me, and after meat,
We'll canvass every quiddity[3] thereof;
For ere I sleep I'll try what I can do:
This night I'll conjure though I die therefor. *Exeunt.*

[Scene II. *Before* FAUSTUS' *House.*]
Enter TWO SCHOLARS.

FIRST SCHOLAR. I wonder what's become of Faustus that was
wont to make our schools ring with *sic probo*[1]?

SECOND SCHOLAR. That shall we know, for see here comes
his boy.

Enter WAGNER.

FIRST SCHOLAR. How now, sirrah! Where's thy master? 5

WAGNER. God in heaven knows!

SECOND SCHOLAR. Why, dost not thou know?

WAGNER. Yes, I know. But that follows not.

---

[1] (line 152) Roger Bacon (1214-1294), English philosopher and scientist
(character in Greene's *Friar Bacon and Friar Bungay*).   [2] Pietro d'Abano,
alchemist of thirteenth century (?).   [3] Fine point.

---

[1] (line 2) Thus I prove.

FIRST SCHOLAR. Go to, sirrah! Leave your jesting, and tell us
where he is.　　　　　　　　　　　　　　　　　　　　　　10

WAGNER. That follows not necessary by force of argument,
that you, being licentiate, should stand upon 't; therefore,
acknowledge your error and be attentive.

SECOND SCHOLAR. Why, didst thou not say thou knew'st?

WAGNER. Have you any witness on 't?　　　　　　　　15

FIRST SCHOLAR. Yes, sirrah, I heard you.

WAGNER. Ask my fellow if I be a thief.

SECOND SCHOLAR. Well, you will not tell us?

WAGNER. Yes, sir. I will tell you; yet if you were not dunces,
you would never ask me such a question; for is not he *corpus*　20
naturale[1]? and is not that *mobile*?[1] Then wherefore should you
ask me such a question? But that I am by nature phlegmatic,
slow to wrath and prone to lechery (to love, I would say), it
were not for you to come within forty foot of the place of
execution, although I do not doubt to see you both hanged　25
the next sessions. Thus having triumphed over you, I will set
my countenance like a precisian[2], and begin to speak thus:—
Truly, my dear brethren, my master is within at dinner, with
Valdes and Cornelius, as this wine, if it could speak, would
inform your worships; and so the Lord bless you, preserve　30
you, and keep you, my dear brethren, my dear brethren. *Exit.*

FIRST SCHOLAR. Nay, then, I fear he has fallen into that
damned art, for which they two are infamous through the
world.

SECOND SCHOLAR. Were he a stranger, and not allied to　35
me, yet should I grieve for him. But come, let us go and inform
the Rector[3], and see if he by his grave counsel can reclaim him.

FIRST SCHOLAR. O, I fear me nothing can reclaim him.

SECOND SCHOLAR. Yet let us try what we can do. *Exeunt.*

---

[1] Physical body, movable.　　[2] Puritan.　　[3] University head.

[Scene III. *A grove.*]

Enter FAUSTUS *to conjure.*

FAUSTUS. Now that the gloomy shadow of the earth
Longing to view Orion's drizzling look,
Leaps from th' antarctic world unto the sky,
And dims the welkin with her pitchy breath,
Faustus, begin thine incantations,   5
And try if devils will obey thy hest,
Seeing thou hast prayed and sacrificed to them.
Within this circle is Jehovah's name,
Forward and backward anagrammatized,
The breviated names of holy saints,   10
Figures of every adjunct[1] to the Heavens,
And characters of signs and erring stars[2],
By which the spirits are enforced to rise.
Then fear not, Faustus, but be resolute,
And try the uttermost magic can perform.   15

Sint mihi Dei Acherontis propitii! Valeat numen triplex Jehovae!
Ignei, aerii, aquatani spiritus, salvete! Orientis princeps Belzebub,
inferni ardentis monarcha, et Demogorgon, propitiamus vos, ut ap-
pareat et surgat Mephistophilis. Quid tu moraris? Per Jehovam,
Gehennam, et consecratum aquam quam nunc spargo, signumque   20
crucis quod nunc facio, et per vota nostra, ipse nunc surgat nobis
dicatus Mephistophilis![3]

[1] Star.   [2] Planets.   [3] May the Gods of Acheron be propitious to
me. May the triple authority of Jehovah succeed. Spirits of fire, air, water,
hail! Belzebub, Prince of the East, ruler of the burning lower region, and
Demogorgon, we propitiate you, that Mephistophilis may appear and rise.
Why do you delay? By Jehovah, Gehenna, and the holy water which I
now sprinkle, and the sign of the cross which I now make, and by our
prayers, may Mephistophilis himself, summoned, now arise for us.

Enter [MEPHISTOPHILIS] *a* DEVIL.

I charge thee to return and change thy shape;
Thou art too ugly to attend on me.
Go, and return an old Franciscan friar;   25
That holy shape becomes a devil best.   *Exit* DEVIL.
I see there's virtue in my heavenly words;
Who would not be proficient in this art?
How pliant is this Mephistophilis,
Full of obedience and humility!   30
Such is the force of magic and my spells.
[Now,] Faustus, thou art conjuror laureate,
Thou canst command great Mephistophilis:
Quin regis Mephistophilis fratris imagine.[1]

Re-enter MEPHISTOPHILIS [*like a Franciscan Friar*].

MEPHISTOPHILIS. Now, Faustus, what would'st thou have me
do?   35
FAUSTUS. I charge thee wait upon me whilst I live,
To do whatever Faustus shall command,
Be it to make the moon drop from her sphere,
Or the ocean to overwhelm the world.
MEPHISTOPHILIS. I am a servant to great Lucifer,   40
And may not follow thee without his leave;
No more than he commands must we perform.
FAUSTUS. Did he not charge thee to appear to me?
MEPHISTOPHILIS. No, I came hither of mine own accord.
FAUSTUS. Did not my conjuring speeches raise thee? Speak!   45
MEPHISTOPHILIS. That was the cause, but yet per accident;
For when we hear one rack[2] the name of God,
Abjure the Scriptures and his Savior Christ,

----

[1] For indeed you have power in the image of your brother Mephistophilis.   [2] Torture (i. e., in anagrams).

We fly in hope to get his glorious soul;
Nor will we come, unless he use such means   50
Whereby he is in danger to be damned:
Therefore the shortest cut for conjuring
Is stoutly to abjure the Trinity,
And pray devoutly to the Prince of Hell.

 FAUSTUS. So Faustus hath   55
Already done; and holds this principle,
There is no chief but only Belzebub,
To whom Faustus doth dedicate himself.
This word "damnation" terrifies not him,
For he confounds hell in[1] Elysium;   60
His ghost be with the old philosophers!
But, leaving these vain trifles of men's souls,
Tell me what is that Lucifer thy lord?

 MEPHISTOPHILIS. Arch-regent and commander of all spirits.

 FAUSTUS. Was not that Lucifer an angel once?   65

 MEPHISTOPHILIS. Yes, Faustus, and most dearly loved of God.

 FAUSTUS. How comes it then that he is prince of devils?

 MEPHISTOPHILIS. O, by aspiring pride and insolence;
For which God threw him from the face of Heaven.

 FAUSTUS. And what are you that you live with Lucifer?   70

 MEPHISTOPHILIS. Unhappy spirits that fell with Lucifer,
Conspired against our God with Lucifer,
And are for ever damned with Lucifer.

 FAUSTUS. Where are you damned?

 MEPHISTOPHILIS. In hell.   75

 FAUSTUS. How comes it then that thou art out of hell?

 MEPHISTOPHILIS. Why this is hell, nor am I out of it.
Think'st thou that I who saw the face of God,
And tasted the eternal joys of Heaven,

---

[1] Does not differentiate.

Am not tormented with ten thousand hells,   80
In being deprived of everlasting bliss?
O Faustus, leave these frivolous demands,
Which strike a terror to my fainting soul.

  FAUSTUS. What, is great Mephistophilis so passionate
For being deprived of the joys of Heaven?   85
Learn thou of Faustus manly fortitude,
And scorn those joys thou never shalt possess.
Go bear these tidings to great Lucifer:
Seeing Faustus hath incurred eternal death
By desperate thoughts against Jove's deity,   90
Say he surrenders up to him his soul,
So he will spare him four and twenty years,
Letting him live in all voluptuousness;
Having thee ever to attend on me;
To give me whatsoever I shall ask,   95
To tell me whatsoever I demand,
To slay mine enemies, and aid my friends,
And always be obedient to my will.
Go and return to mighty Lucifer,
And meet me in my study at midnight,   100
And then resolve[1] me of thy master's mind.

  MEPHISTOPHILIS. I will, Faustus.   *Exit.*

  FAUSTUS. Had I as many souls as there be stars,
I'd give them all for Mephistophilis.
By him I'll be great Emperor of the world,   105
And make a bridge through the moving air,
To pass the ocean with a band of men;
I'll join the hills that bind the Afric shore,
And make that [country] continent to[2] Spain,
And both contributory to my crown.   110

_____

[1] Inform.   [2] Adjoining.

The Emperor shall not live but by my leave,
Nor any potentate of Germany.
Now that I have obtained what I desire,
I'll live in speculation of this art
Till Mephistophilis return again.   *Exit.* 115

[Scene IV. *A street before* FAUSTUS' *House.*]

Enter WAGNER *and the* CLOWN.

WAGNER. Sirrah, boy, come hither.

CLOWN. How, "boy"! Swowns, "boy"! I hope you have seen
many boys with such pickadevaunts[1] as I have. "Boy," quotha!

WAGNER. Tell me, sirrah, hast thou any comings in?

CLOWN. Ay, and goings out too. You may see else.   5

WAGNER. Alas, poor slave! See how poverty jesteth in his
nakedness! The villain is bare and out of service, and so hungry
that I know he would give his soul to the devil for a shoulder
of mutton, though it were blood-raw.

CLOWN. How? My soul to the Devil for a shoulder of   10
mutton, though 't were blood-raw! Not so, good friend. By'r
Lady, I had need have it well roasted and good sauce to it, if
I pay so dear.

WAGNER. Well, wilt thou serve me, and I'll make thee go
like *Qui mihi discipulus*[2]?   15

CLOWN. How, in verse?

WAGNER. No, sirrah; in beaten silk and staves acre[3].

CLOWN. How, how, Knave's acre[4]! Ay, I thought that was
all the land his father left him. Do you hear? I would be sorry
to rob you of your living.   20

WAGNER. Sirrah, I say in stavesacre.

---

[1] Pointed beards.   [2] Who is my pupil (a song).   [3] Larkspur (used
to kill lice).   [4] London street with poor shops.

CLOWN. Oho! Oho! Stavesacre! Why, then, belike if I were
your man I should be full of vermin.

WAGNER. So thou shalt, whether thou beest with me or no.
But, sirrah, leave your jesting, and bind yourself presently 25
unto me for seven years, or I'll turn all the lice about thee into
familiars[1], and they shall tear thee in pieces.

CLOWN. Do you hear, sir? You may save that labor; they are
too familiar with me already. Swowns! they are as bold with
my flesh as if they had paid for my meat and drink.   30

WAGNER. Well, do you hear, sirrah? Hold, take these guilders.

Gives money.

CLOWN. Gridirons! What be they?

WAGNER. Why, French crowns.

CLOWN. Mass, but for the name of French crowns, a man
were as good have as many English counters. And what 35
should I do with these?

WAGNER. Why, now, sirrah, thou art at an hour's warning,
whensoever and wheresoever the Devil shall fetch thee.

CLOWN. No, no. Here, take your gridirons again.

WAGNER. Truly I'll none of them.   40

CLOWN. Truly but you shall.

WAGNER. Bear witness I gave them him.

CLOWN. Bear witness I give them you again.

WAGNER. Well, I will cause two devils presently to fetch thee
away—Baliol and Belcher.   45

CLOWN. Let your Baliol and your Belcher come here, and
I'll knock them, they were never so knocked since they were
devils. Say I should kill one of them, what would folks say?
"Do you see yonder tall fellow in the round slop[2]? —he has
killed the devil." So I should be called Kill-devil all the 50
parish over.

---

[1] Familiar spirits.   [2] Loose breeches

Enter TWO DEVILS; *and the* CLOWN *runs up and down crying.*

WAGNER. Baliol and Belcher! Spirits, away! *Exeunt* DEVILS.

CLOWN. What, are they gone? A vengeance on them, they have vile long nails! There was a he-devil, and a she-devil! I'll tell you how you shall know them: all he-devils has horns, and all she-devils has clifts and cloven feet.   55

WAGNER. Well, sirrah, follow me.

CLOWN. But, do you hear—if I should serve you, would you teach me to raise up Banios and Belcheos?

WAGNER. I will teach thee to turn thyself to anything; to a dog, or a cat, or a mouse, or a rat, or anything.   60

CLOWN. How! a Christian fellow to a dog or a cat, a mouse or a rat! No, no, sir. If you turn me into anything, let it be in the likeness of a little pretty frisky flea, that I may be here and there and everywhere. Oh, I'll tickle the pretty wenches' plackets[1]; I'll be amongst them, i' faith.   65

WAGNER. Well, sirrah, come.

CLOWN. But, do you hear, Wagner?

WAGNER. How!—Baliol and Belcher!

CLOWN. O Lord! I pray, sir, let Banio and Belcher go sleep.

WAGNER. Villain, call me Master Wagner, and let thy   70 left eye be diametarily fixt upon my right heel, with *quasi vestigias nostras insistere*[2].   *Exit.*

CLOWN. God forgive me, he speaks Dutch fustian. Well, I'll follow him, I'll serve him; that's flat.   *Exit.*

[Scene V.]

Enter FAUSTUS *in his Study.*

FAUSTUS. Now, Faustus, must
Thou needs be damned, and canst thou not be saved.
What boots it then to think of God or Heaven?

---

[1] Slits in skirts.   [2] As if to step in our tracks.

Away with such vain fancies, and despair;
Despair in God, and trust in Belzebub.   5
Now go not backward; no, Faustus, be resolute.
Why waverest thou? O, something soundeth in mine ears:
"Abjure this magic, turn to God again!"
Ay, and Faustus will turn to God again.
To God?—He loves thee not.   10
The God thou serv'st is thine own appetite,
Wherein is fixed the love of Belzebub;
To him I'll build an altar and a church,
And offer lukewarm blood of new-born babes.

Enter GOOD ANGEL *and* EVIL [ANGEL].

GOOD ANGEL. Sweet Faustus, leave that execrable art.   15
FAUSTUS. Contrition, prayer, repentance! What of them?
GOOD ANGEL. O, they are means to bring thee unto Heaven.
EVIL ANGEL. Rather illusions, fruits of lunacy,
That makes men foolish that do trust them most.
GOOD ANGEL. Sweet Faustus, think of Heaven, and heavenly
    things.   20
EVIL ANGEL. No, Faustus, think of honor and of wealth.

Exeunt [ANGELS].

FAUSTUS. Of wealth!
Why, the signiory of Emden[1] shall be mine.
When Mephistophilis shall stand by me,
What God can hurt thee, Faustus? Thou art safe;   25
Cast no more doubts. Come, Mephistophilis,
And bring glad tidings from great Lucifer;—
Is 't not midnight? Come, Mephistophilis;
Veni, veni, Mephistophile!

---

[1] Rich port town.

Enter MEPHISTOPHILIS.

Now tell me, what says Lucifer thy lord?   30

  MEPHISTOPHILIS. That I shall wait on Faustus whilst he lives,
So he will buy my service with his soul.

  FAUSTUS. Already Faustus hath hazarded that for thee.

  MEPHISTOPHILIS. But, Faustus, thou must bequeath it solemnly,
And write a deed of gift with thine own blood,   35
For that security craves great Lucifer.
If thou deny it, I will back to hell.

  FAUSTUS. Stay, Mephistophilis; and tell me what good
Will my soul do thy lord.

  MEPHISTOPHILIS.   Enlarge his kingdom.

  FAUSTUS. Is that the reason why he tempts us thus?   40

  MEPHISTOPHILIS. *Solamen miseris socios habuisse doloris.*[1]

  FAUSTUS. Why, have you any pain that[2] torture others?

  MEPHISTOPHILIS. As great as have the human souls of men.
But tell me, Faustus, shall I have thy soul?
And I will be thy slave, and wait on thee,   45
And give thee more than thou hast wit to ask.

  FAUSTUS. Ay, Mephistophilis, I give it thee.

  MEPHISTOPHILIS. Then Faustus, stab thine arm courageously.
And bind thy soul that at some certain day
Great Lucifer may claim it as his own;   50
And then be thou as great as Lucifer.

  FAUSTUS [*Stabbing his arm*]. Lo, Mephistophilis, for love of
      thee
I cut mine arm, and with my proper blood
Assure my soul to be great Lucifer's,
Chief lord and regent of perpetual night!   55
View here the blood that trickles from mine arm.
And let it be propitious for my wish.

---

[1] For the wretched it is a comfort to have had fellows in misery.
[2] You who.

MEPHISTOPHILIS. But, Faustus, thou must
Write it in manner of a deed of gift.

FAUSTUS. Ay, so I will. [*Writes.*] But, Mephistophilis,   60
My blood congeals, and I can write no more.

MEPHISTOPHILIS. I'll fetch thee fire to dissolve it straight.

Exit

FAUSTUS. What might the staying of my blood portend?
Is it unwilling I should write this bill?
Why streams it not that I may write afresh?   65
Faustus gives to thee his soul. Ah, there it stayed.
Why should'st thou not? Is not thy soul thine own?
Then write again, *Faustus gives to thee his soul.*

Re-enter MEPHISTOPHILIS *with a chafer of coals.*

MEPHISTOPHILIS. Here's fire. Come, Faustus, set it on.

FAUSTUS. So now the blood begins to clear again;   70
Now will I make an end immediately.   [*Writes.*]

MEPHISTOPHILIS [*Aside*]. O what will not I do to obtain his
soul.

FAUSTUS. *Consummatum est*[1]: this bill is ended,
And Faustus hath bequeathed his soul to Lucifer—
But what is this inscription on mine arm?   75
Homo, fuge![2] Whither should I fly?
If unto God, he'll throw me down to hell.
My senses are deceived; here's nothing writ:—
I see it plain; here in this place is writ
Homo, fuge! Yet shall not Faustus fly.   80

MEPHISTOPHILIS. I'll fetch him somewhat to delight his mind.

Exit.

Re-enter [MEPHISTOPHILIS] *with* DEVILS, *giving crowns and rich
apparel to* FAUSTUS, *and dance, and then depart.*

FAUSTUS. Speak, Mephistophilis, what means this show?

---

[1] It is finished. See John 19:30.   [2] Man, fly.

MEPHISTOPHILIS. Nothing, Faustus, but to delight thy mind
    withal,
And to show thee what magic can perform.

FAUSTUS. But may I raise up spirits when I please?   85

MEPHISTOPHILIS. Ay, Faustus, and do greater things than these.

FAUSTUS. Then there's enough for a thousand souls.
Here, Mephistophilis, receive this scroll,
A deed of gift of body and of soul:
But yet conditionally that thou perform   90
All articles prescribed between us both.

MEPHISTOPHILIS. Faustus, I swear by hell and Lucifer
To effect all promises between us made.

FAUSTUS. Then hear me read them: *On these conditions following.*
First, that Faustus may be a spirit in form and substance. Sec-   95
ondly, that Mephistophilis shall be his servant, and at his com-
mand. Thirdly, that Mephistophilis shall do for him and bring him
whatsoever [he desires]. Fourthly, that he shall be in his chamber or
house invisible. Lastly, that he shall appear to the said John Faustus,
at all times, in what form or shape soever he please. I, John   100
Faustus of Wittenberg, Doctor, by these presents do give both body
and soul to Lucifer, Prince of the East, and his minister, Mephistoph-
ilis; and furthermore grant unto them, that four-and-twenty years
being expired, the articles above written inviolate, full power to fetch
or carry the said John Faustus, body and soul, flesh, blood, or goods,   105
into their habitation wheresoever. By me, John Faustus.

MEPHISTOPHILIS. Speak, Faustus, do you deliver this as your
    deed?

FAUSTUS. Ay, take it, and the Devil give thee good on't.

MEPHISTOPHILIS. Now, Faustus, ask what thou wilt.

FAUSTUS. First will I question with thee about hell.   110
Tell me, where is the place that men call hell?

MEPHISTOPHILIS. Under the heavens.

FAUSTUS. Ay, but whereabout?

MEPHISTOPHILIS. Within the bowels of these elements,
Where we are tortured and remain for ever; 115
Hell hath no limits, nor is circumscribed
In one self place; for where we are is hell,
And where hell is, there must we ever be:
And, to conclude, when all the world dissolves,
And every creature shall be purified, 120
All places shall be hell that is not Heaven.

FAUSTUS. Come, I think hell's a fable.

MEPHISTOPHILIS. Ay, think so still, till experience change thy
   mind.

FAUSTUS. Why, think'st thou then that Faustus shall be damned?

MEPHISTOPHILIS. Ay, of necessity, for here's the scroll 125
Wherein thou hast given thy soul to Lucifer.

FAUSTUS. Ay, and body too; but what of that?
Think'st thou that Faustus is so fond¹ to imagine
That, after this life, there is any pain?
Tush; these are trifles, and mere old wives' tales. 130

MEPHISTOPHILIS. But, Faustus, I am an instance to prove the
   contrary,
For I am damned, and am now in hell.

FAUSTUS. How! Now in hell!
Nay, an this be hell, I'll willingly be damned here;
What? walking, disputing, &c.? 135
But, leaving off this, let me have a wife,
The fairest maid in Germany;
For I am wanton and lascivious,
And cannot live without a wife.

MEPHISTOPHILIS. How—a wife? 140
I prithee, Faustus, talk not of a wife.

FAUSTUS. Nay, sweet Mephistophilis, fetch me one, for I will
   have one.

¹ Silly.

MEPHISTOPHILIS. Well—thou wilt have one. Sit there till I
come: I'll fetch thee a wife in the Devil's name.   *Exit.*

Re-enter MEPHISTOPHILIS *with a* DEVIL *dressed like a woman, with
fireworks.*

MEPHISTOPHILIS. Tell, Faustus, how dost thou like thy wife? 145
FAUSTUS. A plague on her for a hot whore!
MEPHISTOPHILIS. Tut, Faustus,
Marriage is but a ceremonial toy;
And if thou lovest me, think no more of it.
I'll call thee out the fairest courtesans   150
And bring them every morning to thy bed;
She whom thine eye shall like, thy heart shall have,
Be she as chaste as was Penelope,
As wise as Saba[1], or as beautiful
As was bright Lucifer before his fall.   155
Here, take this book, peruse it thoroughly: *Gives a book.*
The iterating of these lines brings gold;
The framing of this circle on the ground
Brings whirlwinds, tempests, thunder and lightning;
Pronounce this thrice devoutly to thyself,   160
And men in armor shall appear to thee,
Ready to execute what thou desir'st.
  FAUSTUS. Thanks, Mephistophilis; yet fain would I have a
book wherein I might behold all spells and incantations, that I
might raise up spirits when I please.   165
  MEPHISTOPHILIS. Here they are, in this book. *Turns to them.*
  FAUSTUS. Now would I have a book where I might see all
characters and planets of the heavens, that I might know their
motions and dispositions.
  MEPHISTOPHILIS. Here they are too.   *Turns to them.*   170

---

[1] The Queen of Sheba.

FAUSTUS. Nay, let me have one book more,—and then I have
done,—wherein I might see all plants, herbs, and trees that
grow upon the earth.

MEPHISTOPHILIS. Here they be.

FAUSTUS. O, thou art deceived.   175

MEPHISTOPHILIS. Tut, I warrant thee. *Turns to them. Exeunt.*

[Scene VI. *The Same.*]

Enter FAUSTUS *and* MEPHISTOPHILIS.

FAUSTUS. When I behold the heavens, then I repent,
And curse thee, wicked Mephistophilis,
Because thou hast deprived me of those joys.

MEPHISTOPHILIS. Why, Faustus,
Thinkest thou Heaven is such a glorious thing?   5
I tell thee 'tis not half so fair as thou,
Or any man that breathes on earth.

FAUSTUS. How provest thou that?

MEPHISTOPHILIS. 'Twas made for man, therefore is man more
    excellent.

FAUSTUS. If it were made for man, 'twas made for me;   10
I will renounce this magic and repent.

Enter GOOD ANGEL *and* EVIL ANGEL.

GOOD ANGEL. Faustus, repent; yet God will pity thee.

EVIL ANGEL. Thou art a spirit; God cannot pity thee.

FAUSTUS. Who buzzeth in mine ears I am a spirit?
Be I a devil, yet God may pity me;   15
Ay, God will pity me if I repent.

EVIL ANGEL. Ay, but Faustus never shall repent.

                                       Exeunt [ANGELS].

FAUSTUS. My heart's so hardened I cannot repent.
Scarce can I name salvation, faith, or heaven,

But fearful echoes thunder in mine ears   20
"Faustus, thou art damned!" Then swords and knives,
Poison, gun, halters, and envenomed steel
Are laid before me to despatch myself,
And long ere this I should have slain myself,
Had not sweet pleasure conquered deep despair.   25
Have I not made blind Homer sing to me
Of Alexander's love and Œnon's death?
And hath not he that built the walls of Thebes
With ravishing sound of his melodious harp,
Made music with my Mephistophilis?   30
Why should I die then, or basely despair?
I am resolved: Faustus shall ne'er repent.
Come, Mephistophilis, let us dispute again,
And argue of divine astrology.
Tell me, are there many heavens above the moon?   35
Are all celestial bodies but one globe,
As is the substance of this centric earth?
    MEPHISTOPHILIS. As are the elements, such are the spheres
Mutually folded in each other's orb,
And, Faustus,   40
All jointly move upon one axletree
Whose terminine is termed the world's wide pole;
Nor are the names of Saturn, Mars, or Jupiter
Feigned, but are erring stars.
    FAUSTUS. But tell me, have they all one motion, both *situ* 45
et tempore?[1]
    MEPHISTOPHILIS. All jointly move from east to west in twenty-
four hours upon the poles of the world; but differ in their mo-
tion upon the poles of the zodiac.
    FAUSTUS. Tush!   50

_____

[1] In position and in time.

These slender trifles Wagner can decide;
Hath Mephistophilis no greater skill?
Who knows not the double motion of the planets?
The first is finished in a natural day;
The second thus: as Saturn in thirty years; Jupiter in twelve; 55
Mars in four; the Sun, Venus, and Mercury in a year; the moon
in twenty-eight days. Tush, these are freshmen's suppositions.
But tell me, hath every sphere a dominion or *intelligentia*[1]?

MEPHISTOPHILIS. Ay.

FAUSTUS. How many heavens, or spheres, are there? 60

MEPHISTOPHILIS. Nine: the seven planets, the firmament, and
the empyreal heaven.

FAUSTUS. Well, resolve me in this question: Why have we
not conjunctions, oppositions, aspects, eclipses, all at one time,
but in some years we have more, in some less? 65

MEPHISTOPHILIS. *Per inæqualem motum respecta totius.*[2]

FAUSTUS. Well, I am answered. Tell me who made the world.

MEPHISTOPHILIS. I will not.

FAUSTUS. Sweet Mephistophilis, tell me.

MEPHISTOPHILIS. Move me not, for I will not tell thee. 70

FAUSTUS. Villain, have I not bound thee to tell me anything?

MEPHISTOPHILIS. Ay, that is not against our kingdom; but
this is.

Think thou on hell, Faustus, for thou art damned.

FAUSTUS. Think, Faustus, upon God that made the world.

MEPHISTOPHILIS. Remember this. 75

FAUSTUS. Ay, go, accursed spirit, to ugly hell.
'Tis thou hast damned distressed Faustus' soul.
Is 't not too late?

---

[1] An intelligence: an intelligent being or spirit. [2] Because of motion
unequal in relation to that of the whole.

Re-enter GOOD ANGEL *and* EVIL ANGEL.

EVIL ANGEL. Too late.

GOOD ANGEL. Never too late, if Faustus can repent. 80

EVIL ANGEL. If thou repent, devils shall tear thee in pieces.

GOOD ANGEL. Repent, and they shall never raze thy skin.

Exeunt [ANGELS].

FAUSTUS. Ah, Christ, my Savior,
Seek to save distressed Faustus' soul.

Enter LUCIFER, BELZEBUB, *and* MEPHISTOPHILIS.

LUCIFER. Christ cannot save thy soul, for he is just; 85
There's none but I have interest in the same.

FAUSTUS. O, who art thou that look'st so terrible?

LUCIFER. I am Lucifer,
And this is my companion-prince in hell.

FAUSTUS. O Faustus, they are come to fetch away thy soul! 90

LUCIFER. We come to tell thee thou dost injure us;
Thou talk'st of Christ contrary to thy promise;
Thou should'st not think of God: think of the Devil,
And of his dam, too.

FAUSTUS. Nor will I henceforth; pardon me in this, 95
And Faustus vows never to look to Heaven,
Never to name God, or to pray to him,
To burn his Scriptures, slay his ministers,
And make my spirits pull his churches down.

LUCIFER. Do so, and we will highly gratify thee. Faustus, 100
we are come from hell to show thee some pastime. Sit down,
and thou shalt see all the Seven Deadly Sins appear in their
proper shapes.

FAUSTUS. That sight will be pleasing unto me,
As Paradise was to Adam the first day 105
Of his creation.

LUCIFER. Talk not of Paradise nor creation, but mark this show: talk of the Devil, and nothing else.—Come away!

Enter the SEVEN DEADLY SINS.

Now, Faustus, examine them of their several names and dispositions.   110

FAUSTUS. What art thou—the first?

PRIDE. I am Pride. I disdain to have any parents. I am like to Ovid's flea[1]: I can creep into every corner of a wench; sometimes, like a periwig, I sit upon her brow; or like a fan of feathers, I kiss her lips; indeed I do—what do I not? But,   115 fie, what a scent is here! I'll not speak another word, except the ground were perfumed, and covered with cloth of arras.

FAUSTUS. What art thou—the second?

COVETOUSNESS. I am Covetousness, begotten of an old churl in an old leathern bag; and might I have my wish I   120 would desire that this house and all the people in it were turned to gold, that I might lock you up in my good chest. O, my sweet gold!

FAUSTUS. What art thou—the third?

WRATH. I am Wrath. I had neither father nor mother: I   125 leapt out of a lion's mouth when I was scarce half an hour old; and ever since I have run up and down the world with this case[2] of rapiers wounding myself when I had nobody to fight withal. I was born in hell; and look to it, for some of you shall be my father.   130

FAUSTUS. What art thou—the fourth?

ENVY. I am Envy, begotten of a chimney sweeper and an oyster-wife. I cannot read, and therefore wish all books were burnt. I am lean with seeing others eat. O that there would come a famine through all the world, that all might die, and   135

---

[1] In a poem, probably medieval, attributed to Ovid.   [2] Pair.

I live alone! Then thou should'st see how fat I would be. But must thou sit and I stand! Come down with a vengeance!

FAUSTUS. Away, envious rascal! What art thou—the fifth?

GLUTTONY. Who, I, sir? I am Gluttony. My parents are all dead, and the devil a penny they have left me, but a bare pension, 140 and that is thirty meals a day and ten bevers[1]—a small trifle to suffice nature. O, I come of a royal parentage! My grandfather was a Gammon of Bacon, my grandmother a Hogshead of Claret-wine; my godfathers were these, Peter Pickleherring, and Martin Martlemas-beef[2]. O, but my godmother, she 145 was a jolly gentlewoman, and well beloved in every good town and city; her name was Mistress Margery Marchbeer. Now, Faustus, thou hast heard all my progeny, wilt thou bid me to supper?

FAUSTUS. No, I'll see thee hanged; thou wilt eat up all 150 my victuals.

GLUTTONY. Then the Devil choke thee!

FAUSTUS. Choke thyself, glutton! Who art thou—the sixth?

SLOTH. I am Sloth. I was begotten on a sunny bank, where I have lain ever since; and you have done me great injury 155 to bring me from thence. Let me be carried thither again by Gluttony and Lechery. I'll not speak another word for a king's ransom.

FAUSTUS. What are you, Mistress Minx, the seventh and last?

LECHERY. Who, I, sir? I am one that loves an inch of 160 raw mutton[3] better than an ell of fried stockfish; and the first letter of my name begins with Lechery.

LUCIFER. Away to hell, to hell! *Exeunt the* SINS.
Now, Faustus, how dost thou like this?

FAUSTUS. O, this feeds my soul! 165

---

[1] Light repast between meals.   [2] Salt beef, hung up on St. Martin's Day, November 11.   [3] Slang for whore.

LUCIFER. Tut, Faustus, in hell is all manner of delight.

FAUSTUS. O might I see hell, and return again. How happy
were I then!

LUCIFER. Thou shalt; I will send for thee at midnight.
In meantime take this book; peruse it thoroughly,　　　170
And thou shalt turn thyself into what shape thou wilt.

FAUSTUS. Great thanks, mighty Lucifer!
This will I keep as chary as my life.

LUCIFER. Farewell, Faustus, and think on the Devil.

FAUSTUS. Farewell, great Lucifer! Come, Mephistophilis.　175

Exeunt omnes.

Enter WAGNER[1].

WAGNER. Learned Faustus,
To know the secrets of astronomy,
Graven in the book of Jove's high firmament,
Did mount himself to scale Olympus' top,
Being seated in a chariot burning bright,　　　180
Drawn by the strength of yoky dragons' necks.
He now is gone to prove cosmography,
And, as I guess, will first arrive at Rome,
To see the Pope and manner of his court,
And take some part of holy Peter's feast,　　　185
That to this day is highly solemnized.　　　*Exit.*

[Scene VII. *The* POPE'S *Privy Chamber.*]

Enter FAUSTUS *and* MEPHISTOPHILIS.

FAUSTUS. Having now, my good Mephistophilis,
Past with delight the stately town of Trier[2],
Environed round with airy mountain-tops,

---

[1] In some editions chorus. In some editions, also, the materials of Scene
VIII are introduced here.　　　[2] Treves.

With walls of flint, and deep entrenched lakes,
Not to be won by any conquering prince; 5
From Paris next, coasting the realm of France,
We saw the river Maine fall into Rhine,
Whose banks are set with groves of fruitful vines;
Then up to Naples, rich Campania,
Whose buildings fair and gorgeous to the eye, 10
The streets straight forth, and paved with finest brick,
Quarter the town in four equivalents.
There saw we learned Maro's[1] golden tomb,
The way he cut, an English mile in length,
Through a rock of stone in one night's space; 15
From thence to Venice, Padua, and the rest,
In one of which a sumptuous temple stands,
That threats the stars with her aspiring top,
Thus hitherto has Faustus spent his time.
But tell me, what resting-place is this? 20
Hast thou, as erst I did command,
Conducted me within the walls of Rome?
   MEPHISTOPHILIS. Faustus, I have; and because we will not be
     unprovided,
I have taken up his Holiness' privy-chamber for our use.
   FAUSTUS. I hope his Holiness will bid us welcome. 25
   MEPHISTOPHILIS. Tut, 'tis no matter, man, we'll be bold with
     his good cheer.
And now, my Faustus, that thou may'st perceive
What Rome containeth to delight thee with,
Know that this city stands upon seven hills
That underprop the groundwork of the same, 30
[Just through the midst runs flowing Tiber's stream,
With winding banks that cut it in two parts,]

---

[1] Virgil, considered a magician in the Middle Ages.

Over the which four stately bridges lean,
That make safe passage to each part of Rome:
Upon the bridge called Ponto Angelo 35
Erected is a castle passing strong,
Within whose walls such store of ordnance are,
And double cannons, framed of carved brass,
As match the days within one complete year;
Besides the gates and high pyramides, 40
Which Julius Cæsar brought from Africa.

FAUSTUS. Now by the kingdoms of infernal rule,
Of Styx, of Acheron, and the fiery lake
Of ever-burning Phlegethon, I swear
That I do long to see the monuments 45
And situation of bright-splendent Rome.
Come therefore, let's away.

MEPHISTOPHILIS. Nay, Faustus, stay; I know you'd fain see
the Pope,
And take some part of holy Peter's feast,
Where thou shalt see a troop of bald-pate friars, 50
Whose *summum bonum*[1] is in belly-cheer.

FAUSTUS. Well, I'm content to compass then some sport,
And by their folly make us merriment.
Then charm me, that I
May be invisible, to do what I please
Unseen of any whilst I stay in Rome.

MEPHISTOPHILIS *charms him.*

MEPHISTOPHILIS. So, Faustus, now
Do what thou wilt, thou shalt not be discerned.

[1] Highest good.

Sound a sennet[1]. Enter the POPE *and the* CARDINAL OF LORRAIN *to the banquet, with* FRIARS *attending.*

POPE. My Lord of Lorraine, wilt please you draw near?

FAUSTUS. Fall to, and the devil choke you an[2] you spare!   60

POPE. How now! Who's that which spake?—Friars, look about.

FIRST FRIAR. Here's nobody, if it like your Holiness.

POPE. My lord, here is a dainty dish was sent me from the Bishop of Milan.

FAUSTUS. I thank you sir.   *Snatches it.* 65

POPE. How now! Who's that which snatched the meat from me? Will no man look? My Lord, this dish was sent me from the Cardinal of Florence.

FAUSTUS. You say true; I'll ha't.   *Snatches it.*

POPE. What, again! My lord, I'll drink to your Grace.   70

FAUSTUS. I'll pledge your Grace.   *Snatches the cup.*

CARDINAL OF LORRAIN. My lord, it may be some ghost newly crept out of purgatory, come to beg a pardon of your Holiness.

POPE. It may be so. Friars, prepare a dirge to lay the fury of this ghost. Once again, my lord, fall to.   75

The POPE *crosseth himself.*

FAUSTUS. What, are you crossing of yourself?
Well, use that trick no more, I would advise you. *Cross again.*
Well, there's the second time. Aware the third, I give you fair warning.

Cross again, and FAUSTUS *hits him a box of the ear; and they all run away.*

Come on, Mephistophilis, what shall we do?

MEPHISTOPHILIS. Nay, I know not. We shall be cursed with bell, book, and candle.   80

---

[1] Sequence of trumpet notes.   [2] If.

FAUSTUS. How! bell, book, and candle,—candle, book, and
bell,
Forward and backward to curse Faustus to hell!
Anon you shall hear a hog grunt, a calf bleat, and an ass bray,
Because it is Saint Peter's holiday.

Re-enter all the FRIARS *to sing the Dirge.*

FIRST FRIAR. Come, brethren, let's about our business   85
with good devotion.

Sing this:

Cursed be he that stole away his Holiness' meat from the table!
Maledicat Dominus[1]!
Cursed be he that struck his Holiness a blow on the face!
Maledicat Dominus!
Cursed be he that took Friar Sandelo a blow on the pate!
Maledicat Dominus!   89
Cursed be he that disturbeth our holy dirge! *Maledicat Dominus!*
Cursed be he that took away his Holiness' wine! *Maledicat
Dominus! Et omnes sancti*[2]! *Amen!*

[MEPHISTOPHILIS *and* FAUSTUS] *beat the* FRIARS, *and fling fireworks
among them; and so exeunt.*

[Scene VIII. *An Inn Yard.*]

Enter ROBIN *the Ostler with a book in his hand.*

ROBIN. O, this is admirable! Here I ha' stolen one of Dr.
Faustus' conjuring books, and i' faith I mean to search some
circles[3] for my own use. Now will I make all the maidens in
our parish dance at my pleasure, stark naked before me; and
so by that means I shall see more than e'er I felt or saw yet.   5

---

[1] May the Lord curse [him].   [2] And all the saints.   [3] With vulgar
double meaning.

Enter RALPH *calling* ROBIN.

RALPH. Robin, prithee come away; there's a gentleman tarries to have his horse, and he would have his things rubbed and made clean. He keeps such a chafing with mistress about it; and she has sent me to look thee out. Prithee come away.

ROBIN. Keep out, keep out, or else you are blown up; 10 you are dismembered, Ralph; keep out, for I am about a roaring piece of work.

RALPH. Come, what dost thou with that same book? Thou canst not read.

ROBIN. Yes, my master and mistress shall find that I can 15 read, he for his forehead, she for her private study; she's born to bear with me, or else my art fails.

RALPH. Why, Robin, what book is that?

ROBIN. What book! Why, the most intolerable book for conjuring that e'er was invented by any brimstone devil. 20

RALPH. Canst thou conjure with it?

ROBIN. I can do all these things easily with it: first, I can make thee drunk with ippocras[1] at any tabern in Europe for nothing; that's one of my conjuring works.

RALPH. Our Master Parsons says that's nothing. 25

ROBIN. True, Ralph; and more, Ralph, if thou hast any mind to Nan Spit, our kitchenmaid, then turn her and wind her to thy own use as often as thou wilt, and at midnight.

RALPH. O brave Robin, shall I have Nan Spit, and to mine own use? On that condition I'll feed thy devil with horse- 30 bread as long as he lives, of free cost.

ROBIN. No more, sweet Ralph; let's go and make clean our boots, which lie foul upon our hands, and then to our conjuring in the Devil's name. *Exeunt.*

---

[1] Sugared and spiced wine.

[Scene IX. *An Inn.*]

Enter ROBIN *and* RALPH *with a silver goblet.*

ROBIN. Come, Ralph, did not I tell thee we were for e'
made by this Doctor Faustus' book? *Ecce signum*[1], here's a sim
purchase[2] for horsekeepers; our horses shall eat no hay as lo
as this lasts.

Enter the VINTNER.

RALPH. But, Robin, here comes the vintner.

ROBIN. Hush! I'll gull him supernaturally. Drawer, I h
all is paid: God be with you. Come, Ralph.

VINTNER. Soft, sir; a word with you. I must yet have a gol
paid from you, ere you go.

ROBIN. I, a goblet, Ralph; I, a goblet! I scorn you, and
you are but a &c.[3] I, a goblet! Search me.

VINTNER. I mean so, sir, with your favor.　　　　*Searches h*

ROBIN. How say you now?

VINTNER. I must say somewhat to your fellow. You,

RALPH. Me, sir! me, sir! Search your fill.

VINTNER *searches him.*

Now, sir, you may be ashamed to burden honest men
with a matter of truth.

VINTNER. Well, t'one of you hath this goblet about y

ROBIN [*Aside*]. You lie, drawer, 'tis afore me.—Sirrah y
I'll teach ye to impeach honest men; stand by; I'll scour y
for a goblet! Stand aside you had best, I charge you in
name of Belzebub. Look to the goblet, Ralph. [*Aside to* RALI

VINTNER. What mean you, sirrah?

ROBIN. I'll tell you what I mean. [*Reads.*] *Sanctobulorum*

---

[1] Behold the sign.　　　[2] "Racket."　　　[3] The actor could fill in li
vituperation.

riphrasticon—Nay, I'll tickle you, vintner. [*Aside to* RALPH.] 25
Look to the goblet, Ralph. *Polypragmos Belseborams framanto*
pacostiphos tostu, Mephistophilis, &c.[1]   [*Reads.*]

Enter MEPHISTOPHILIS, *sets squibs at their back* [*and then exit*].
They run about.

VINTNER. *O nomine Domini!*[2] What meanest thou, Robin?
Thou hast no goblet.

RALPH. *Peccatum peccatorum!*[3] Here's thy goblet, good 30
vintner.

Gives the goblet to VINTNER, *who exit.*

ROBIN. *Misericordia pro nobis!*[4] What shall I do? Good Devil,
forgive me now, and I'll never rob thy library more.

Re-enter to them MEPHISTOPHILIS.

MEPHISTOPHILIS. Monarch of hell, under whose black survey
Great potentates do kneel with awful fear,
Upon whose altars thousand souls do lie,
How am I vexed with these villains' charms!   35
From Constantinople am I hither come
Only for pleasure of these damned slaves.

ROBIN. How from Constantinople? You have had a great
journey. Will you take sixpence in your purse to pay for
your supper, and begone?

MEPHISTOPHILIS. Well, villains, for your presumption, I transform thee into an ape, and thee into a dog; and so begone.

Exit.

ROBIN. How, into an ape? That's brave! I'll have fine sport
with the boys. I'll get nuts and apples enow.

RALPH. And I must be a dog.

ROBIN. I' faith thy head will never be out of the pottage pot.

Exeunt.

---

[1] Invented words, meaningless.   [2] In the name of the Lord.   [3] Sin
of sins.   [4] Mercy for us.

Enter CHORUS.

CHORUS. When Faustus had with pleasure ta'en the view
Of rarest things, and royal courts of kings,
He stayed his course, and so returned home;   50
Where such as bear his absence but with grief,
I mean his friends and near'st companions,
Did gratulate his safety with kind words,
And in their conference· of what befell,
Touching his journey through the world and air,   55
They put forth questions of astrology,
Which Faustus answered with such learned skill,
As they admired and wondered at his wit.
Now is his fame spread forth in every land;
Amongst the rest the Emperor is one,   60
Carolus the Fifth, at whose palace now
Faustus is feasted 'mongst his noblemen.
What there he did in trial of his art,
I leave untold—your eyes shall see performed.   *Exit.*

[Scene X. *The* EMPEROR'S *Court.*]

Enter EMPEROR, FAUSTUS, *and a* KNIGHT *with attendants.*

EMPEROR. Master Doctor Faustus, I have heard strange report
of thy knowledge in the black art, how that none in my em-
pire nor in the whole world can compare with thee for the
rare effects of magic; they say thou hast a familiar spirit, by
whom thou canst accomplish what thou list. This, therefore,   5
is my request, that thou let me see some proof of thy skill,
that mine eyes may be witnesses to confirm what mine ears
have heard reported; and here I swear to thee by the honor
of mine imperial crown, that, whatever thou doest, thou shalt
be no ways prejudiced or endamaged.   10
KNIGHT. [*Aside.*] I' faith he looks much like a conjuror.

FAUSTUS. My gracious sovereign, though I must confess myself far inferior to the report men have published, and nothing answerable[1] to the honor of your imperial majesty, yet for that love and duty binds me thereunto, I am content to do whatsoever your majesty shall command me. 15

EMPEROR. Then, Doctor Faustus, mark what I shall say.

As I was sometime solitary set
Within my closet, sundry thoughts arose
About the honor of mine ancestors, 20
How they had won by prowess such exploits,
Got such riches, subdued so many kingdoms,
As we that do succeed, or they that shall
Hereafter possess our throne, shall
(I fear me) ne'er attain to that degree 25
Of high renown and great authority;
Amongst which kings is Alexander the Great,
Chief spectacle of the world's pre-eminence,
The bright shining of whose glorious acts
Lightens the world with his[2] reflecting beams, 30
As, when I heard but motion[3] made of him,
It grieves my soul I never saw the man.
If, therefore, thou by cunning of thine art
Canst raise this man from hollow vaults below,
Where lies entombed this famous conqueror, 35
And bring with him his beauteous paramour,
Both in their right shapes, gesture, and attire
They used to wear during their time of life,
Thou shalt both satisfy my just desire,
And give me cause to praise thee whilst I live. 40

FAUSTUS. My gracious lord, I am ready to accomplish your request so far forth as by art, and power of my Spirit, I am able to perform.

---

[1] Equal.   [2] Its.   [3] Mention.

KNIGHT. [*Aside.*] I' faith that's just nothing at all.

FAUSTUS. But, if it like your Grace, it is not in my 45
ability to present before your eyes the true substantial bodies
of those two deceased princes, which long since are consumed
to dust.

KNIGHT. [*Aside.*] Ay, marry, Master Doctor, now there's a
sign of grace in you, when you will confess the truth. 50

FAUSTUS. But such spirits as can lively resemble Alexander and
his paramour shall appear before your Grace in that manner
that they best lived in, in their most flourishing estate; which
I doubt not shall sufficiently content your imperial majesty.

EMPEROR. Go to, Master Doctor, let me see them pres- 55
ently[1].

KNIGHT. Do you hear, Master Doctor? You bring Alexander
and his paramour before the Emperor!

FAUSTUS. How then, sir?

KNIGHT. I' faith that's as true as Diana turned me to a stag!

FAUSTUS. No, sir, but when Actæon died, he left the 60
horns for you. Mephistophilis, begone.   *Exit* MEPHISTOPHILIS.

KNIGHT. Nay, an you go to conjuring, I'll begone.   *Exit.*

FAUSTUS. I'll meet with you anon for interrupting me so.
Here they are, my gracious lord.

Re-enter MEPHISTOPHILIS *with* [SPIRITS *in the shape of*] ALEXANDER
and his PARAMOUR.

EMPEROR. Master Doctor, I heard this lady while she 65
lived had a wart or mole in her neck. How shàll I know
whether it be so or no?

FAUSTUS. Your Highness may boldly go and see.

Exeunt [Spirits].

EMPEROR. Sure these are no spirits, but the true substantial
bodies of those two deceased princes. 70

[1] Immediately.

FAUSTUS. Will 't please your Highness now to send for the knight that was so pleasant with me here of late?

EMPEROR. One of you call him forth.   *Exit* Attendant.

Re-enter the KNIGHT *with a pair of horns on his head.*

How now, sir knight! Why I had thought thou had'st been a bachelor, but now I see thou hast a wife, that not only gives thee horns, but makes thee wear them. Feel on thy head. 75

KNIGHT. Thou damned wretch and execrable dog,
Bred in the concave of some monstrous rock,
How darest thou thus abuse a gentleman?
Villain, I say, undo what thou hast done!

FAUSTUS. O, not so fast, sir; there's no haste; but, good, 80
are you remembered how you crossed me in my conference
with the Emperor? I think I have met with you for it.

EMPEROR. Good Master Doctor, at my entreaty release him;
he hath done penance sufficient.

FAUSTUS. My gracious lord, not so much for the injury 85
he offered me here in your presence, as to delight you with
some mirth, hath Faustus worthily requited this injurious knight;
which, being all I desire, I am content to release him of his
horns; and, sir knight, hereafter speak well of scholars. Mephistophilis, transform him straight. [MEPHISTOPHILIS *removes* 90
the horns.] Now, my good lord, having done my duty I humbly
take my leave.

EMPEROR. Farewell, Master Doctor; yet, ere you go,
Expect from me a bounteous reward.   *Exeunt.*

[Scene XI. *A Green, then the House of* FAUSTUS.]

Enter FAUSTUS *and* MEPHISTOPHILIS.

FAUSTUS. Now, Mephistophilis, the restless course
That Time doth run with calm and silent foot,
Short'ning my days and thread of vital life,

Calls for the payment of my latest years;
Therefore, sweet Mephistophilis, let us   5
Make haste to Wittenberg.

MEPHISTOPHILIS. What, will you go on horseback or on foot?

FAUSTUS. Nay, till I'm past this fair and pleasant green,
I'll walk on foot.

Enter a HORSE-COURSER[1].

HORSE-COURSER. I have been all this day seeking one   10
Master Fustian; mass, see where he is! God save you, Master
Doctor!

FAUSTUS. What, horse-courser! You are well met.

HORSE-COURSER. Do you hear, sir? I have brought you forty
dollars for your horse.   15

FAUSTUS. I cannot sell him so; if thou likest him for fifty, take
him.

HORSE-COURSER. Alas, sir, I have no more.—I pray you speak
for me.

MEPHISTOPHILIS. I pray you let him have him; he is an   20
honest fellow, and he has a great charge, neither wife nor child.

FAUSTUS. Well, come, give me your money. [HORSE-COURSER
gives FAUSTUS *the money*.] My boy will deliver him to you.
But I must tell you one thing before you have him; ride him
not into the water at any hand.   25

HORSE-COURSER. Why, sir, will he not drink of all waters?

FAUSTUS. O yes, he will drink of all waters, but ride him
not into the water; ride him over hedge or ditch, or where
thou wilt, but not into the water.

HORSE-COURSER. Well, sir.—Now I am made man for   30
ever. I'll not leave my horse for forty. If he had but the quality
of hey-ding-ding, hey-ding-ding[2], I'd make a brave living on

---

[1] Horse trader.   [2] Could dance to music.

him: he has a buttock as slick as an eel. [*Aside.*] Well, God
b'wi' ye, sir, your boy will deliver him me. But hark ye, sir;
if my horse be sick or ill at ease, if I bring his water to   35
you, you'll tell me what it is?   *Exit* HORSE-COURSER.

FAUSTUS. Away, you villain; what, dost think I am a horse-
doctor?
What art thou, Faustus, but a man condemned to die?
Thy fatal time doth draw to final end;   40
Despair doth drive distrust unto my thoughts:
Confound these passions with a quiet sleep.
Tush, Christ did call the thief upon the cross;
Then rest thee, Faustus, quiet in conceit. *Sleeps in his chair.*

Re-enter HORSE-COURSER, *all wet, crying.*

HORSE-COURSER. Alas, alas! Doctor Fustian, quotha? Mass,   45
Doctor Lopus[1] was never such a doctor. Has given me a pur-
gation has purged me of forty dollars; I shall never see them
more. But yet, like an ass as I was, I would not be ruled by
him, for he bade me I should ride him into no water. Now I,
thinking my horse had had some rare quality that he would   50
not have had me known of, I, like a venturous youth, rid him
into the deep pond at the town's end. I was no sooner in the
middle of the pond, but my horse vanished away, and I sat
upon a bottle[2] of hay, never so near drowning in my life. But
I'll seek out my Doctor, and have my forty dollars again, or   55
I'll make it the dearest horse!—O, yonder is his snipper-snapper.
Do you hear? You hey-pass[3], where's your master?

MEPHISTOPHILIS. Why, sir, what would you? You cannot
speak with him.

HORSE-COURSER. But I will speak with him.   60

MEPHISTOPHILIS. Why, he's fast asleep. Come some other time.

---

[1] Dr. Lopez, Queen Elizabeth's physician, hanged on a charge of having
conspired to poison her.   [2] Bundle.   [3] Juggler.

HORSE-COURSER. I'll speak with him now, or I'll break his glass windows about his ears.

MEPHISTOPHILIS. I tell thee he has not slept this eight nights.

HORSE-COURSER. An he have not slept this eight weeks, 65 I'll speak with him.

MEPHISTOPHILIS. See where he is, fast asleep.

HORSE-COURSER. Ay, this is he. God save you, Master Doctor! Master Doctor, Master Doctor Fustian!—Forty dollars, forty dollars for a bottle of hay! 70

MEPHISTOPHILIS. Why, thou seest he hears thee not.

HORSE-COURSER. So ho, ho!—so ho, ho! [*Hollas in his ear.*] No, will you not wake? I'll make you wake ere I go.

Pulls FAUSTUS *by the leg, and pulls it away.*

Alas, I am undone! What shall I do?

FAUSTUS. O my leg, my leg! Help, Mephistophilis! Call 75 the officers. My leg, my leg!

MEPHISTOPHILIS. Come, villain, to the constable.

HORSE-COURSER. O lord, sir, let me go, and I'll give you forty dollars more.

MEPHISTOPHILIS. Where be they? 80

HORSE-COURSER. I have none about me. Come to my ostry[1] and I'll give them you.

MEPHISTOPHILIS. Begone quickly.

HORSE-COURSER runs away.

FAUSTUS. What, is he gone? Farewell he! Faustus has his leg again, and the horse-courser, I take it, a bottle of hay for 85 his labor. Well, this trick shall cost him forty dollars more.

Enter WAGNER.

How now, Wagner, what's the news with thee?

---

[1] Inn.

WAGNER. Sir, the Duke of Vanholt doth earnestly entreat your company.

FAUST. The Duke of Vanholt! An honorable gentleman, 90 to whom I must be no niggard of my cunning. Come, Mephistophilis, let's away to him. *Exeunt.*

[Scene XII. *Court of the* DUKE.]

Enter the DUKE OF VANHOLT, *the* DUCHESS [FAUSTUS, *and* MEPHISTOPHILIS].

DUKE. Believe me, Master Doctor, this merriment hath much pleased me.

FAUSTUS. My gracious lord, I am glad it contents you so well. —But it may be, madam, you take no delight in this. I have heard that great-bellied women do long for some dainties 5 or other. What is it, madam? Tell me, and you shall have it.

DUCHESS. Thanks, good Master Doctor; and for I see your courteous intent to pleasure me, I will not hide from you the thing my heart desires; and were it now summer, as it is January and the dead time of the winter, I would desire 10 no better meat than a dish of ripe grapes.

FAUSTUS. Alas, madam, that's nothing! Mephistophilis, begone. [*Exit* MEPHISTOPHILIS.] Were it a greater thing than this, so it would content you, you should have it.

Re-enter MEPHISTOPHILIS *with the grapes.*

Here they be, madam; wilt please you taste on them? 15

DUKE. Believe me, Master Doctor, this makes me wonder above the rest, that being in the dead time of winter, and in the month of January, how you should come by these grapes.

FAUSTUS. If it like your Grace, the year is divided into two circles over the whole world, that, when it is here winter 20 with us, in the contrary circle it is summer with them, as in

India, Saba, and farther countries in the East; and by means
of a swift spirit that I have, I had them brought hither, as ye
see—How do you like them, madam; be they good?

DUCHESS. Believe me, Master Doctor, they be the best 25
grapes that I e'er tasted in my life before.

FAUSTUS. I am glad they content you so, madam.

DUKE. Come, madam, let us in, where you must well reward
this learned man for the great kindness he hath showed to you.

DUCHESS. And so I will, my lord; and whilst I live, rest 30
beholding for this courtesy.

FAUSTUS. I humbly thank your Grace.

DUKE. Come, Master Doctor, follow us and receive your
reward.   *Exeunt.*

[Scene XIII. *A Room in the House of* FAUSTUS.]

Enter WAGNER, *solus.*

WAGNER. I think my master means to die shortly,
For he hath given to me all his goods;
And yet, methinks, if that death were near,
He would not banquet and carouse and swill
Amongst the students, as even now he doth,   5
Who are at supper with such belly-cheer
As Wagner ne'er beheld in all his life.
See where they come! Belike the feast is ended.

Enter FAUSTUS, *with two or three* SCHOLARS [*and* MEPHISTOPHILIS].

FIRST SCHOLAR. Master Doctor Faustus, since our conference
about fair ladies, which was the beautifullest in all the world, 10
we nave determined with ourselves that Helen of Greece was
the admirablest lady that ever lived; therefore, Master Doctor,
if you will do us that favor, as to let us see that peerless dame of
Greece, whom all the world admires for majesty, we should
think ourselves much beholding unto you.   15

FAUSTUS. Gentlemen,
For that I know your friendship is unfeigned,
And Faustus' custom is not to deny
The just requests of those that wish him well,
You shall behold that peerless dame of Greece, 20
No otherways for pomp and majesty
Than when Sir Paris crossed the seas with her,
And brought the spoils to rich Dardania.
Be silent, then, for danger is in words.

Music sounds, and HELEN *passeth over the stage.*

SECOND SCHOLAR. Too simple is my wit to tell her praise, 25
Whom all the world admires for majesty.

THIRD SCHOLAR. No marvel though the angry Greeks pursued
With ten years' war the rape of such a queen,
Whose heavenly beauty passeth all compare.

FIRST SCHOLAR. Since we have seen the pride of Nature's
works, 30
And only paragon of excellence,
Let us depart; and for this glorious deed
Happy and blest be Faustus evermore.

FAUSTUS. Gentlemen, farewell—the same I wish to you.

Exeunt SCHOLARS. *Enter an* OLD MAN.

OLD MAN. Ah, Doctor Faustus, that I might prevail 35
To guide thy steps unto the way of life,
By which sweet path thou may'st attain the goal
That shall conduct thee to celestial rest!
Break heart, drop blood, and mingle it with tears,
Tears falling from repentant heaviness 40
Of thy most vile and loathsome filthiness,
The stench whereof corrupts the inward soul
With such flagitious crimes of heinous sins

As no commiseration may expel,
But mercy, Faustus, of thy Savior sweet,   45
Whose blood alone must wash away thy guilt.

FAUSTUS. Where art thou, Faustus? Wretch, what has thou
    done?

Damned art thou, Faustus, damned; despair and die!
Hell calls for right, and with a roaring voice
Says "Faustus! Come! Thine hour is [almost] come!"   50
And Faustus [now] will come to do thee right.

       MEPHISTOPHILIS *gives him a dagger.*

OLD MAN. Ah stay, good Faustus, stay thy desperate steps!
I see an angel hovers o'er thy head,
And, with a vial full of precious grace,
Offers to pour the same into thy soul: 55
Then call for mercy, and avoid despair.

FAUST. Ah, my sweet friend, I feel
Thy words do comfort my distressed soul.
Leave me a while to ponder on my sins.

OLD MAN. I go, sweet Faustus, but with heavy cheer,   60
Fearing the ruin of thy hopeless soul.   *Exit.*

FAUSTUS. Accursed Faustus, where is mercy now?
I do repent; and yet I do despair;
Hell strives with grace for conquest in my breast:
What shall I do to shun the snares of death?   65

MEPHISTOPHILIS. Thou traitor, Faustus, I arrest thy soul
For disobedience to my sovereign lord;
Revolt[1], or I'll in piecemeal tear thy flesh.

FAUSTUS. Sweet Mephistophilis, entreat thy lord
To pardon my unjust presumption,   70
And with my blood again I will confirm.
My former vow I made to Lucifer.

---

[1] Turn back.

MEPHISTOPHILIS. Do it now then quickly, with unfeigned
  heart,
Lest danger do attend thy drift.

  FAUSTUS *stabs his arm and writes on a paper with his blood.*

FAUSTUS. Torment, sweet friend, that base and crooked age[1],
That durst dissuade me from my Lucifer,   76
With greatest torments that our hell affords.
MEPHISTOPHILIS. His faith is great, I cannot touch his soul;
But what I may afflict his body with
I will attempt, which is but little worth.   80
FAUSTUS. One thing, good servant, let me crave of thee,
To glut the longing of my heart's desire,—
That I might have unto my paramour
That heavenly Helen, which I saw of late,
Whose sweet embracings may extinguish clean   85
These thoughts that do dissuade me from my vow,
And keep mine oath I made to Lucifer.
MEPHISTOPHILIS. Faustus, this or what else thou shalt desire
Shall be performed in twinkling of an eye.

             Re-enter HELEN.

FAUSTUS. Was this the face that launched a thousand ships,
And burnt the topless towers of Ilium?   91
Sweet Helen, make me immortal with a kiss.   *Kisses her.*
Her lips suck forth my soul; see where it flies!—
Come, Helen, come, give me my soul again.
Here will I dwell, for Heaven be in these lips,   95
And all is dross that is not Helena.

             Enter OLD MAN.

I will be Paris, and for love of thee,
Instead of Troy, shall Wittenberg be sacked;

  [1] Old man.

And I will combat with weak Menelaus,
And wear thy colors on my plumed crest;   100
Yea, I will wound Achilles in the heel,
And then return to Helen for a kiss.
Oh, thou art fairer than the evening air
Clad in the beauty of a thousand stars;
Brighter art thou than flaming Jupiter   105
When he appeared to hapless Semele;
More lovely than the monarch of the sky
In wanton Arethusa's[1] azured arms;
And none but thou shalt be my paramour.   *Exeunt.*
    OLD MAN. Accursed Faustus, miserable man,   110
That from thy soul exclud'st the grace of Heaven,
And fly'st the throne of his tribunal seat!

Enter DEVILS.

Satan begins to sift me with his pride[2]:
As in this furnace God shall try my faith,
My faith, vile hell, shall triumph over thee.   115
Ambitious fiends, see how the heavens smiles
At your repulse, and laughs your state to scorn!
Hence, hell! for hence I fly unto my God.   *Exeunt.*

[Scene XIV. *The Same.*]

Enter FAUSTUS *with the* SCHOLARS.

FAUSTUS. Ah, gentlemen!
FIRST SCHOLAR. What ails Faustus?
FAUSTUS. Ah, my sweet chamber-fellow, had I lived with
thee, then had I lived still! But now I die eternally. Look comes
he not, comes he not?   5

---

[1] Arethusa is one of the Hesperides; the reference is probably to sunset.
[2] Cf. Luke 22:31.

SECOND SCHOLAR. What means Faustus?

THIRD SCHOLAR. Belike he is grown into some sickness by being over solitary.

FIRST SCHOLAR. If it be so, we'll have physicians to cure him. 'Tis but a surfeit. Never fear, man.   10

FAUSTUS. A surfeit of deadly sin that hath damned both body and soul.

SECOND SCHOLAR. Yet, Faustus, look up to Heaven; remember God's mercies are infinite.

FAUSTUS. But Faustus' offences can never be pardoned;   15 the serpent that tempted Eve may be saved, but not Faustus. Ah, gentlemen, hear me with patience, and tremble not at my speeches! Though my heart pants and quivers to remember that I have been a student here these thirty years, oh, would I had never seen Wittenberg, never read book! And what   20 wonders I have done, all Germany can witness, yea, the world; for which Faustus hath lost both Germany and the world, yea Heaven itself, Heaven, the seat of God, the throne of the blessed, the kingdom of joy; and must remain in hell for ever, hell, ah, hell, for ever! Sweet friends, what shall become of Faustus,   25 being in hell for ever?

THIRD SCHOLAR. Yet, Faustus, call on God.

FAUSTUS. On God, whom Faustus hath abjured! On God, whom Faustus hath blasphemed! Ah, my God, I would weep, but the Devil draws in my tears. Gush forth blood instead of   30 tears! Yea, life and soul! Oh, he stays my tongue! I would lift up my hands, but see, they hold them, they hold them!

ALL. Who, Faustus?

FAUSTUS. Lucifer and Mephistophilis. Ah, gentlemen, I gave them my soul for my cunning!   35

ALL. God forbid!

FAUSTUS. God forbade it indeed; but Faustus hath done it. For vain pleasure of twenty-four years hath Faustus lost eternal joy and felicity. I writ them a bill with mine own blood; the date is expired, the time will come, and he will fetch   40 me.

FIRST SCHOLAR. Why did not Faustus tell us of this before, that divines might have prayed for thee?

FAUSTUS. Oft have I thought to have done so; but the Devil threatened to tear me in pieces if I named God; to fetch both body and soul if I once gave ear to divinity; and now 'tis   45 too late. Gentlemen, away! lest you perish with me.

SECOND SCHOLAR. Oh, what shall we do to save Faustus?

FAUSTUS. Talk not of me, but save yourselves, and depart.

THIRD SCHOLAR. God will strengthen me. I will stay with Faustus.   50

FIRST SCHOLAR. Tempt not God, sweet friend; but let us into the next room, and there pray for him.

FAUSTUS. Ay, pray for me, pray for me! and what noise soever ye hear, come not unto me, for nothing can rescue me.

SECOND SCHOLAR. Pray thou, and we will pray that God   55 may have mercy upon thee.

FAUSTUS. Gentlemen, farewell! If I live till morning I'll visit you; if not—Faustus is gone to hell.

ALL. Faustus, farewell.

Exeunt SCHOLARS. *The clock strikes eleven.*

FAUSTUS. Ah Faustus,   60
Now hast thou but one bare hour to live,
And then thou must be damned perpetually!
Stand still, you ever-moving spheres of Heaven,
That time may cease, and midnight never come;
Fair Nature's eye, rise, rise again and make.   65
Perpetual day; or let this hour be but
A year, a month, a week, a natural day,
That Faustus may repent and save his soul!

O *lente, lente, currite noctis equi!*[1]
The stars move still[2], time runs, the clock will strike,   70
The Devil will come, and Faustus must be damned.
O, I'll leap up to my God! Who pulls me down?
See, see where Christ's blood streams in the firmament!
One drop would save my soul—half a drop: ah, my Christ!
Ah, rend not my heart for naming of my Christ!   75
Yet will I call on him: O spare me, Lucifer!—
Where is it now? 'Tis gone; and see where God
Stretcheth out his arm, and bends his ireful brows!
Mountain and hills come, come and fall on me,
And hide me from the heavy wrath of God!   80
No! no!
Then will I headlong run into the earth;
Earth gape! O no, it will not harbor me!
You stars that reigned at my nativity,
Whose influence hath allotted death and hell,   85
Now draw up Faustus like a foggy mist
Into the entrails of yon laboring clouds,
That when they vomit forth into the air,
My limbs may issue from their smoky mouths,
So that my soul may but ascend to Heaven.   90

The watch strikes.

Ah, half the hour is past! 'Twill all be past anon!
O God!
If thou wilt not have mercy on my soul,
Yet for Christ's sake whose blood hath ransomed me,
Impose some end to my incessant pain: 95
Let Faustus live in hell a thousand years—
A hundred thousand, and at last be saved!

---

[1] "O slowly, slowly run, horses of the night." Ovid, *Amores*, I, 13.
[2] Continue to move.

O, no end is limited to damned souls!
Why wert thou not a creature wanting soul?
Or why is this immortal that thou hast?   100
Ah, Pythagoras' metempsychosis[1]! were that true,
This soul should fly from me, and I be changed
Unto some brutish beast! All beasts are happy,
For, when they die,
Their souls are soon dissolved in elements;   105
But mine must live, still to be plagued in hell.
Curst be the parents that engendered me!
No, Faustus; curse thyself, curse Lucifer
That hath deprived thee of the joys of Heaven.

The clock striketh twelve.

O, it strikes! Now, body, turn to air,   110
Or Lucifer will bear thee quick to hell. *Thunder and lightning.*
O soul, be changed into little water-drops,
And fall into the ocean—ne'er be found.
My God! my God! look not so fierce on me!

Enter DEVILS.

Adders and serpents, let me breathe awhile!   115
Ugly hell, gape not! Come not, Lucifer!
I'll burn my books!—Ah Mephistophilis!

Exeunt [DEVILS *with* FAUSTUS].

Enter CHORUS.

[CHORUS.] Cut is the branch that might have grown full
   straight,
And burned is Apollo's laurel bough,

---

[1] Transmigration of souls.

That sometime grew within this learned man.　　　120
Faustus is gone; regard his hellish fall,
Whose fiendful fortune may exhort the wise
Only to wonder at unlawful things,
Whose deepness doth entice such forward wits
To practice more than heavenly power permits.　*Exit.*　125
　Terminat hora diem, terminat author opus.[1]

---

[1] The hour ends the day; the author ends his work.

Rinehart Editions